Thank You for Raping Me

By Athena Ives

I have tried to recreate events, locales, and conversations from my memories of them. In order to maintain their anonymity in some instances I have changed the names of individuals and places, I may have changed some identifying characteristics and details such as physical properties, occupations, and places of residence.

Copyright © 2021 by Athena Ives

Author Photo by Jodie Royak

For more information: Dr.Athena.Ives@gmail.com.

ISBN 978-0-9980417-2-8 (Hard Copy)

ISBN 978-0-9980417-4-2 (eBook)

www.AthenaIves.com

Acknowledgments

I dedicate this book to the two most important people in my life, my Person and my Cinni Mini. Always and Forever Agapē.

Introduction

The title of the book probably caught your attention and evoked some form of strong emotion. The first edition of *Thank You for Raping Me* was written during a time in my life where I was on a journey to embrace all of myself. It was the first time I shared many things about what I experienced, from childhood until now. During the audiobook recording process, I realized that there were some things I didn't fully explain or left out, and other things, that should have been kept between myself and the individual involved. That is why I chose to come out with a second edition. The title of the book I chose to keep because I still feel the same way. It is a powerful message I want to use to inspire others on their journey to find purpose and meaning in their pain.

So why that title? Millions of people around the world have been raped. Even more have experienced some form of extreme trauma. Over the years I have found healing through research and science; understanding more about why these types of things happen. Our culture and belief systems play a major role. While I am a firm believer that everything happens for a reason, it still wasn't enough. Finding a purpose helped, but wasn't enough. When I was a child, I had this unexplainable belief that I was destined or created for something extraordinary. My child mind thought perhaps it was my ability to play soccer or my strength and one day I would be conducting special ops missions to rescue children. I made extreme sacrifices, chose the most challenging paths, and had a voice in my head that was relentless if I did something wrong, pushing me to make it right. If I told a lie or did something bad, I couldn't live with it. I had to tell the truth. Perhaps it was due to the fact that I had so many secrets I was hiding from the world. Not secrets of things I had done wrong, but other people's secrets. There were also secrets I kept because I knew that no one would believe me. At a young age I developed an ability to sense evil in people. There was no tangible evidence or proof, but I could feel it in my soul. I was rarely wrong and it often took years to find out that I had been right. I also had an ability to sense the good in people, a good other people rarely saw. This was a blessing and a curse.

For most of my childhood I was in survival mode. Always on high alert, similar to what it feels like on a patrol in Fallujah. It took most of my life to come close to understanding the impact this had on my brain and every molecule of my life. I couldn't understand why so many horrific things happened to me when all I did was try to be the best person I could be. I loved God, I was the best sibling, daughter, and friend I could possibly be. I think the worst thing I did as a child was throw rotting pumpkin at a boy that was bullying me. No matter how hard I tried it never seemed to be enough for anyone in my life. As I got older, I came so close to reaching my dreams, but each time, I wasn't enough. It had nothing to do with the effort I put in, it had to do with a force outside of my control. A freak accident, being at the wrong place at the wrong time. After each dream was destroyed, I found another to replace it. Relentless in my quest to reach my destiny of becoming someone great, a superhero.

We all have different definitions of heroes. For many it's the men and women that serve our country in the military. For others it's an athlete who came from nothing and became a legend. To some, a hero is a parent or role model. Even though these heroes are very different, they have many of the same characteristics in common, and all of it has to do with choices. Heroes aren't all strong men with capes. They are individuals that chose the hard path, did what they felt was right, and never stopped fighting for what they believed in. A hero doesn't come home and take off their cape. They don't lay down on the battlefield and give up while their brothers and sisters fight on. Being a hero is a choice.

My story isn't a fairy tale. All though my story isn't finished, it will never have a happily ever after ending. My journey to become the superhero I am now is not a journey I would wish on anyone. No one in their right mind wants to be raped. No one asks to be betrayed, see their children die, lose their dream job. Bad things happen to all of us. None of us are safe from pain, trauma, or heartbreak. We do not have a choice in becoming a victim, but we do have a choice in staying one.

The difference between a superhero and a villain is the choices they make. A superhero experiences a trauma or is given an ability and they CHOOSE to use it for good. A villain does the opposite. I had a choice. I could have allowed being raped and the trauma I experienced to make me hateful, a drug addict, or a killer. Instead

I chose to use that trauma for good. I gained superhuman strength from the painful experiences I have survived and like a superhero, I chose to use it to help people. My life isn't a happy one. This story is raw, brutally honest, truthful and will take you on my journey through some of the most painful moments a human can survive. I chose the title to not only prepare the reader, but to scream from the front page that I AM NOT A VICTIM. I chose to be thankful for what happened to me because it gave me the strength, experience, empathy and knowledge I needed to help so many others like me. To show them they aren't alone. To show them that your family can hurt you more than can be explained by science or any belief you have. To show you that no matter the pain you have experienced, you can use it for good. That it is ok to be vulnerable when you need to be. To give you hope that your pain had a purpose and you can use it to save others.

Table of Contents

x

Chapter 1

My debut into this world began in my father's hands. My parents had strange beliefs about childbirth, which they never explained, and tried their best to have all of their children at home. They had no midwife and several of my siblings almost died in the process. I will never forget, years later when my younger brother was born, seeing my father rushing to the car holding my mother who was covered in blood. She almost died due to complications and she had to be rushed to the hospital.

I was the third child and first daughter in the family. Being the only redhead in a family of blonds I never felt like I belonged. People would often question if I was adopted or perhaps the result of an affair. This feeling of not belonging was not just limited to my hair color. It started slowly and was barely noticeable during my early years. As I grew and developed cognitive skills, the difference between myself and my siblings became increasingly apparent.

My unwillingness to conform and become a mindless lemming that followed all instructions was just the start. My mother didn't work and my father was barely able to pay the bills working with computers. The pity stares we received when my mother would be standing in line at the grocery store with five children under the ages of 12 and a stack of food stamps would make my skin crawl. My mother had married young, around 20 years old. The beautiful, hippie surfer, woman posing in daisy crowns and always smiling, my mother's former self, was gone. A submissive, weak, tolerant shell was left.

Perhaps those pity stares at the store were for how trapped and exhausted she looked. My father, a tall, handsome, dark haired man, had transitioned from a California surfer, skating empty pools with some of the legends of the skateboarding industry, to a Jesus freak. When he took on a task or a belief, he gave everything he had. Despite my great dislike for the man, I do have numerous similar traits that I am grateful for, and one of them is effort. If he believed in something, he wouldn't let anything change his mind. Every breath he took followed his beliefs, and when he was saved, his entire life changed due to his new religious beliefs.

My parents every decision was guided by their distorted views of the Bible. I say my parents, but really, whatever my father said went and my mother had no voice of her own. They decided to shelter us from the sins of the world by homeschooling my siblings and I. You would think that such a religious family would attend church regularly. However, my father disagreed with just about every single religious affiliation in our area. We would attend a local church occasionally, but those were typically followed with rants about how ignorant the pastor was.

From the age of five, a soccer ball rarely left my feet. Memories of my early childhood are foggy, to say the least, but I recall spending hours and hours in our pool or playing soccer. Neither of my parents went to college, which caused extreme financial difficulties. Despite these financial constraints, my parents had another child. When my sister was born the dynamics between my brothers and I changed drastically. They worshiped this little blond haired, blue eyed baby and I became the target for bullying and torment. This particularly was due to the attention I received from my father because of my soccer skills.

When I wasn't swimming in our pool or doing schoolwork, I was off running around with my two older brothers playing barefoot soccer with the other boys in the neighborhood. At seven years old, I met my reality with my brothers. I stepped on a bee during a barefoot soccer game and my brothers left me crying in the middle of the soccer field. Unable to get the stinger out, I hobbled the half mile home to find my brother's doting over my little sister. Acceptance never came from my brothers. Everything from twisting my wrist to almost drowning me was their pattern of tolerating me. My gut told me something was wrong. I saw how other older brothers treated their sisters, protectively. Even though I longed for that kind of protection, it forced me to stand on my own two feet. If I couldn't depend on my older brothers or my parents to protect me, I knew that I had to protect myself. I would never have a safety blanket or be able to look over my shoulder for help. At an early age I was forced to depend on myself. No matter how difficult a task, I always found a way out and how to do it alone.

My life consisted of home schooling, soccer, swimming and God. When my father couldn't tolerate the church we were going to any longer, he began to scour the religious realm of different churches and pastors in an attempt to find one that met his own beliefs. He would get tapes of pastors he agreed with and would play them as a form of church in our home every Wednesday and Sunday. We also had to read the Bible every morning and every evening as soon as we were old enough to read. These pastors always sounded so angry and I never quite understood how they could say, 'Love thy neighbor' one moment and the next, that all homosexuals were going to burn in hell for all eternity.

Do you ever smell something that takes you back to a place or a memory? Every time I smell jasmine, it reminds me of a night blooming jasmine tree that grew right outside my window. It also reminds me of how little of my childhood I actually remember. This brings up a never-ending debate on repressed memories. Repressed memories are caused by your body protecting itself from events that you were not able to cope with. Some people believe that you need to dig up those memories through numerous methods for you to determine if there are any underlying issues that are preventing you from healing. Some believe that your body was protecting itself and to let those memories stay buried. The fact that I can only remember snapshots of my past lead me to believe that I blocked out a large part of my childhood. Do I really want to dig them up?

Chapter 2

At the age of 10, I was ripped from my home in sunny California and taken to an extreme weather mosquito filled Michigan where I knew no one. I was taken away from my relatives, warm weather, pool, and soccer league. My father had chosen this miserable state because he found one pastor whose teachings were on par with his beliefs. I didn't realize it then, but my father had joined a religious cult.

My parents and most of the members at this cult church had strict beliefs preventing us from participating in any of the following on the Lord's Day: watching TV, reading secular books, playing or watching any type of sport, doing homework. The rules for females were much stricter and we were viewed as being less than males. We were forced to wear modest clothing similar to Amish attire. We were punished for laughing too loudly, spending too much time with the opposite sex no matter the context, and we weren't allowed to speak publicly. We had to ask a man to speak for us. All of us were restricted from interacting with anyone outside the church. We were allowed to spend time with those on the approved friends list. These friends were typically restricted to the pastor's children.

When you are part of a cult, whether by choice or being forced, you don't truly realize how dangerous everything is until you get out. Even though I could sense the evil surrounding me, I didn't fully grasp the depths of evil permeating throughout that church. When we first started attending, I immediately did not fit in. My parents had received endless calls from nosy members complaining either about my choice of clothing, me falling asleep during the long prayers and boring sermons, excessive goofing, or for associating with too many of the boys. I was a tomboy and I related more to the boys my age.

I remember the sound of spankings echoing from the boiler room during hell fire and damnation sermons. That is where you were taken if you stepped out of line. The pastors of the church always wore these thick wool suits and required the chapel to be kept at a freezing temperature no matter the season. I recall wearing pants under my skirts because of the cold and on one occasion, I smuggled in my comforter from home. I strutted down the aisle like a queen wrapped in her royal robes. I did this not only because I was freezing my ass off, but also to make a statement. Instead of saying, "Hey assholes, turn on the heat. My warmth didn't last long as I was yanked out of my seat and dragged down the aisle to the boiler room. The spankings at home I received were even worse. I remember being forced to get naked in front of my father, even at 16-years-old, to receive my bare bottom spanking. The times he used his bare hand were worse than any form of spanking tool he used.

They had sermons about women losing weight to please their husbands and there were weigh-ins that followed. It was only the women and girls that were shamed. Public shaming was common

6

and many women developed eating disorders. Wives would call my parents to complain that their husband was struggling with lust and I should dress less provocatively. I was 12/13 years old and dressed like a tomboy or a nun. Every time that phone would ring on a Sunday afternoon I would cringe because it would usually be about me. I grew large breasts at an early age and had an athletic body so anything I wore was seen as provocative.

There was an active sex trafficking and child bride ring from the Dominican Republic. Grown women would be forced to write down their prayer requests to be read by another man (or even her teenage son) because even the sound of her voice was sinful. Pastors not fulfilling their duties as mandated reporters in order to protect the men that were abusing their daughters or wives. Pastors required oversight meetings which included showing proof of income and their contributions to the church in tithes.

Sexual abuse and victims were never believed. Children were forced at 3 years old to sit still and quiet for hours. If they fussed, they were beaten. They required extreme isolation. We were not allowed to associate with other denominations. All other denominations were going to hell and if you associated with them you were going to hell, punished, and forced to repent or be excommunicated. We took vacations together to approved of places which usually were conferences that cost money that went to fill their pockets. We were not able to question anything said by pastors or other church authority. You were the one who was sinning by questioning them and were in danger of going to hell. They taught and enforced parent to break their children's spirit in to save them from sin by beating them into submission. The women and children were supposed to obey and not question. Pastors who lacked any type of degree would ignore genuine mental health disorders, like schizophrenia, and treat them with prayer.

The one positive I did take away from this cult was meeting an incredibly resilient girl named Joy, who quickly became my best friend. We both shared one thing in common, a hate for the church and my father. We both preferred sleepovers at Joy's house because her mother was much more lenient than mine and she never felt comfortable around my father. Joy's mother was Black and her father was White. This was one reason that my parents restricted the amount of time we spent together. They would never admit to being racists, but my father's side has a long line of KKK members. It was an unspoken understanding that we would never be allowed to date anyone of color. Growing up I never understood the concept of racism. To me, disliking someone for the color of their skin was just idiotic. She could have been blue and I wouldn't have cared.

When we moved to Michigan, my father immediately became involved with the area youth soccer organization AYSO and signed my two older brothers, myself, and my younger sister up to play. He also became involved in coaching my team as well as my brothers. During my first season, it became obvious that the level of play was significantly lower than the level of play in California. Because of this, I scored on average around four goals per game. The parents on the opposing team would almost get in fistfights with my father because I was humiliating their team. My father's solution was placing me in the goal, but I had such a desire to score that I would take the ball all the way up the field and score.

After two seasons of this, my father decided to put me in the all-boys league. Not only did I hold my own, I made the national all boys select team that would be participating in the national AYSO soccer tournament. This caused an extreme amount of jealousy with my siblings that would only grow with my increasing soccer success. While my soccer skills made me feel that my father cared about me and loved me, I knew it was dependent on how well I played.

Have you ever fought so hard for conditional love you begin to think that it's the only type of love anyone could ever have for you? There are not many positive things to say about my father, but he did give me the incredible opportunity to know and show that I could do anything the boys could do. This molded me into the independent and ability confident woman I became. I lived for those moments when I would score a goal or walk off the field at halftime to see his proud grin. There were times when he wasn't pleased with my playing, but those were rare because of the effort I put in. My soccer ability was the only thing that I could do to make him proud of me, to make him love me.

If he wasn't the coach of a team I was playing for, he would be in the stands or on the sideline at every game. He would brag about me to others right in front of my brothers. This added to the hatred my brothers had for me. They would come up with ways to hurt me and make themselves feel better.

My mother and I had extremely strained relationship. I somewhat held her responsible for the mental abuse I received on a constant basis from my father. I would come to her crying when he would comment on my appearance or weight in a belittling manner and she would side with him. She also never stood up for myself and my siblings, despite disagreeing with some of the disciplinary actions my father used. We had a wooden paddle my father had made sitting on the mantle as a constant warning to not step out of line. Mister Spank and a frowning face was written on it in a black Sharpie. One of her favorite methods of punishment was to twist my wrists like my brothers would do to inflict pain. Parents need to understand and take responsibility for the damage they do to their children by not protecting them or believing them. How many children were raped or abused by a family member and the mother or father turned a blind eye or even worse, blamed the child?

When I reached the eighth grade, my parents decided that they would enroll me into the public school system. My mother had no educational background and I was falling behind. I went to a school that was infested with rich white kids. This was a school where name brand clothes and the cars you were dropped off in either made you popular or an outcast. I was dropped off in a 13-seater, child-molester van, wearing my brother's hand-me-down clothes and shoes that were too big. You can imagine my popularity status. I didn't make any friends that year and I received a humiliating GPA of 2.1.

Chapter 3

Freshman year, I joined my two older brothers in the same high school. One was a junior and the other in his senior year. My oldest brother, Jacob, was on the varsity team, but he rarely got any playing time. I got along with him more than any of the other siblings. My father was the main reason that Jacob and I didn't have a close relationship. I felt bad for Jacob, especially when my father would belittle him after a game and use me as an example of how he should play. Jacob did not have it easy. He was a tall, good looking blond that looked a lot like my father. Despite his physical appearance and good looks, my father made it impossible for Jacob to develop any type of self-confidence. Cain, the second oldest, was a master manipulator from the time he could speak. He displayed numerous psychopathic traits. On the rare occasions he was caught doing something wrong, he would avoid punishment by either lying or shifting the blame to another undeserving person. His blond hair turned brown as he got older and he resembled my mother. Cain was her favorite and she let him get away with everything.

Both of my older brothers had an extraordinary ability to memorize things, almost photographic. Even though they rarely studied, they both were 4.0 students. I, on the other hand, would study for hours and barely pass my classes. My freshman year marked a significant turning point in the relationship I had with my father. Prior to this, I was treated like one of his sons. For several years I played two age groups up on Jacob and Cain's team so my father could coach all three of us at the same time. Once I hit my freshman year, this completely changed. It turned into 'You belong in the kitchen; you need to be a young lady and marry a pastor; you can't act like that. Why can't you be more like your sister? Why can't you cook like your sister? You're too fat and muscular. Guys don't like that. They want you thin and beautiful like your sister. You need to be graceful and ladylike. You can only wear skirts to church, no more pants.

Because crying was seen as a weakness, I would hide my head in my pillow and did my best to never let anyone see me cry. Part of me wanted to scream at my father and tell him how much I hated him and wanted him dead. I still don't know why I held back so much. Then again, I felt trapped and saw no way out! In my own way I rebelled. I loved being one of the guys and had no desire to be the type of woman he wanted me to be. I began to despise him and would pretend I was a terrible cook to get out of helping in the kitchen.

At my school I wasn't one of the popular kids, but I also wasn't a constant target for bullies. I wasn't a jock or a brainy nerd. I marched to the beat of my own drum. I had several acquaintances in numerous different clicks, so I never really fit in anywhere. I would spend my lunch time working on my homework for the next day. I did this because I would either have soccer after school or, during the off season, I worked as a grocery bagger.

There was one girl named Delilah who came from a very wealthy family and was part of the popular crowd. We had choir together and soon became good friends. Delilah's family attended a church that my parents didn't necessarily approve of but thankfully, after introducing her and telling them all about her, I was occasionally allowed to sleepover. I would invite her to sleepover at my house, but she never felt comfortable.

This next chapter is dealing with my rape as a child and it is going to be extremely graphic. I felt that it was very important to not sugar coat this at all. It is a horrific crime that happened to myself and millions of children around the world. It happens every single day. The least we can do is listen to these stories and learn from them. Stop sugarcoating them. Stop allowing these predators, these evil child rapists to get away with it. We have to share our truth. We have to stop sheltering family members. We have to put the blame on the evil monsters out there that are hurting children instead of blaming the victims. It is going to be extremely graphic so please take that into consideration. It can bring up a lot of painful memories as it has for myself.

Chapter 4

At the age of 12 or 13, the exact age I couldn't exactly say, my older brother Cain began raping me. My first sexual experience took place before I had a first kiss, before I fell in love, and with a monster that was supposed to protect me from these very evils. The first time was something that I will never be able to erase from my memory, no matter how much I try. It was a hot summer night and I decided to sleep in the basement due to the extreme Michigan heat. I have always been a heavy sleeper, but one night something woke me up. I froze when I felt my panties being pulled off slowly and carefully to avoid waking me. There was a dim light from the VCR and I slightly opened my eyes enough to see my brother Cain's brown hair. My heart was pounding so loud I didn't know what to do. I lay there frozen with fear.

Cain had always been a physically violent person and I feared what would happen if I even moved. My siblings and I hated waking Cain up in the morning because he would wake up swinging. There were even holes in the walls of his room from his angry outbursts and punching through the drywall. I also developed a fear of drowning because of his violent and explosive behavior. When I was around eight, Cain, Jacob and I were playing in our swimming pool. I playfully dunked Cain, which resulted in him returning the act and holding me under the water until I almost drowned. On another occasion, when my two front teeth had finally grown in, Cain overreacted again and shoved me. My face collided with the edge of the pool, causing me to almost bite through my lower lip and chipping my two front teeth. My parents didn't have dental coverage, so it would take me fifteen years to fix my teeth. Every time I looked in the mirror and I saw my chipped teeth, I remembered what he had done to me.

I also contribute my claustrophobia to Cain. We were in the basement making forts and I was pretending to be a mummy. I placed a sleeping bag over my head and began walking around, making wailing noises. The next thing I know, I felt hands around my ankles and landed hard on the ground, face down. I felt Cain get on top of me, making it difficult to breathe. Panic set in and I begged Cain to let me out of the sleeping bag. He laughed and refused to let me out. The more I struggled, the harder it was to breathe. It felt like I was in there for hours and the only reason he finally let me out was because I pissed myself. My brothers also used to lock me in our cellar pantry and turn out the light and would only open the door if I yelled loud enough for my mom to hear.

Outdoor activities involved snowball fights and those got very violent. If I threw a snowball at one of my brothers, they would have to one up me. This would often involve them taking rocks or ice balls and packing the snow around it. I would end up with gashes in my face or bruises where they met their mark. Now, don't get me wrong, I initiated some of these encounters and didn't always care about the aggressive play we had. I wanted to be included, but when Jezebel would play with us, they would never overdo it with her. She was their little princess and they treated her like one.

Some of you may find this next part to be too graphic and disturbing, but I feel it is important to share with people what really happened. I believe that too many times people categorize molestation, sexual assault and even rape in a way that sugarcoats the events. A sexual assault could be an unwanted ass grab or someone holding you down and ripping off your clothes. Very different encounters, which is why I feel it's important to share the details. To my mother, who said I never fully explained in detail what your son did to me, now you know!!!

The fear of a violent reaction and not knowing what was going on kept me frozen and pretending to be asleep. After pulling down my panties, he spread my legs slightly and I felt his breath on my inner thighs. He started with his tongue and then started shoving his fingers inside me. I was prepubescent and had never even put in a tampon. My brother was going down on me and fingering me while I lay their frozen in terror. To my disgust, he would take his fingers out and I could hear him lick them before he roughly shoved them back inside me. His sharp fingernails cutting inside me, tears started streaming down my cheeks and pooling inside my ears.

I only moved to pull my panties and shorts on when I heard him go into the laundry room and start masturbating. The sick bastard not only raped me, he went and masturbated because he was so aroused. You sick fuck. I lay frozen on my back tears, soaking my pillow, terrified to make a sound, or he would come back for more.

I felt weak, ashamed and confused. After what seemed like

hours, I went upstairs to the bathroom and tried to scrub away the filth with a washcloth. I was too afraid to take a shower and wake my father up, so I quickly snuck back into my boiling hot room and silently cried into my pillow. No sleep came that night. In the nights after I awoke with every creak that old house made. After that night, I did everything I could not to sleep in the basement. He started to hide under my bed, hoping to catch me changing clothes. He also would hide in the shower trying to watch me go to the bathroom. From then on, I would have to clear the bathroom and my bedroom, making sure this monster wasn't lying in wait for me. Whenever I caught him, he would lie and say he was playing hide and seek.

The nights when I was forced to sleep in the basement and I couldn't tell my parents why I didn't want to, were some of the longest nights of my life. I would lay paralyzed in fear, terrified to fall asleep. I would try and leave a movie on low enough that my parents couldn't hear and in hopes to prevent my brother from coming down. I couldn't stand the silence because I would freak out every sound I heard in the house. I would fall asleep watching the movie and would be woken up to the same scenario over and over again. I don't know how many times this happened or when it eventually stopped, but it went on for a long time. Looking back, I believe that my innocent mind blocked out many more encounters that may have been much worse.

Chapter 5

Due to the rape, emotional abuse from my father, and a long list of mental and physical abuse from my parents, I began to contemplate suicide. I would go to the library and research different methods. My only escape was soccer, but that wasn't enough. I had no support system. Not one person knew what was really going on, not even Joy. To make things even more challenging, the jealousy my brothers had been developing for years, increased in high school. Their little sister was a starter on the varsity soccer team as a freshman, and our father would talk openly about how much better I was than they were.

My father also encouraged tension between my younger sister Jezebel and I. He would constantly bring up how she was more attractive than I was, and he had a deluded notion that I was somehow jealous of her. I wasn't jealous of her looks. I had no desire to be anything like her. She was fake, manipulative, backstabbing and had no concept of who she was. If there was any jealousy, it was on her part. She would take the few clothes I had and always tried to dress like me. All the music I liked she would listen to. However, if anyone more popular than me disliked that music, she would say how stupid it was and would make fun of me for listening to it.

I envied my classmates at school with older brothers that made their high school years easier. I would watch these protective big brothers hug their younger sisters in front of their lockers, take them to prom if they didn't have a date, have lunch with them, and come to their defense if anyone ever tried to bully them. Mine did the opposite. They avoided me like the plague and would often make fun of me in front of their friends in the hallway. Even though I looked up to Jacob and had a better relationship with him at home, he still wouldn't defend me even if someone was making fun of me or giving me a difficult time.

On one occasion, Cain was having a birthday party at a local water park. I was doing everything I could to avoid him and was hiding in the back of our van. After years of emotional abuse, I had very little self-confidence in my appearance. Wearing my first two-piece bathing suit, I tried to hide my insecurities by acting confident with my body. While I was talking with Joy, Cain came walking up with my new crush. Cane made a joke in front of everyone that I look like a dude in a bathing suit and commented on how much pizza I ate. I didn't have an ounce of fat on me, but I felt like an obese and ugly redhead.

My crushes on boys were very different than most girls my age. The feelings weren't sexually related. They were more about friendship and wanting so badly to have someone love me like I saw in the movies or in the hundreds of books I read. Quite often when someone has an unwanted sexual encounter, their body becomes a means to enact revenge on the offending sex. The loss of control over choosing a sexual partner often leads them to be overly promiscuous. Others end up hating the opposite sex and avoid sex altogether. I started to believe that no man would ever truly love me and they would only want to have sex with me, use me, and then leave when they got what they wanted. However, I never gave up hope. Something inside me refused to allow the world to change me, and I knew that I deserved an amazing mind-blowing Hollywood type love story where a man would love me unconditionally.

Instead of letting anyone see me cry I went and hid in the back of our van. Not knowing I was there, Cain and my crush got in the front seat to talk away from our parents' ears. They were discussing the recent bomb threat we had in our school and began plotting to make one themselves. Then the topic turned to me. Cain told his friend that I liked him and they both had a good laugh. They went on to talk about how ugly I was and how stupid I looked in my bathing suit. With tears streaming down my face, I prayed that they would leave and did everything I could to not let them hear me. After they left I stayed hidden long enough to ensure I didn't look like I had been crying. I went back to the party, smiling and laughing like nothing had happened. I had become very good at masking what was truly going on and lying to myself about what was really going on in my life.

The cruel boys in high school added to the poor self-esteem I already had. While sitting in science class, one of the popular boys leaned over and asked me if I was a virgin. I ignored him and continued to take notes, my cheeks starting to heat and turn red with embarrassment. Blushing was one thing I had not yet managed to control. This only encouraged him and he kept trying to get me to respond. When I didn't, he told me he knew I was still a virgin because, quote, no one would ever fuck someone as ugly as you, especially one with a fire crotch.

My brothers and I did agree on one thing. We didn't want our father in our lives. I remember sitting in our van on Sunday at church, all of us plotting different ways to kill him. We thought of running him over in the parking lot with the van or poisoning his coffee.

My suicidal thoughts started to transition to forming a plan. I read articles I found at the library on different methods of suicide. I didn't want to die; I just didn't want to ever wake up again. I would daydream about dying in a fire trying to rescue a child, or about being killed in a battle saving my fellow soldiers. Every time we got in a car, I prayed I would die and that Cain and my father would as well. These thoughts became worse when soccer season ended and I spent more time at home. I researched how many pills and what types, what the body goes through, and how painful it would be. I even walked across a street without looking, praying a car would kill me instantly.

Chapter 6

When my parents came and told my siblings and I that we were going to have another addition to the family, we were angry. They were poor, on and off food stamps, and my mother was in her 40s. We already were made fun of constantly for our large family. For the seven of us, we had one shower. Why would they bring another child they couldn't afford into this world?

The day finally came and for some reason, my mother wanted me to be in the hospital room with her and my father. I remember being utterly horrified and grossed out by the birth. Then I had this incredible, life altering feeling of unconditional love for this beautiful little girl. She was the most beautiful baby I had ever seen. The moment I held Marie, my life changed and I stopped having any thoughts of suicide. I had found my soul mate.

Marie and I were inseparable. I would wake up if I heard her cry at night, feed her a bottle or sing her to sleep. As she got older, she would crawl into my bed to sleep with me. I took care of her as soon as I got home from school and spent all my free time with her. She used to sit in my lap and pick my cuticles until they bled. Oddly, it was comforting. The physical pain, combined with my love for her helped numb the ongoing abuse and the memories I was desperately trying to forget. My love for her continued to grow with every breath I had, every time I sang her to sleep, and every time she fell asleep in my arms. Instead of crying when my world was falling apart, I would go hold her. Smelling her freshly bathed head, feeling her silky-smooth skin, soaking in the unconditional love I felt that radiated with her every breath, kept me alive. She saved my life by loving me. The power of unconditional love is an incredible, powerful tool. It can be used to destroy or *heal*, and I am forever grateful for the bond we share.

Abuse can come in so many different shapes and forms, both visible and invisible. Not only was I experiencing ongoing sexual abuse, but the emotional abuse from my family, mainly my father, and often physical abuse from my mother, added to everything else I was experiencing. Marie was my coping mechanism. When my father told me I was fat, when my brothers picked on me, when I was picked on at school for my red hair, I would just hold her and all of those feelings of hurt would dissipate. The sound of her heartbeat, the smell of her hair, her breath on my skin, was like medicine to my soul.

When my maternal grandpa passed away, my family drove all the way from Michigan to California. We were poor with a very large family so we couldn't afford to fly or even get a hotel to make the trip less arduous. Our road trips were anything but glamorous. Our family, of now eight, piled into our van with no air conditioning and no fun stops along the way. Despite the miserable conditions, I was so excited to see my cousins! I also loved spending time with my grandma and my favorite aunt and uncle. My aunt and uncle lived in a multimillion-dollar home in Rancho Santa Fe, California. This beautiful home had a massive backyard, guest house, and luxurious pool featuring a waterfall and a hot tub. I had several cousins that were a few years younger than me, but we all got along very well.

After the funeral, I was scolded by my mother for not crying and accused of being wicked, for not showing more emotion. She warned me that I better be on my best behavior or I wouldn't be allowed to spend the night with my cousins. After a massive potluck with all my relatives, I was evaluating the decadent dessert table and wished I could have had tried all of them. In my family we were never allowed to leave food on our plate as this was considered wasteful. My mother was also a dreadful cook. On several occasions the food would be so terrible, Cain, who had a weak stomach, would vomit the food on his plate. My father would make him eat his own vomit, saying that Cain did this on purpose and would only throw up the food he didn't want. DELUSIONAL!

With this in mind, I knew that I couldn't take a few pieces of different desserts to try them all, because I would have to finish the entire piece. So, I cut half of one piece of chocolate cake and another half piece of my grandmother's amazing lemon meringue pie. I was laughing and talking with my cousins who were piling several different desserts onto their plates. As I went to grab a fork, my father came over, grabbed my arm, took the plate out of my hand and loudly told me, "You're in training! What did I tell you about your weight and getting fat? You can only have one piece. Which one do you want?" The room became silent. My relatives were trying to hide how uncomfortable the situation was. I tried to walk away, but he held onto my arm and asked me again which piece I wanted. I told him I didn't want any of it with a bit of an attitude in my voice as I was trying to disguise how embarrassed I was.

This made him even more angry. He pulled me aside and told me that I was no longer allowed to spend the night as I had been an embarrassment to him and disrespected him in front of my relatives. As soon as he let go, I fled the room with marks from his grip on my arm. My Aunt Em, who had witnessed it all, came and found me. She sat down on the floor of the laundry room with me and put her arms around me. I desperately wished I could have traded places with my cousins.

My father's constant degrading comments on my weight and appearance caused such negative self-esteem issues I still struggle with them today. Have you ever known something in your head but your heart still makes you doubt? I know in my head that I'm not ugly and fat, but I still see an unattractive person with a body I am never content with. I must remind myself constantly that those were lies. It is like rewiring your brain to get rid of the lies or change your incorrect thoughts. It is something I work on daily and I still have moments of doubt.

Aunt Em, my mother's youngest sister, had quite the history with my parents. She married my uncle, who was a very wealthy businessman, 15 years her senior. She followed in my grandma's footsteps, who also married my grandpa, who was 15 years her senior. My aunt told me that when my father asked my grandpa for my mother's hand, he didn't give his blessing and he and my grandmother begged for my mother not to marry him. They also pleaded with my mother not to marry him.

She told me that when I was a toddler, my family was evicted from our home and we were living in a motor home on their property. I was too young to remember, but she told me that she had my uncle call Child Protective Services on my father. According to her, my father would spank me and my brothers, who weren't older than six to the point where we had bruises covering our butts. She told me that these spankings were brutal and more like beatings. After seeing blood in mine and Cain's diapers, they called CPS. My aunt wasn't sure how it was possible, but CPS only took us for a few nights before returning us. My distrust in the justice system and in adults to believe children or protect them in general, began very early on.

Years later, my father's sister, Aunt Sally, told me that when she was a teenager, she remembered sitting in our trailer with my mother, crying and trying to block out the sounds of our screams. To this day, I will never understand why my relatives, knowing about all of this, never confronted him or did anything more about it. Instead, they avoided the situation and turned a blind eye. I believe that my aunts told me about these beatings and sexual abuse in hopes that I wouldn't blame my mother. However, my mother chose to drown out the sounds of her own children screaming in pain, with a pillow. She is equally to blame. Or perhaps they felt guilty and want me to know that they tried to help in their own way. Really? You saw your nieces and nephews being traumatized and you did nothing.

Marie, soccer, and Joy helped me get through many of those

difficult years. Joy and I would see each other every Sunday when I didn't fake sick to avoid going. Despite how close we were, I never told her about Cain. She knew what a monster my family was, but I wouldn't even admit to myself what he had done. I had never even written about it in my own journal. Joy's siblings were the opposite. I got along with all of them. They were what kept her going and helped her get through the numerous illnesses she had. Joy was the only friend I had that saw me play soccer in high school. She would try and come to as many games as she could and was my biggest fan.

Chapter 7

Delilah and I continued to become better friends. We didn't spend much time together outside of school due to my busy schedule, and my parents wouldn't often let me spend the night. However, in the fall season when I wasn't playing soccer, I joined the cross-country team to stay in shape for soccer. Delilah also joined. Her parents loved me and would always invite me over when I was allowed. They thought I was a good influence on Delilah and I was. I pushed her to do better in school, comforted her when the wrong guys she dated hurt her, and we never got in trouble. Her father would come and cheer both of us on at our cross-country meets.

I also sang in the choir with Delilah for all four years of high school. My parents never made it to any of my cross-country meets or choir concerts. Delilah's Parents were always there encouraging me and they grew to dislike my family for how they treated me. Delilah's dad loved my determination and would constantly try to encourage Delilah to work harder in her running, but she didn't care about that. She was more into boys and fashion. In the four years I played soccer in high school, Delilah never came to one single game. She made it to almost every home football and basketball games though. Looking back, I would call our friendship significantly one sided. However, she was one of the only friends I had other than Joy, and it *helped* to have someone at school.

During my senior year, my sister Jezebel was a freshman at my high school. Despite our issues and how poorly she treated me, I did my best to protect her and look out for her. I treated her like I wish my brothers had treated me. I used to wake her up in the morning with coffee mixed with hot chocolate. On her birthday and Valentine's Day, I surprised her with a dozen red roses and balloons. I did this because she had mentioned how lucky the girls were with boyfriends that got them roses. On the card with the roses I put that it was from a secret admirer. She knew they were from me, but told her friends that they were from a boy. I continued this for the rest of her high school years. On one occasion when I was in college, I skipped class and brought her a cute stuffed monkey with roses. I went out of my way to make her feel welcome, safe, and the opposite of what my brothers made me feel.

Jacob ended up moving out after he received an academic full ride scholarship to a very prestigious school. He didn't make the soccer team which devastated him. He moved out against my parents' wishes and rebelled against everything they had taught him. He became an alcoholic, skipped classes, started smoking, and his life started to spin out of control. This destructive path became worse after his girlfriend broke up with him to go out with his best friend. He drank excessively and skipped so many classes they took away his full-ride scholarship.

Refusing to go back home. He joined the army. When he was is in boot camp, I wrote him every single week. I tried to do what

I thought he would appreciate under those circumstances. I wanted him to not feel alone and was trying to make up for the lack of love from my parents.

Jacob was a genius. He could quote a sentence he read one time out of a history book, over a year later. He missed a perfect ACT score by a couple of points. It was no surprise when he tested so high the Army put him into a special counterintelligence field and sent him off to an intense language school where he learned to speak fluent Russian. After graduating with honors, he was stationed in Germany. I admired him and wished I could be as smart as he was.

Cain graduated with a 4.0 but decided not to attend college. He was kicked out of the house after sneaking out numerous times, getting caught for smoking, and getting into a physical altercation with my father. He moved to California and stayed with my aunt and uncle for around a year. He ended up becoming involved with a gang, drugs, and street racing. He was causing too many problems for my uncle and they asked him to leave. He fled the state after he found out that he had a warrant out for his arrest.

After coming back to Michigan, he started selling drugs and was living in a tent in some park. His tent was burned down by some of the drug dealers that were retaliating against something he had done. I am not sure of the specifics but the same gang kidnapped him. As they were beating him inside the car, he barely escaped by trying to smash the windshield with his kicks. This distracted them and he ended up jumping out of the moving car.

He got back on his feet after selling more drugs and was living with a mutual friend I had known from the church.

Have you ever experienced what I like to call the prodigal son effect? It happens when you don't get in trouble and do the right thing, but all the attention goes to the problem child. All the money to help them get out of trouble. Too often parents focus on punishment or the problem child instead of rewarding the deserving child. My parents never had to tell me to do my homework and my teachers loved me, opposite for Cain. I was a very good kid but never received any praise from my parents.

During my final week of high school, Delilah invited me to a party that she had heard about. She told me that it was hosted by a friend of mine, but when we showed up, I realized that she had tricked me and it was my brother's place. I was so uncomfortable I ended up getting drunk for the first time. Being drunk helped and made the situation more tolerable. Sometime during the night, I remember turning down the music so Delilah, who was 'White Girl Wasted', could call us a ride. Cain got pissed that the music was turned down and tried to make me give him the remote. When I wouldn't, he grabbed me by my throat, lifted me up and slammed me into the wall. I dropped the remote and he let me go.

I went to find Delilah so we could leave. At that point I was ready to walk home. I found her passed out on the porch. A boy she was seeing at the time arrived to take us home. I spent the night at her house. We had a choir festival the next morning and I had gotten permission to spend the night.

My senior year, Joy was involved in a horrific car accident.

She was pulling out of a restaurant but couldn't see the oncoming traffic due to the cars blocking her view. She made the right hand turn when semi hit the driver's side where she was. She was rushed to the hospital with broken ribs, a broken left arm and a shattered femur. Joy was in the hospital for several weeks and I would visit her almost every single day. Her resilient spirit never complained about the hand that she was dealt.

Chapter 8

Marie had taken over as a love of my life, but soccer was still my passion. The sport's physical demands required me to run and work out daily during the off season. I not only had to juggle school and soccer training, but also earning money because my father was in and out of jobs. I would have to pay for my own dental or medical co-pays, soccer equipment and clothes. At the age of 12, I worked around the neighborhood shoveling snow. In the summer I would mow lawns or help with home repairs for money. My father would attend almost every single game in high school and even became involved with the announcing.

The Women's varsity coach was also the Men's varsity coach. My brother and I had the same coach. This led to my father and coach constantly butting heads. My father would confront my coach with his unsolicited opinions and I ended up paying for it by being placed on the wing or back as a defender when all I wanted to do was be a forward and score. During my high school career, I averaged around two point five goals per game. My sophomore and junior years, I earned all-conference, MVP, and numerous other awards. Other than the moments I spent with Marie; the soccer field was my only escape. I would forget everything but the incredible feeling I would get after scoring or playing an amazing game.

During the off season, I received a seasonal call from the Olympic development team coach trying to recruit me. Every season I had to give them the same response "Sorry Coach, my father won't let me play on Sunday." Not only was he keeping me from my dream of playing in the Olympics, my coaches hated him which ultimately negatively impacted my career. My father wouldn't let me play on the Olympic development team because they played on Sunday, and because I couldn't play on Sunday, I wasn't allowed on the team.

I lived for those Friday night home games when there would be a light mist, the stadium lights shining down, a decent sized crowd, the smell of grass, and the sound of the ball being passed back and forth. My senior year I was the captain and I wore the captain's band with pride on my right upper calf above my shin guard. Because my coach hated my father, he did nothing to help with college recruitment. My senior year, I was one of the first females in school history I knew of to make all state in soccer. My coach had called several local colleges to help with recruiting some of the other seniors on my team. He never made one single call for me.

After one game, I had a college coach come up to me who had been called by my coach to watch some of the other seniors play. She saw me play and didn't want the other players, she wanted me. She approached me after the game and told me she wanted me to play for her team. They already had tryouts, but my ability was apparent to her and she told me there was no need to try out. I was offered a full ride scholarship to play for a small Catholic college not far from where I lived. Even though I dreamed of playing for UCLA or North Carolina State, because I didn't have any help being recruited and my school wasn't very well known for their soccer athletes, this wasn't an option. I accepted the scholarship and started intense training for the upcoming season.

That summer, after my high school graduation, I played on a semiprofessional team which helped prepare me for a higher level of play with much better caliber players. My college team began practices before the beginning of the school year. I was one of five freshmen that were new to the team. I was the youngest on the team and the Men's soccer coach already knew who I was. He hired me the summer before my freshman year as a skills coach and I got to know several of the men that played for his team. I hadn't played with men in a while and I remember how much I missed it compared to the female teams. During some pickup games I played with them, I held my own with these guys, earning their respect. Both coaches had high hopes for me.

The Women's coach was a short, openly lesbian, soccer alumni with a fiery temper. The feeling of pride in my hard work somewhat replaced the love I never received from my family. It was a kind of love I had control over, and in a way it made me work so much harder.

On September 9th, 1999, I was in class when someone mentioned what an unlucky day it was going to be. I ignored the comment. I was pumped for my first home game and was beyond excited to be given a starting position. We were tied one to one with ten minutes left in the game. I was playing a phenomenal game. With three minutes to go my cleat hit a divot in the grass and I heard a snap. I felt excruciating pain in my knee and fell, unable to get up. I knew my career was over and I would never be the same again. I was heartbroken.

This was the first time in my soccer career where I didn't get up immediately so my father knew something was wrong. He didn't come to the sideline to see if I was all right. Instead, he waited in the van to take me home. Sitting in the front seat, my knee the size of a cantaloupe, I desperately needed words of encouragement. He never told me it would be all right or asked if I was OK. He just stated, "Well, it looks like you tore your ACL. You'll have surgery, but it looks like your career is over."

I hated him! I wanted to jump over that seat, strangle him and tell him what a monster he was. The physical pain was unlike anything I had ever experienced. Refusing to let him see my devastation, I turned my head to the window, unable to stop the tears. I was silent for the rest of the ride home. I felt like my soul was leaving my body and my hopes and dreams were going with it. My way out from this hell and the cult seemed to be closed forever.

I had not only torn my ACL; I tore every single ligament in my knee and shredded my meniscus. Several weeks later, I had an outpatient ACL graft surgery. On the ride home, the morphine was wearing off and I had only been sent home with Vicodin. For the next month I was in and out of consciousness from the extreme pain. The pain was so bad I could barely get up and go to the bathroom and went from screaming in pain and sobbing to vomiting the saltine crackers I had tried to eat. I would sob for hours and even asked my mother to go get me a gun to kill myself and I was dead serious. It was a pain I had never experienced for that long before. I had experienced extreme pain, but nothing that lasted weeks without letting up. I couldn't keep down anything and had lost a ton of weight.

The memories of being raped and the years of emotional abuse from my father came back like Satan, whispering in my ear. The first love of my life, soccer, and my only foreseeable way out, had been ripped from me and left my body mangled. My dreams of playing in the World Cup were crushed. I began physical therapy less than two months after my surgery and did everything I could to get back on the field. I followed every instruction from the physical therapist and even paid out of my own pocket for extra sessions. Every session would end with stretching and tearing apart the scar tissue. I would bury my face in the massage table, hiding the tears of extreme pain. There were several other grown men that were there for an ACL injury. I would hear them crying and cursing the therapist when they were getting stretched. My therapist told me that he had never seen anyone take so much pain and not complain like I did. I would leave every session with a puddle of sweat on the massage table from the pain.

When I was going through this intense physical therapy, my father bought me a gift. He had gotten me one of my favorite movies *Ever After* with Drew Barrymore, and he told me that I reminded him of Cinderella. I couldn't believe what I was hearing. Who was this man? Then he proceeded to tell me, "You are like Cinderella in the movie, ugly, homely looking and chunky. And the prince overlooked all of that because of her great personality. Your sister is the beautiful stepsister. All the men wanted her, but she was a bitch." I was a size four with thirteen percent body fat. Those words gave me the drive to defy him even more in my own way. Defy him by doing everything in my power to become the best version of myself I could be. I would never give him the satisfaction of seeing me fail.

Chapter 9

Tensions escalated between my parents and I. On several occasions I asked if I could spend the night with some of my teammates in the dorm, which they refused to allow. When I would get upset and get "an attitude", they would punish me by revoking my driving privileges and I would have to get a ride to class. When I approached my father about buying a car with money I had earned, he replied, "No, you don't need a car, you can use ours." When I informed him that I didn't want him to keep controlling me by taking the car away, he became angry and sternly told me, "If you don't want to use our car and you don't want to be controlled, then pack your bags and leave." I turned around, walked into my room, closed the door and packed two suitcases. You want to control me? Try to break me? Not anymore! I used every hurtful word, every beating, every humiliation to escape from that toxic place that was never my home.

Back in high school my senior year, I had met a girl named Charity. We hit it off right away. I called her and asked her if I could sleep on her couch. She lived in a two bedroom with another girl about a mile from my school. She didn't hesitate and came right away to take me away from that unhealthy, toxic environment. My only sad thought about leaving was Marie. She cried and begged me to stay. It absolutely crushed me, but I knew that in order to show her how to one day be strong, I had to be strong myself. Plus, the monster Cain wasn't living there anymore. I used the money I had saved for my car and helped with rent and groceries. For the first time in my life, I had freedom.

I didn't become an alcoholic, experiment with drugs, or become a promiscuous as my brothers had done. Instead, I ended up improving my grades, became financially independent, kept up rehabbing my knee and started the long process of finally being able to start healing. I made the Dean's list and my school invited all the parents to an appreciation lunch. My father ended up coming and the only words he said to me were "Nothing has changed. What you are doing is wrong and we will continue to keep you from your sister until you repent and come home." The only reason he came was to show off that he had a daughter on the Dean's list and to try and talk to the Men's soccer coach. The Men's coach was the head of a select soccer league my father was trying to get involved with.

When my sophomore year started, I returned to the team and struggled due to my knee and the amount of damage my injury had inflicted. My days involved school and an hour in the training room. Before every game and practice, I would arrive to the training room for twenty minutes of heat, a tearful stretching session where I would be white knuckled and writhing in pain, followed by a twenty-minute ice bath. Later in the season, I suffered a few broken ribs and had to spend even more time in the training room getting my ribs wrapped.

My father never came to any more of my games. It was an odd

feeling going from seeing him at every single game, that sense of feeling loved only when I played well, to having no one in the crowd that had come to see me play. Would it have been easier to quit, give up, run back to my family and have an easier life? Absolutely. Why do you think that so many people never find success? It is so much easier to give up when things become difficult. The world tried to take my first love, soccer. My brother raped me taking my innocence. My father tried to take away the belief that anyone could ever love me. My stubbornness refused to allow me to quit. I had come too far and overcome more by the time I was eighteen than most people experienced in a lifetime.

My other roommate, Sarah, had several friends in common with Cain, and I found out that he was homeless again. I wasn't aware at the time of his involvement stealing and selling drugs. I offered to allow him to sleep on my couch after asking my roommates. You may question why the hell I would allow this monster into my home? I had become a master of pushing my memories down so far, I began to believe the lies myself. In fact, I overly tried to act as if the opposite were true. In order to force myself to forget, I would do the opposite. Similar to when you are crying inside but you put a smile on your face. It helped me believe the lie even more. I told myself that him raping me never happened.

I even let him borrow my car! After letting him borrow it, I got in to drive to school the next day for a final. The car was dead because he left the lights on all night. I had to call a friend for a ride to school and almost missed my final. When I confronted him, all he said was "It's a piece of shit car. I thought the lights went off on their own."

Another time, he didn't like my sound system, so he tried to install a stereo, I later found out he had stolen. The first time I had ever been pulled over was his fault. He messed up the fuses and my tail lights were out. I received a repair and report ticket which he told me he would take care of if I allowed him to use my car when I was gone on spring break.

When I returned from spring break, my car was gone and so was Cain. After making a few calls, I found out that my car was impounded. Cain had blown a tire on the freeway and when he was trying to change the tire, a police officer stopped to help. The officer ran Cain's information and Cain had an arrest warrant. Not only was my car impounded and needed a new tire, there was a major gash in the hood and the taillight he had promised to fix was still out. I had to pay to get the car out of impound, a new tire, get the taillights fixed, and had to pay the late fee for the ticket.

Years down the road, I discovered that Cain had used my car as a getaway vehicle to rob vets for ketamine. His friends ended up getting caught and going to prison, but somehow, he got away with it as he always did. He never apologized even after he got out of jail and I finally put my foot down and told him he couldn't stay with me anymore.

I was fighting depression from the abuse, not being able to see Marie, and my soccer career was falling apart. I was 19 years old and I still had never kissed a boy. I started to become more and more depressed with my life. I was having constant flashbacks and nightmares of what my brother had done. The words of my father, "you're fat and homely looking. You can't eat that. You'll never find a man. You sure didn't get the looks in the family." Those words haunted me. Every item of food I ate, I hated myself for it. It began where I would eat too much, which felt good going down, but I would feel sick and guilty right away. After these moments of weakness, I would make myself vomit. I made every excuse under the sun. Dancers do it. I don't do it every day. What's worse? Being fat or getting sick? The only thing I had ever been good at, playing soccer, was taken away from me. The only thing I felt I had remaining was my athletic body. Due to my knee injury and the increase in alcohol consumption, I had put on a few pounds. I look back at the photos now and I wish I had that body. Six pack, toned legs, thirteen percent body fat... But all I saw was a fat, unattractive body, an ugly face, and someone no man found attractive.

During my third soccer season I was still recovering from my knee injury. I knew that I would never play the same again. I was still a great player, but it was obvious I wouldn't go much further in my soccer career, my knee was just too badly damaged. My coach had given up on me and it was apparent she developed a strong dislike for me. She had become the coach of my former high school and ended up coaching my sister Jezebel. My father and her constantly butted heads and he would call her a butch dike to her face. She would take out her dislike for him on me and cut my playing time drastically, despite me being tied with the lead goal scorer on our team. During our homecoming game, we were down one to zero and my coach finally put me in. I ended up scoring a few minutes after, but she subbed me out right after. She subbed me in during the second half with ten minutes left in the game. We were tied one to one and I scored the winning goal.

The university awarded one male and female athlete with the honor of being Athlete of the Month. There would be an article featuring that athlete in the school paper. The athlete would receive a plaque and would be invited to dinner with the dean. The previous season, one of our top players had made Athlete of the Month and my coach had made a huge deal about it. She had given a speech to us all and even went and purchased a new soccer bag with the player's name and number stitched in it. A week after the homecoming game where I scored the winning goal, I received a phone call from the dean congratulating me on being selected for Athlete of the Month. I had a full-page article in our paper. All the girls on the team came and congratulated me on all my hard work. When we are all gathered for a team meeting prior to the game, one of the girls in the team asked the coach if she knew that I had made Athlete of the Month. My coach responded, "There is no I in team" and went back to discussing game strategy. I knew at that moment my career was done at that school.

Towards the end of the school year, I was cramming for finals and had been invited by a classmate to study. The study session turned into drinks and my friend's roommate, who I had a thing for, had just broken up with his girlfriend and every girl on campus was talking about it. He was a very attractive basketball player, and when he made a move, I was shocked. My first kiss ended up being a drunken make out session, a and a few inexperienced teeth bumps.

When he started to pull off my shorts, I asked him to stop and he got pissed. I told him I wasn't ready and he sat up and put his shirt on. It was around 3:00 a.m. and I was still too drunk to drive home. He then asked me to leave because he was trying to get back with his girlfriend and he didn't want anyone finding out about me. He said his girlfriend might be coming in the morning to get some of her things so I needed to leave. He didn't even bother walking me out. I didn't know what to do so I went out to the front porch and sat on their couch. I curled up in a ball, freezing my ass off in the middle of December, snow on the ground, and I cried myself to sleep this moment.

My first kiss, him *making* me leave, reinforced my belief that men only wanted one thing for me. Did I give up all hope and become a whore or swear off men altogether? My past experiences with men would have given me every reason to do so. What did they know? They chose girls that spent hours in the mirror *instead* of working on improving what was in their head or their heart. They spent more time picking out clothes and on their looks. Most people would have never been able to endure the bullshit I had and still come out on top.

Because I had lost my soccer scholarship my junior year, I couldn't afford to keep going to school, so I dropped out. I got a job as a server at an Italian fine dining restaurant. I decided to save up my money and move back to my hometown, San Diego.

On the day I was to leave and start a new life in California, my father called and asked me to lunch. I sat and listen to him go on and on about what a mistake I was making. He told me that every good thing that had happened to me, my full-ride, soccer skills, dean's list grades, happened because I obeyed and listen to him and followed God's law. "Look what happened to your knee and your soccer career when you disobeyed me. If you go to California against my will, you will fail. You will be miserable and come back repentant of your ways. I wish you had never been born!" Without another word, he stood up, leaving his uneaten meal and walked out.

Chapter 10

After moving in with my maternal grandmother, I found a job at Starbucks and met a good friend named Jeff. Finally, I not only lived in a place with someone that loved me, but I had freedom and friends. A few months after arriving back home to San Diego, my family decided to come out for a visit. There was a massive family argument due to my relatives standing up to my parents for the first time about how badly they treated me. In the end, my grandma kicked them out and when they left to go back to Michigan, Jezebel decided to give up college and stay in California. My parents were still using Marie to control and punish me. They wouldn't let me speak to her. Before they left, she clung to me, crying and begging my parents to let her stay with me. My mother came and ripped her out of my arms. It felt as if someone was legally kidnapping my child.

In August, Delilah decided to cash in on a free place to stay in San Diego and came out for a visit. Being there for my 21st birthday was just a bonus. One of the nights Delilah was there, Jeff invited me over and told me to bring my sister and friend. When I hung out with Jeff and the other guys, we didn't do a lot of drinking. That night, however, Delilah and Jezebel busted out the alcohol and things started to get crazy. I didn't drink because I was driving and I had to work early the next morning. Jezebel was throwing herself at all the guys and talking about how hot she was. Delilah was flirting with everyone as well. The last straw was when I looked over to see Delilah and Jezebel making out to impress the guys. I told the girls I was leaving, but they wanted to stay. I left them there doing shots off each other. After I left, Jezebel gave all of the guys there a blow job.

On my 21st birthday, without asking, Jezebel through a party at my grandma's house. She invited a guy she had been dating for a few months and recently dumped. He only came because he was friends with me. After making out with another guy right in front of him, she went and took 21 shots of Bacardi. She bragged that she could drink more than me and she would take the 21 shots for my birthday for me. After finishing the shots, she passed out in her room and vomited on herself. I had to pick her up, carry her to the shower, clean her up, change her, and make sure she didn't have alcohol poisoning.

The next few weeks, Jezebel was out of control. Several nights at three o'clock in the morning, my grandma would come knock on my door and ask if Jezebel was alright. She didn't bother to call and my grandma was always worried about her. After a few weeks of this, my grandma sat us down and told us that living there wasn't going to work out. There had never been any issues until Jezebel arrived. I loved spending time with my grandma!

Jezebel was like a hurricane that comes and goes, destroying everything in her path. A second cousin of ours from Montana wanted to move to San Diego, so the three of us got a two-bedroom apartment a block from the beach. As much as I didn't want to live with Jezebel, I still felt responsible for her. Plus, I couldn't afford living alone. My cousin ended up moving back home and Charity decided to come and take her place. I was so excited to live with her again. In the few months we had lived there, Jezebel had already gained a massive reputation of being the apartment whore. We lived in an apartment complex that consisted mainly of college students.

Jezebel thrived on attention. She would come out and sit on guys laps without an invitation, grab their asses and disappear into their apartment. When she was drinking, she was even worse and she made sure to loudly tell everyone around that she was a virgin. One night I heard a group of guys laughing after she made that comment and I asked them why. They told me that she slept with nearly everyone in the complex and she had the loosest pussy they had ever felt. I actually was a virgin and never had a boyfriend. Well, I considered myself a virgin because I wanted to believe that losing it requires the sex to be consensual.

I met a guy through a work friend and we hit it off. He asked me for my number and called me a few days later asking me out. He took me to dinner and afterwards we went to a pool hall. He was a successful engineer and we had great conversation. We dated for a few weeks, but I wanted to take it very slowly. One day he brought lunch to my work at Starbucks and while we were sitting out front eating, Jezebel, who worked at Sprint at the time in the same shopping center, showed up to get free coffee. Even though I didn't want to, I had to introduce her because she literally sat down at the table interrupting our date. She loved inserting herself into situations where she wasn't invited. When my break ended and I had to go back to work, she stayed outside for another ten minutes talking to my date. After my date came in to say goodbye, Jezebel came in to get her Frappuccino and told me that she was so happy for me and how hot he was.

After a long day of work, I returned home ready to relax. Sitting on my couch with a glass of wine was the guy I was dating. I was surprised and annoyed. I knew I didn't invite him and only one person could have. Jezebel came stumbling out of the kitchen with a full glass of red wine. "Oh, look who I invited" she slurred. I sat down in the three-seater couch next to him. Jezebel came over and didn't sit in the open seat, she squeezed her way in between us, spilling wine on my work pants, which she found hilarious. When I came back into the room after changing, she was standing up, holding out her hand and asking him to give her a back massage. It took everything in me not to smash her face into the wall. To cool off, I went for a walk and he came out after me asking if I was all right. He told me he wasn't expecting her to flirt like that, but he thought she was hot. I told him I never wanted to see him again and that he needed to leave before I punched him in the face.

After a long walk on the beach, I returned to an empty apartment and went to bed. When I woke up the next morning at four o'clock in the morning for an opening shift, I went to get dressed and couldn't find my work pants. I knew I had washed and folded them the previous night in preparation for work. I also knew right away where they were. Since she was little Jezebel would take clothes from my closet no matter how many times, I would tell her to ask first.

I knocked on her door and entered after there was no response. I spotted my work pants crumpled on the floor next to her bed where her and my date were both laying naked together. I slammed the door so hard it shook the apartment. I confronted her when I got home and she told me they didn't do anything and they had just fallen asleep. They went out several more times until she got bored and ended up telling me that he was an asshole. She also felt the need to tell me that I should be thankful that she saved me from that.

I wasn't happy with my living situation and I needed a change. After coming up with a plan to move to London, I bought a scooter and put my car up for sale. I was going to ship my belongings to England and use the money I got for my car to get settled and find work. I had canceled my insurance because I wasn't driving it and put it up for sale.

It was the day before Valentine's Day and Jezebel and I were planning on having a girl's night with dinner and movies. I couldn't get the groceries on my scooter, so I took my car. On my way back from the grocery store, car filled with cold products, my car died going uphill, during rush hour, on a two-way road, with no shoulder. I got out and started calling everyone I knew. No one picked up, including Jezebel. So, I started walking the four miles home. Halfway up the hill, it started raining and I was soaked by the time I got home.

As soon as I walked in, Jezebel arrived and I told her what had happened. I asked her if she could take me to get the groceries for our Valentine's dinner so they wouldn't melt. She got irritated, telling me that she was in a hurry to take her car to my friend Patrick's house so he could change her oil for her. Patrick was a mechanic and I had a thing for him since the day I met him around a year prior. She wouldn't even let me change my clothes. When we arrived to where my car was parked, she stayed in the car and I got out to get the groceries. Instead of getting out to help me, she sat in the car screaming at me that if her car got hit, I would have to pay for it. On the way to Patrick's house, I said, "you know, I have a thing for Patrick, right? I really like him." She responded, "Why? He's so skinny and he's a mechanic."

I found out that Patrick had his car stolen that day, so in order to cheer him up, I invited him over and we could both be miserable car owners together. As soon as we got home, Jezebel immediately started drinking and was all over Patrick. When she pulled the same massage request as before, I walked down the street to the bar before I did something I would possibly regret. I woke up the next morning and was in the kitchen when Patrick snuck out of her room in his boxers, snatching up his clothes, and making his escape as quickly as he could.

Charity had moved back to Michigan and we had a male roommate who I worked with at Starbucks. He knocked on my door and asked me if I was all right. I told him no. I thought he was referring to my car, which I had towed and parked back in the garage. He asked me if I had seen my car and I told him "yes, the transmission went out and I had to have it towed." He responded "no. I mean, did you see it today?" I felt sick. I looked up to the sky before I walked out the door making sure a bomb wasn't going to drop on my head. All four windows were smashed, the car seats were torn up, and the stereo was ripped out. I called the police who didn't do anything and received an estimate for my transmission, which was more than the car was even worth.

Jezebel came into my room and saw me crying and asked me what was wrong. I told her I couldn't believe what she had done. She responded, "It's not my fault. I'm more attractive than you and guys like me more." She then proceeded to tell me she wasn't going to make our Valentine's dinner because she was going on a date with one of the neighbors. I want to go back and punch myself in the face. What the hell was wrong with me? This stupid whore just had sex with two guys she knew I cared about, treated me like shit for most of my life, and had the nerve to tell me it was because she was more attractive. Why? Why did I allow people to treat me this way? Back then I saw it as me being strong and able to handle whatever happened to me without changing who I was. I loved my heart, the way I never let anything break me, and my resilient spirit. Looking back, I would slap some sense into that naive girl, teach her to stand up for herself and never let anyone hurt her again.

Wanting a better career than Starbucks, I went and applied for a job at a preschool. I ended up moving up quickly and after a year, I became an associate pre-kindergarten teacher. I became friends with the lead teacher Amanda and I loved my working with the kids. During this time, Jezebel got back in touch with a former boyfriend that had broken up with her. He joined the Marines and was stationed in Hawaii. He asked her to come and visit him, which she did, and she never came back.

My grandmother had also moved away and a few months later, she ended up in the hospital with a rare blood disease. My relatives asked me to come to the hospital to say goodbye. Because he wasn't going to live through the night. I didn't cry when I saw how much her health had declined. She had lost around 15 pounds and for her small body, that was significant and I hardly recognized her. My cousins, aunts and uncles were all there as well. My aunts and cousins were all crying. I kissed her forehead, held her hand and told her, "You are my hero and I love you. Tell Grandpa hi for me." I didn't cry because I was happy that she wasn't going to suffer and I knew how unhappy she had been since my grandpa died.

Due to the family drama when my relatives asked my parents to leave, there was a great deal of strain between them. They had informed my mother before and after my grandmother's death. My mother told me that she wasn't going to be coming to the funeral due to how they treated my father. No one had any issues with my mother, it was my father they disliked. My parents blamed me for what happened and I don't think my mother ever got over losing her mom and blamed that on me as well. I was relieved that she wasn't going to come.

I started playing soccer on an outdoor Women's league and became friends with two of the girls I had met. My knee still gave me major problems, but I really needed soccer in my life. One of the women was a Marine and the other Navy. I enjoyed hearing all their stories about their military careers. The Marine who didn't play soccer but came to help coach, invited me to numerous barbecues and introduced me to the guys she worked with.

Chapter 11

On Thanksgiving, my new roommate Liz invited me to go with her to her family's house in Arizona. She had also invited a childhood friend named Michael. He was a tall, handsome, white, Marine grunt with an intriguing past and a great smile. There was something about him that I was drawn to. Perhaps it was the fact that he was a ballroom dance instructor and a machine gunner. It reminded me of my two sides. The night before Thanksgiving, Michael asked me to join him for a ride on one of the family quads. After riding around for about a half an hour, he stopped and we sat there talking. As we looked out over the Arizona desert, I laid my head on his back, sitting behind him, listening to him talk about his life.

After our mini vacation was over, we got home late and Michael slept over. It was the first time I had ever slept next to a man that didn't ask me to leave. At one point during the night, he gently held my face and kissed me. A great first kiss that was passionate just enough without being too much to scare me off. The next few weeks, Michael called and messaged me almost daily.

A year before I met Michael, Jacob, who had ended up meeting a German girl while stationed there, told me he was getting married. We had grown a little closer over letters and mix tapes that he would send me. When he told my family he was getting married, the only question they had was, "is she a Christian?" She was actually Catholic who, according to my parents, are all going to hell. Jacob and his fiancée came to California to get married where they knew they had family that would support them. Because of how my parents treated my brother and his new wife, I wrote them a letter and told them not to contact me anymore and what they were doing was wrong. It would be a year before we spoke again.

One evening I told Michael I wasn't feeling well and I wasn't going to be able to go visit him. He ended up borrowing a car, drove over an hour, and surprised me with chicken soup and flowers. For the first time. I allowed someone to go down on me and even though it felt incredible, I had tears running down my face. I was so angry that I couldn't fully enjoy this moment due to the flashbacks running through my head. Michael held me all night running his hands through my hair. It was such an unfamiliar and comforting feeling to be held like that. In the morning I woke up and rolled over. He had this look on his face that I had never seen before. He said, "Babe, I think I'm falling in love with you." I was speechless. I never thought anyone would ever tell me that and I wasn't sure how I felt. I asked him if it would be OK if I told him when I was ready. I was falling for him, but I was dreading knowing that he was leaving in a week to go back home after he got out of the Marine Corps.

In November I called to wish Jezebel a happy birthday. Even after everything she put me through, she was still my sister. She excitedly told me that she just got engaged. I knew of a guy that she had been dating at a whitewater rafting job she had known for a few months, so I thought it was that guy. She told me it was someone else she had met in September. He was a pastor and former Marine captain. She went on to tell me how he proposed. Her fiancé Levite, asked her to take a walk with him and took her to a tree that he had carved WYMM (will you marry me) and gave her a sapphire ring. She told me that he had bought this ring six years ago, knowing one day he would give it to his wife. He also bought a pair of shoes for his future wife during the same time, without even knowing her shoes eyes. I guess he had been shopping for a wife with the right size feet.

Jezebel told me after she said yes, he took her back to his apartment and washed her feet. Levite told her, "Just as Jesus washed his disciples' feet. So I will wash yours." I had no *idea* what to say. I was trying so hard not to laugh hysterically. They were getting married in December and asked me to be the maid of honor. I didn't want to go, but I told her I would. Once again, why the hell did I say yes? Why did I constantly forgive her and allow her to treat me like she did as if nothing happened? The main reason I said yes was because I wanted to see Marie. When I was telling Michael about how nervous I was to go, he offered to go with me. Things were happening so quickly. Was I really falling in love with him too, or was it just a new and incredible feeling?

On the day of the wedding, Michael and I arrived at the church. I was nervous for so many reasons. When I saw Marie, I wanted to put her in my suitcase and take her back with me. After giving me a huge hug, she started dragging me through the church showing me everything. I saw my younger brother John talking with a man in his dress blues and recognized him from the pictures Jezebel sent me. I walked over. "You must be Levite. Welcome to the family", I said going in for a hug. He stuck out his hand for a handshake instead. I ignored his rude gesture and introduced myself. "Oh, you're that sister", he said when I told him that I was from California. From this moment on, every single time I spoke to this man or had anything to do with him, he always did his best to insult me. My sister had found someone exactly like my father.

I found Jezebel in a back room doing her hair. I made sure that Michael was all right and had Marie show him around. My heart melted, seeing her grab his hand and drag him down the hall. Jezebel was wearing a plane, hippie-style, cream colored wedding dress with an empire waist and no shoes. Why would you not wear shoes if you are getting married in a church? This was so unlike her. We grew up talking about weddings and she always wanted a big wedding in a church with a huge white flowing dress and sparkly shoes. I, however, said I wanted to have a wedding on a beach, with bare feet, a simple dress, and all my friends could come camp out and bring a dish because who the heck would I want to pay for a caterer on your own wedding?

I had also picked a very unusual song. It's an instrumental Irish song on the Coors album at the very end. The only people that knew about the song were Jezebel and my Cousins because I played it for them numerous times. It was my wedding song and Jezebel knew it. As we were standing to walk down the aisle, my song, MY WEDDING SONG started playing! I don't know why anything surprised me at that point. I turned and looked at her. "You took my song?" I was fighting back tears of rage. She stammered and replied, "No Levite chose the song." You Lying Whore!

Before leaving, Michael and I were standing, talking to the married couple. Levite asked what Michael did and Michael told him that he was a Sergeant in the Marine Corps. Levite looked down on anyone that wasn't an officer. He smiled and looked at me and said, "Oh, I get it now. You're one of those girls." He was referring to the numerous women that go after Marines for their paycheck and medical. I wanted to hit him, but Michael pulled me away and we left.

A few weeks after returning from Michigan, Michael moved back home. I wanted so badly to make it work between us, but he was going to school in Illinois. They had much better benefits that extend beyond the GI Bill. He was also helping raise his nephew because his sister was a single mother in the Navy. I was looking into jobs in his area and even apartments. Despite my hatred for the cold weather, we talked daily on the phone, but it had started becoming less and less due to his added responsibilities, and as I would soon find out, lack of interest.

To distract me from missing Michael, I joined a coed indoor soccer team that Liz told me about. One player in particular caught my eye. He was a bald, white, muscular, attractive Marine named Charles. I overheard that he was married, but getting divorced. He invited us to go to Mission Beach that weekend and ride his jet skis. I was still wrapped up in the growing distance and lack of messages from Michael. I spent most of the day on the beach with my phone wishing he would call. Yes, I used to be that girl waiting on a guy. Charles came over after getting off the jet ski and asked me if I wanted a turn. I told him I was waiting for my boyfriend to call. He laughed and he told me not to wait too long and to get out and have fun. I took what he said to heart and went for a ride.

The messages and phone calls from Michael continued to decrease, and I was worried that he was doubting I would wait for him. So, I increased my efforts to relocate, which only intensified the distance between us. I hadn't yet learned that smothering the guy would do the opposite and he ended up pushing me away. He told me he didn't want me to give up everything I had in California for him. Around the six-month time of being together, he came to visit. Michael had made plans to go visit a buddy and his wife that were still in the Marine Corps. Wanting to spend more time with him I foolishly invited myself. On the drive up I asked him what was going on and didn't fall for his response that nothing was wrong. He ended up telling me that everything he used to love about me he now hated and that he was never in love with me. I sat through a night with his friends, doing everything in my power to not cry or show that anything was wrong. I felt numb.

On the hour ride home, he didn't say a word to me. As soon as we walked in the door, I came unglued. Every fucked-up thing a man had ever done to me came to surface and the floodgates opened. I became that drama queen sobbing while burning our photos. As I was lying in bed sobbing, Michael finally came in, the Michael I knew. He held me as I cried. I cried for the years of abuse, what my brother did and for the twenty-three years of holding it all in. I broke down and told Michael, the first person I ever told, what my brother had done to me. I had lied to myself and everyone I knew for all of those years. I am not sure if I told him because I wanted him to feel so bad that he would stay, or if I knew that this moment would never come again. He kissed my forehead, telling me how sorry he was and held me as I cried myself to sleep.

The next morning, I woke up and he was gone. He left on an early flight two days early and I never saw him again. I went to my indoor game that night and one of the girls on the team asked me how my weekend was. I responded, "Not so great. I got dumped." Charles overheard and in a smart-ass way responded, "Well, that sucks." I lashed back "Damn, why don't you kick me when I'm down? That's fucked up." He immediately felt bad. "I didn't mean it like that", he said, stumbling on his words. I realized he wasn't being mean and we dropped it.

I want to take a moment and talk about the lifelong damage that child sexual abuse has, especially in regards to relationships. When a child is sexually assaulted, there are lasting effects that impact all aspects of their life into adulthood. As you can see, I was extremely immature when it came to relationships. The fear and anxiety that came from childhood abuse impacted this relationship and my future relationships as well. That's why I find it so frustrating when judges hand out such light sentences to rapists. They don't understand the impact that this has on you for the rest of your life. Every first kiss, every first hug, every first intimate encounter, you have flashbacks. It destroys the beauty, the purity and the love between two people. Two consenting people that care about each other. Even though this relationship ended in not the most pleasant manner, I still can take something positive out of it and be grateful for what I learned out of the relationship. It was a huge turning point in my life! For the first time I was actually able to be honest with myself and finally tell the truth about what my brother had done to me. And for that I will forever be grateful.

Chapter 12

I was confused, hurt, angry and unsure how to deal with a breakup. I had never had to deal with someone saying they loved me, feeling like they truly did, and then losing it. Not only losing it, but for them to tell me that they never loved me and the things they loved about me, they actually hated.

Liz and my other roommates took me to Mexico for a day trip to cheer me up. It helped take my mind off things and I drank enough tequila to help numb my mind. On our way back from Mexico, I received a phone call from an unknown number. It was Charles. He had gotten my number from the indoor soccer roster and was asking what I was up to. He and some friends ended up meeting us at our house when we got back. I had been drinking all day and was very drunk. Charles was also very intoxicated. He ended up apologizing for the comments he had made, but he was happy that I was now single. He went on to tell me that he was almost divorced and was very attracted to me. I was too drunk to grasp the situation and I was surprised because I didn't think he liked me. I was also attracted to him, but I still had feelings for Michael.

The next morning, we all had breakfast and before he left, Charles asked me to go to a movie. I was still hesitant, but I also knew I needed to move on. Plus, it made me feel good that I had an attractive option just a few days after being dumped. It was a foreign feeling to have men attracted to me. I told Charles I wanted to but wasn't ready for a relationship. After hanging out during group events, he invited just me to a baseball game. After a couple beers, he gathered enough courage and asked if he could kiss me. By this time, I had started to let down my walls and let him kiss me. After that first kiss, I was smitten. I fought my feelings for him and would constantly tell him that I didn't want anything serious. But truthfully, I was falling for him. He was relentless and soon we were inseparable.

When we weren't working, we spent most of our free time together. He made me feel sexy, beautiful and unleashed a sexual passion I had never had with Michael. His obvious lust for my body, combined with this apparent caring for me, helped me not only overcome the breakup with Michael but even more incredibly, my distrust of men. I thought that he would be the only one that truly loved me, start a family with me and be the first I allowed to have sex with me. I was still confused about my beliefs on sex and was still waiting.

Even though we didn't have sex, we decided to spice things up a bit in the bedroom. Charles took me to Hustler and bought me my first vibrator. It gave me my first orgasm and Charles loved using it on me. I had never felt anything like it before, I thought maybe I was damaged goods. Despite his best effort, Charles could never make me climax. My lack of ability to climax with my boyfriend had a lot to do with the mental damage from my first sexual experience being with my brother.

Sexual abusers are accountable for much more than the physical act. They can cause irreparable damage that follows you for the rest of your life. They can take away your ability to enjoy a healthy sex life with a partner of your choice. They can leave such scars that render you unable to climax with someone you love. I hated my brother for what he had done to me, and I was reminded every night by the look on my boyfriend's face when he felt that he wasn't a good enough lover.

I was in such a great place mentally, physically and emotionally for one of the first times in my life. Finally, I had enough courage to confront my brother and tell my family what had happened. I will be forever grateful to Charles for that. I still wasn't strong enough to do it over the phone, so I wrote my brother a letter. I wrote one to him and one to his wife. I had heard that they were having problems.

Years later, she told me that he ended up in jail twice for domestic violence. He even knocked her out one night while pregnant with their daughter. Due to her pregnancy, my parents forced him to marry her if he wanted any help from them at all. I was concerned for her because I knew how manipulative my brother could be. I wrote her a letter because I knew they had a daughter together and I was concerned for her safety when she got older. I don't know why I was concerned at the time because I had no knowledge of anyone else who he had abused, but I still had this uneasy feeling.

After sending the letter. I waited several days and then called my mother. I told her over the phone about what Cain had done to me. At first, she cried, but then she started questioning me. Why didn't you say anything? What exactly happened? Are you sure? Maybe you just made it up. How long did it go on? I had only talked about the rape with three people before her, Michael, Charles and my friend Amanda. I wasn't ready to get into details, especially with my mother. Our sex talk happened when I was around sixteen, after I had been raped and had already seen videos and knew the basics of sex. She told me that women do not enjoy sex until they are around 35 and only enjoyed a little. Sex is a duty toward your husband and not something you enjoy. Try explaining to your Bible thumping mother that hated sex about how your own brother went down on you and raped you. Maybe it was just because of the vagueness of my information or perhaps the truth was just too much for her to handle, but nothing ever happened after I told her. It went back to the same as it was before. As if I had never told her.

After being let go from my kindergarten teaching job, I was not happy and I needed a better career path than the meager salary of a teacher. They had let me go after I refused to hide the fact that the school was going to put a cell phone tower inside the playground disguised as a cross. They told us we couldn't tell the parents and I had several pregnant mothers in my class. I refused to keep my mouth shut and I was fired for it.

I dreamed of having a career as an FBI agent, but I would need to finish up my bachelor's degree to do that. I couldn't afford to have my own apartment, let alone travel or returned to school. I began exploring my options. I had always wanted to join the military, but my full-ride to play soccer in college kept me from joining. I talked to Charles about joining the Marine Corps. He took me to a recruiting office and I began the process. Charles had mixed feelings about me joining because he knew what the Marine Corps was like and what the men in it were like. He knew that I could be stationed anywhere and we even talked about the differences in rank and the problems that may cause. However, he was supportive in whatever choice I made, but I still felt that tension.

I tried to talk to him one night to see what was going on with him because I felt a shift between us. I told him I was in love with him and wanted badly for him to open up and talk to me about what he was thinking. He finally gave me an answer. "What do you want to hear? That my wife ripped out my heart and I care more about you than I ever cared about her. I can't go through that again." I told him I loved him and I would give him space. That I would prove to him that I wasn't like her. I never would hurt him like she did and would never cheat on him. I asked if it was because we hadn't had sex yet, and I even told him that I was ready. He said it had nothing to do with that and he only wanted to cross that line when I was ready, not feeling like he pushed me over it. The lengths we will go for people we love. If I could tell myself anything with the knowledge I now have, it would be: if he loves you, none of this would matter. Don't change your beliefs, your morals, or anything else to keep a person that doesn't want you. To love yourself and let them love you if they choose to.

I had not officially signed any papers, but I had a possible date for boot camp, which is around two months away. Charles gave me advice on how to train for the physical test and I began working out every day at his gym before he came home from work. Then

I would have dinner ready and spend the evening with him. On football Sunday, I loved to cook for him and his friends would come over. There were several times we would get off work at the same time and we would go run together. I was nervous about joining, but excited at the same time.

In October, I was feeling the pressure of finances as I had taken a massive pay cut when I got fired. Charles offered to let me stay with him until I left for boot camp. I was hesitant, but not much would change as we almost were already living together. I moved out of Liz's house and in with Charles. I asked Liz if I could keep most of my stuff in boxes in her garage and she didn't mind. I only brought my work clothes and other necessities and tried my best to not get in the way or make him feel overwhelmed.

After I moved in, we went to a house party put on by some of his coworkers I didn't know. During the ride over I knew something was wrong. I put on my game face and acted like everything was fine. We were all drinking and I was trying to talk to some of the wives at the party, but I just didn't fit in. Around two hours into the party, I couldn't find Charles anywhere and his truck was gone. I asked around and found out that he had gone to pick up some people. I was more upset that he drove after drinking and was worried about him. He was gone for almost an hour and when I called him, he didn't pick up his phone.

I was sitting by myself watching the beer pong game, trying to distract my thoughts when Charles finally walked in with a blond female. He told me she needed a ride and he was just being nice.

I was frustrated, hurt, scared and angry. What did I do to deserve this? I was nothing like his ex. I would never cheat on him. I gave him everything a man wanted minus the sex, but I made sure he was always satisfied.

I went outside to gather my thoughts and one of his friends came out to see if I was all right. He told me that I didn't deserve to be treated like that, which made me realize how obvious Charles attitude and demeanor had changed towards me. I drank more to numb my mind that was running a mile a minute. I even went in and introduced myself to the girl and asked Charles to be my partner for the next beer pong game. I was sitting in the kitchen talking with one of the wives when I saw Charles start playing beer pong with the girl he had picked up. I walked outside and asked him "I thought we were going to be partners." He responded "but she doesn't know anyone." I wanted to tell him that I didn't know anyone either, and I was his damn girlfriend. Instead of causing a drunk scene, I retreated to another room and fell asleep crying on some stranger's couch.

We didn't say much on the ride home the next morning. It was Halloween and we had made plans to pass out candy together. He left me at the apartment telling me had to go help out a friend move. I went and bought candy and got dressed up excited about spending my favorite holiday with him. He never came back. I messaged him to see when he was coming back to hand out candy. He told me that he was going to stay at his friend's house and pass out candy there. I spent the night by myself crying and devastated, knowing it was over, but not wanting to admit it.

The next morning, Charles came home and told me he couldn't do it anymore and asked me to move out. It had been less than five days. Less than five days since I moved in and he wanted me out. I had a meltdown and was sobbing while packing up my car. When he offered to help me pack, I coldly told him to fuck off in between gasping sobs. I wouldn't let him ease his conscience by helping me. I called Liz and asked her if I could move back in. My room had been rented out, but the couch was still available.

He stood outside my car as I was getting ready to drive away, asking me not to drive and to calm down. When will men ever realize telling a woman to calm down has the opposite effect. It is like telling someone that what their feeling is wrong and it downplays the pain they put you through! I told him that he no longer had any right to ask me for anything and I drove away. To make things even more painful, he had asked me to the Marine Corps ball months before. I had already bought a beautiful dress and I was so excited to go. I asked our mutual friend Jenna to come over on the night of the ball to watch movies or maybe go out. I didn't want to be alone that night. She said yes but last minute she canceled, telling me she didn't feel good and was going to bed early. I spent the night crying and pathetically checking MySpace to see any pictures he posted. The next day at work, I went to leave a message on Jenna's page.

My heart was crushed. She had posted photos of the Marine Corps ball. She had gone as Charles date. Every picture of them was like salt in an open wound. I felt betrayed, angry and crushed. I held back the tears of rage and continued to work. After I calmed down, I confronted her about what she had done. Just when I had been doing so well and started standing up for myself, I regressed. I was afraid that my belief that no one would ever love me was true and that I would end up alone. I was willing to allow people to hurt me because I was terrified my worst fears were coming true.

The next week, in hopes of getting Charles back, I told my recruiter that I had a change of heart and was going to put off joining. I let Charles know and he only told me to do what was best for me. My thought process was that me joining was the issue and maybe if he saw what I was willing to give that up, he would give me another chance. What the hell was I thinking? Give me another chance. I had done nothing but love him, show him I cared and be the best possible partner I could be. Can I please go back and slap myself?

Weeks went by and I kept trying and only succeeded in pushing him away. Jenna had apologized about lying to me and going with Charles to the ball. She told me that she felt bad that he was going alone so when he asked her, she agreed. She lied to me because she didn't want to hurt me. Like a pathetic fool I forgave her. She invited me to her birthday party she was having at Chili's. I showed up early to help her set up and was so glad to be out of the house and distracted from my depressed mood.

As I was sitting at the table waiting for my food to arrive, I heard an all too familiar voice. I froze, scared to turn around. Eventually I did, only to see Charles walking in with his arm around the waist of a busty, chunky blond who disturbingly resembled his ex-wife. My mind automatically started judging myself. Is that why he broke up with me? Was he not attracted to me? For so long my thought process was extremely self-deprecating and destructive. My progress and healing had gone backwards and was unbelievably difficult when I was surrounded by selfish people that only used me and tossed me aside after I had served my purpose, I glared at Jenna, "I can't believe you didn't tell me he was coming." She had even known he was bringing a date. She shrugged, her blond hair whipping around as she turned away to attend to her guests. I wanted to grab her by the throat and slam her face into the wall. I was done with her. Finally, she had pushed me too far, even too far from my over forgiving, passive nature.

I got up and walked to the bathroom. I had to pass Charles on the way there and he whispered in my ear that he had gotten my messages and how good I looked. His familiar smell, that hand that used to hold me and make me feel safe, the closeness of those lips that used to passionately kiss me, made the tears start to come. I ignored his comment and fled to the bathroom. After regaining my composure, I returned to the table and forced myself to eat a few chips even though I had lost my appetite. Charles and his new lady were sitting directly across from me and she was all over him. Why did I allow this torture to continue? Part of me wanted to show him I could *care* less about him with this new chick, but the other part of me didn't want to allow anyone to change the loving and compassionate person I was.

After around five minutes, I couldn't take it any longer. I placed a twenty-dollar bill on the table to pay for my drink and chips. I didn't feel like waiting around for the change. Jenna came running out to apologize and I told her to fuck off. God, It felt so good to stand up for myself and show her that I was done with her abuse. I never spoke to her again, despite her continued efforts.

Chapter 13

One evening, Joy's mother called to let me know that Joy had been diagnosed with multiple sclerosis. I was heartbroken and angry at God for putting her through all of this. Even though we hadn't been as close as we used to, or talked as often, I still considered her one of my forever friends. She had already gone through so much spina bifida, a massive car accident, all of her other medical issues, and now this. She was an incredible woman with a resilient attitude, a beautiful soul, and a loving heart. Why did all these bad things happen to her?

After hearing this news and what had just happened with Charles, I needed a change. I knew Charles had moved on and I needed to as well. I went back to the recruiter and told him I wanted to leave at the next possible date. There was no goodbye party. I packed my belongings and left. The next day I joined the other Marine poolees on a flight to Parris Island, South Carolina for Marine Corps recruit training. A few of us went to have our last dinner at Friday's in the airport. It was such a disappointing last meal and the chicken I ordered tasted strange.

March, 2006, I stepped off the bus and onto the famous yellow footprints. During the bus ride I had started feeling sick to my stomach, not from nerves, but something much worse. I felt lightheaded and nauseous as I stood on the yellow footprints. The next few hours became a blur of screaming, running here and there and standing for hours. They brought us into medical and we went through the shot gauntlet. This gauntlet consisted of painted footprints marking where to stop. Medics were on each side and would stab you in the arm with numerous different immunizations. While we were standing there waiting, after receiving around twelve shots, I began having cold and hot flashes. I ended up blacking out. I woke up to a drill instructor (DI) standing over me screaming, "Get the fuck up. This isn't nap time!"

Thank God we were ordered to sit right after or I would have been taken to medical and I didn't want to start my first day of boot camp looking weak. We were then taken to a squad bay. A large open dorm filled with bunk beds and a large bathroom with open showers. When they began the piss test, I couldn't hold back the nausea and instead of peeing, I vomited in the toilet of the open stall. Remembering the funny taste of that damn chicken, I suspected food poisoning and wanted to die. Possibly suspecting I was vomiting on purpose because I was afraid of popping for drugs, the DIs had me stand in the piss line for what seemed like hours. They kept forcing me to chug water. Being the only recruit left to pee, I had a team of female DIs taking turns screaming at me as I chugged water. When I couldn't hold the water down, I would sprint to the toilet and vomit. I was finally able to hold down enough water to provide a small amount of urine and collapsed onto the woolly green comforter that was expertly folded with perfect corners covering the mattress.

Thankfully, I kept down breakfast the next day and by dinner I had gained my strength back. A week or so after arriving to boot camp, I was missing my Cinni Mini, my nickname for Marie. Growing up we had nicknames for each other. She called me Batman because I protected her and was her superhero. I called her Cinni Mini because she loved the McDonald's Cinni Mini buns. I kept a photo of us with me in my breast pocket to give me the strength I needed. I decided to write my family and let them know where I was. I knew they wouldn't be happy, but they never were with any of the choices I made. The only reason I stayed in touch with my family was to keep in contact with Marie.

I found training, especially the physical training, quite easy. My years of soccer helped prepare me. Despite never picking up a weapon, I learned quickly how to take it apart, put it back together, and how to shoot. I hated drill but I loved the Marine Corps mixed martial arts program. Those classes got us away from the DIs and their never-ending screaming and playing stupid games. Many of the girls would get so frustrated that some of them would even start crying. I knew it was part of the process. Breaking us down to make us all equal so we would learn to follow instructions without question.

They would send us to chow and when we returned to our squad bay, it looked like a tornado had gone through it. If any foot lockers were ever left unlocked, they would dump them over and kick the contents everywhere, throw the mattresses off the bunks ruining the perfectly made beds, and whatever else they could find to throw around. They would have us run back and forth, picking things up and putting it on the other side of the squad bay. My view of these games was it was better than sitting on the ground with our legs crossed. This hurt my knee beyond words! Plus, it was an opportunity to get some cardio in.

A month into it, we had already gone through several guides. A guide is the leader of the platoon and had many responsibilities. The first three guides were fired right away after making some stupid mistakes or falling behind in runs or hikes. There was one girl that had been guide for almost three weeks. She was an ROTC recruit, meaning in her high school she was part of a Marine program that began training high school students. She knew how to drill, grew up shooting weapons, and she knew most of the Marine Corps knowledge and history before even arriving to Parris Island. However, she wasn't fit at all. She could barely run a thirty-minute 5k (the length of our required fitness run test), could only do fifty crunches and couldn't do the arm thing for more than twenty seconds. She barely passed our physical fitness test (PFT).

I was focused on a perfect score. During the time I was in the Marines, to get a perfect score I would need to run a 5k in under 21 minutes, get a 70 second arm hang, and do 100 crunches in under two minutes. Our first PFT was for practice and I ran a 22:30 5k, did 100 crunches, and a 50 second arm hang. I had never done much upper body conditioning and I knew I needed to improve on this. I practiced my arm hang every night during our square-away time. This was a time for you to prepare your uniform, write letters home, clean your weapon, make sure your foot locker was clean and whatever else needed to get done. I wrote a letter to Liz telling her about how easy the fitness was, how I hated being around so many girls and, I'm ashamed to say, I talked smack about our fat and out of shape guide.

Because I had spent most of my square away time doing push-ups and arm hangs, I ran out of time. I hid the letter in my Marine Corps Book of Knowledge that we were given to study and planned on finishing it later. Just my luck, the DIs found it when they went through our books. While we were in class, they told us to get up and leave our books to go pick up gear. When I returned to class and opened up my book, my letter to Liz was gone. I was so nervous about the repercussions to follow. They made me stress the entire day. That evening one of our DIs, a short, fiery blond German woman, had a sit down and proceeded to read my letter to the platoon. Not the entire thing, just the section talking smack about our guide and how easy the PT was. My face turned bright red, my heart was beating out of control, and I felt the eyes of every recruit glaring at me and the guide praying for my death. When the DI asked me, "So Recruit Ives, you think you can do a better job?" I stood up and said, "Yes, I know I can." I was made guide the next morning and all hell was unleashed on me.

Before I became guide, I only had one night duty a week (same as everyone else), but they changed it to every single night. I was called up on the quarterdeck to get ITd every time someone screwed up. IT is basically extra exercise used as punishment. However, they were doing me a solid by making me stronger due. I was averaging around 250 push-ups a day and hundreds of mountain climbers. It became so often I didn't even wait to get told. If I heard someone get called up, I would jump up, remove my blouse and join in.

On several occasions, the DIs would go into their office and I would start telling whoever was up there with me, after completing the assigned fitness punishment, "OK, now mountain climbers, don't give up, push harder, now jumping jacks. Come on, you can do this!" I could hear them laugh at my extra exercises inside the office but afterwards they came out straight faced and started screaming. "Who the fuck do you think you are Ives, a DI? Oh, so you want to be a DI now too! Get the fuck back in line."

The main things I struggled with were drill and the dreaded, nightly, duck walk, sweeping. For drill, I caught on quickly with working the guide on, but I had a messed up right wrist. It would act up, causing extreme pain and grip issues after hours of drilling. Yes, the same wrist that had been injured repeatedly by my mother and brothers. Knowing the cause of my wrist injury helped me push past the pain. Every time I started to hurt; I used my anger to get through it.

Not only was I sleep deprived, I was also extremely underfed. As the guide, I was the last to eat and I had to be done as soon as the first recruit was done. The guide had to monitor those in their platoon while in the chow line. Only when everyone in my platoon had gone through could I sit down and inhale my food. I would desperately watch as I stuffed my face, praying the skinny girls who ate quickly would allow me more than 45 seconds to consume enough food to last me until the next meal. I could care less about what I looked like shoving food down my throat. I ended up losing twenty-three pounds by the time I graduated. I knew exactly how much weight I had lost because every night before lights out, we would have a safety and health inspection. This was by far one of the most embarrassing moments for girls that were insecure about their weight. When I first arrived, I was self-conscious, but as I started getting my abs back that I hadn't had since soccer, I gained more self-esteem.

Another humiliating experience was being forced to wear these white granny panties with our last names written on the back in black marker and a hideous white sports bra. One by one, we would be required to stand in front of the DI as the senior DI took down our weight and report any other medical conditions. While turning around in a circle with our hands up, twisting them, we would have to say "this recruit has no medical issues to report at this time". When the larger girls came up, the DIs would poke their muffin tops, telling them that they need to stop eating so much. They would then announce their weight loudly for everyone to hear. Some of the girls would start to cry which would only make it worse.

Before the crucible, I was experiencing sharp pain in my right ankle and was sent to medical. I found out that I had a stress fracture and the doctor wanted to put me on light duty. I refused, not willing to give up my guide position. The Crucible is a test you must pass to earn the title Marine. It pushed you to your limit and beyond. The test lasted around 54 hours, tested you with sleep and food deprivation, challenged you both mentally and physically, and included a 45-mile hike in full gear over the duration of the test. During the hike, the guide lead from the front holding the guidon. I couldn't show any signs of pain or slowing down.

During the test we had an obstacle course involving low crawling on your back under concertina wire. While I was going through this section, live fire going off overhead, I caught my right pinky on a blade. It ripped through my glove, slicing through the nail and up to the tip of my finger. Despite the pain, I kept going and I didn't realize the damage until the blood started seeping through my glove. We had first aid kits with our gear, so I cleaned and wrapped my finger, hiding the injury from any of the DIs. Although it hurt, it was nothing compared to the pain in my ankle. The picture I carried with me of Marie and I, helped give me the strength to finish the crucible.

During final drill practice, I didn't have any band aids and my finger hadn't healed enough. When the DI came to re-position my finger, she broke the wound open and blood started flowing down the guidon making it slide out of position because I couldn't grasp it tight enough. After getting yelled at several times for my hand not being in proper position, the DI noticed the blood. She took me to the sandpit and made me do around forty burpees. The sand helped clot the blood, which I thought was her intent, but then she came up several more times, squeezing the hell out of my finger, trying to make me cry. I never gave her the satisfaction.

A few days before Family Day, the day before graduation, I was called into the senior DIs office. She was an attractive Hispanic woman, around a year older than me. After I reported in and she told me "at ease", she took a long pause, trying to figure out how to tell me what she needed to say. "Recruit Ives, as you know, you are going to have the rare privilege of being our honor graduate. As you learned during graduation practice, the families of the honor graduates are honored during the ceremony and have special reserved seating. This is a great honor. I hope you understand that." I replied, "Yes, ma'am, I do. I am truly honored." She continued. I don't remember the exact words; I only remember that numb feeling and fighting the tears when she told me that no one in my family was coming. Marie had told me in a letter that her and my parents were coming to see me graduate and I was so excited to see her. I also was holding onto this naive hope that my parents would be proud of me for being honor grad.

I was unprepared for the emotional earthquake. It almost brought me to my knees, but I managed to remain standing and keep the tears from coming. I bit my tongue hard. It helped take my focus off the emotional pain and onto the physical pain. The copper taste of blood filled my mouth and I prayed she would dismiss me. "I'm so sorry. I can't even imagine how difficult this news is. If you need to see the chaplain or speak with someone, let me know, you're dismissed." Turning around quickly to flee the office, she became a DI again and sternly said "Recruit Ives, did you forget how to be dismissed?" "Shit. Sorry. I mean, dismissed, Aye ma'am" I said, coming to attention.

The next day I was ordered to report to the commanding officer of the recruit depot. Scared shitless and not knowing what I did wrong, I reported in. You never get called in there unless you had someone die in your family or you seriously screwed up like trying to kill your DI or something. After properly reporting in, I was handed the phone with no explanation. "Hello?" I said not having any idea who was on the other line. "Hi, Athena, this is Captain

Levite, your brother in law. I just want to let you know that no one is going to come to your graduation. It's too far for your parents and we are just too busy with work." I could literally hear the smirk on his face through the phone. "I am aware of that. I was informed yesterday" I replied coldly. What a dick! I loathed even the sound of his judgey, creepy voice. He replied "Oh I heard, I just wanted *to* tell you over the phone, make sure you really grasp the concept that no one is coming to your graduation." My cheeks started turning red with anger and my heart rate increased. All the pent-up emotion I had been holding pushed me over my limit. "You're such a prick. Go to hell" I said, and hung up.

The look on the CO's face was shocked. "I'm so sorry sir! My brother in law who was kicked out of the Marine Corps wanted to rub it in that no one was coming to see me graduate." I could see a look of sympathy in his eyes. "Aren't you honor graduate" he asked? "Yes sir, I am." "Well, I'm sorry to hear that", he said. "Is there anyone else coming to see you that we could put in the family section instead?" Damn it, the emotions started to creep up in my throat. "No, sir. No one is coming to see me graduate." He dismissed me, but before I left he said, "Recruit, I've heard good things about you. I believe you can have a promising career in the Marine Corps. Don't let this get you down or keep you from becoming a great leader of Marines." "I won't, sir. Thank you" I said leaving.

My final PFT came and I had so much anger and hurt me, I used it to push me to my fastest run time ever: 20.13! I came in third place for the run in our battalion of around 120 recruits, and missed being Iron Woman by only three seconds. Even though I was disappointed

I couldn't be Iron Woman and Honor Grad, I knew that I had given it everything I had. Playing competitive soccer had taught me to accept a loss only if I had given it 110 percent.

Family Day was another emotional obstacle I would have to overcome. It was a day I had imagined spending with Marie. Showing her where we slept, the guidon I carried, the confidence course... That in particular I was proud of! The smaller obstacle course was fun and I did very well, but the confidence course, I was the only female, I knew of, in my company that was able to complete the entire thing. When I climbed the rope to finish the course, I felt such a sense of pride and reward for all the hard work and training I had done. Instead, Family Day was spent tagging along like a pet adopted from the pound because no one wanted it. It was a day spent on an emotional roller coaster. The feeling of pride I felt to have a PFC chevron on my sleeve, didn't make up for the knife in my heart pain when seeing all the families crying and hugging their loved ones. After seeing a little girl resembling Marie run and jump into her sister's arms, I had to retreat back to the squad bay. Sitting alone on my rack, I went over the drill card for graduation day. I didn't want to make a single mistake in front of so many people. It was also a distraction from the devil trying to creep back into my mind.

Graduation day came as a typically miserable, hot and humid day. The sand fleas were out in full force crawling into your nose and under your cover. You couldn't swipe them away without a DI screaming in your face. Sweat had already started to drip down my back while standing in line awaiting the order to march onto the parade deck. I'm not sure I can think of any other place on Earth where you could have hundreds of 18 to 22-year-olds standing in complete silence. You could hear the quiet banter from the DIs talking about plans or what scantily clad mother to avoid if you wanted to keep your career. I could smell breakfast from the chow hall which made my stomach growl from hunger, even though it wasn't the best of food. The smell of fresh-cut grass drifted into the air as the ceremony started.

I felt enormous pride as I led our company out onto the blazing hot parade deck. Music played as I concentrated on my steps and listened to my DI giving orders. The male platoons went first. I felt the sting of envy as the families of the honor graduates stood to applaud their son, boyfriend, or brother. The envy turned to anger trying to steal away my day. No! Don't show emotion. Don't cry or let them take this from you. Trying to repair the damage my family did to my heart was an ongoing battle. When it came my turn to receive my award and they announced my name, not one person stood. The bleachers were 15 or so yards away and I could see the family members looking around surprised that no one was there. When they realized that I was the only honor graduate there with no family or friends, one by one they started to stand up and show support for me. As I marched back to my company, I was grateful for the crowd's response, but felt such a feeling of loneliness, I couldn't shake it. The only time I let a tear escape was when I was handed the Eagle, Globe & Anchor, symbolizing I had made it! I became one of the few, the proud. I earned the title Marine.

Chapter 14

After the 10 days of liberty I reported to Camp Geiger, North Carolina for Marine Corps Combat Training, or MCT. We were one of the first Co-Ed platoons. MCT was an intense 29 days of training in land navigation, multiple weapon systems, patrolling, field ops, and plenty of live ranges. I enjoyed MCT very much, minus the disgusting living conditions, the humidity, and the drama with having a coed group made it challenging. Once again, I achieved the honor of being the guide. Being guide with a coed platoon was a challenge! For the first time in my life, I was put in charge of men. The challenge of being a female Marine became very apparent when a male, the same rank as you, had an issue with being told what to do by a female. I wanted to tell them to grow up. They put me in charge for a reason. My hard work, initiative, and other leadership traits were why I was chosen. Not because I was sleeping with the platoon sergeant, which I wasn't. Typically, in any military situation, if a female military member picks up rank or does well in her job, it is automatically assumed that she is sleeping with her supervisor.

North Carolina during the month of June was hot, humid, and infested with mosquitoes. This disastrous combination, combined with the lack of proper showers and constant physical demands, created one of the worst living conditions I've ever been in. You think the smell of death is bad? Try walking into a female Marines Quonset hut under these conditions. You're greeted with a smell so bad that it would knock you off your feet. It was a combination of crotch sweat, body odor, mildew and anchovy-like two-day old period tampons. It was enough to make anyone considering going UA. UA means unauthorized *absence*. Despite taking a baby wipe shower, putting on deodorant and hanging up my sweat soaked cammies, I still never felt clean. Even though I hung up my cammies every night, they would never be dry in the morning due to the extreme humidity.

The head (bathroom) was even worse than the huts. Due to there being so few females we were always given the leftovers. If you are an enlisted female Marine, plan on having your head not only located the furthest away, but also the most disgusting. This one had one working toilet and two urinals. Taking a dump required you to wake up an hour before you were supposed to and a prayer the only toilet wasn't occupied. Learning to pee in a urinal was just one of the skills I picked up.

On the day of our land navigation test, my partner was useless in finding the target points. She ended up giving up and returned to the rally point. Being the determined individual I am, I continued alone and found the targets by myself. Running out of time I tried to hurry back to the rally point. I struggled through the dense overgrowth and the intense humidity/heat. I finally made it back. When I reported into my platoon sergeant, I resembled a drowned Sasquatch. My cammies were dripping from sweat, I had dirt smudged across my face, and tree branches were hanging on for dear life to my boonie cover. "What in the hell Ives? Did you fall in the lake?" "Uhhh...

Yes, Staff Sergeant. I slipped and fell in" I stammered. He looked puzzled as he looked down at my feet. "Then why the fuck are your boots still dry Marine?" "I fell in backwards and kept my boots out of the water. You know, Doc's always telling us how important dry socks are Staff Sergeant." He started to laugh, "Get the hell out of here Ives."

At night, the instructors would often come in and choose girls to "take out the trash". I found out this was code for when the instructors wanted to have sex with the female students in the porta potties. The porta potties were far from clean and I didn't even want to use them to go to the bathroom in, let alone have sex. Not that I knew what having consensual sex was even like, but I could only imagine how disgusting it would be in that condition. One instructor I had caught eyeballing my boobs on more than one occasion when we were in boots and utes, came and told me to help take out the trash. "Respectfully Sergeant, I am working on the gear list. Staff Sergeant asked me to make sure I check all the females. You know, my duties as the guide and all. After all, you did teach me how to be a good leader." This instructor was an attractive man with bright green eyes, an enticing smile, and a soccer player physique. I saw right through his game but the other girls fell for it. My unique cult upbringing helped me see through snakes like him. "OK, good to go Ives. Make sure you don't forget anything" he replied and went on to find another willing participant.

The night shoots were my favorite. I loved looking up at the stars with the night vision goggles (NVGs). It was like something out of Star Wars and the heat sensing goggles, were bad ass! While others bitched and complained about the long hours, I loved feeling like special ops. Even though I knew I would never be able to hold that title due to having a vagina, I still dreamed of becoming one. On our hikes I always led from the front and I felt intense pride in being in such an honored position. My platoon sergeant had a great deal of respect for me and a week before graduation, he came to let me know that I was going to be meritoriously promoted. He was in his early 40s and I found out that he had started later in his life like I had. His hazel eyes were kind and his leadership characteristics inspired respect. He was strict but nurturing. This was something I had never experienced before from a male supervisor. His words telling me he was proud of me, brought back memories of my father and how different this man was from him.

During graduation, I was waiting to be called up to receive my award. Several other guides from the other platoons were called up and received their promotion. When it came time for my platoon, instead of my name they called out the name of one of the females that had repeatedly been seen "taking out the trash". Disappointment seeped in and that negative voice telling me that I was a failure and worthless found its way back in. Why couldn't I catch a break? What was the point in trying anymore when my best just wasn't good enough? After the ceremony, we were released and my platoon sergeant came up to me and pulled me aside. "Ives, I want to apologize. You deserved that promotion. There was nothing I could do. My hands were tied. My instructors fucked up. Private Delgado threatened to tell the command about "taking out the trash" if she didn't get promoted. She slept with all of the instructors. You're an outstanding Marine. Don't let this hold you back. I know you are going to do well wherever you go."

Chapter 15

As we were sitting on our sea-bags (large green duffel bags for our gear) waiting to hear which MOS (Military Occupation Specialty) we were getting, I was chatting with some of the male Marines from my MCT platoon. They told me that they had recognized me from boot camp, but I didn't recall ever seeing them. Then again, I was a five-foot nine redhead with large boobs, kind of hard to miss. I had made friends with a few of them. We patiently waited for our new careers to be announced. They finally announced our MOS numbers James 0337, Rodgers 2832, Heath 1371, Jenson 0311, Patrick 0311, Ives 1371. Our instructors were wandering around chatting with us, giving advice on our new jobs. A Marine named Heath and I were happy that we both had the same MOS, but I had no idea what it actually was.

Heath was a blue-eyed blond boy from Philadelphia. He was easy to talk to and we shared the same hardworking attitude and desire to excel in the Marine Corps. Because I had told the recruiters I wanted to leave as soon as possible for boot camp, I lost my previous seat for intel. They told me that they could put me under the ground support category with several different possibilities. One, included MP Military Police, which is the one I wanted. The instructor informed me that 1371 was a combat engineer, which he had to explain to me.

This young grunt MCT instructor had a bald head and crazy eyes. He excitedly told me that it was the most "bad ass job in the Marine Corps" and he wished he had gotten that. He told me that I would get to do minesweeping, build structures and blow shit up. Hiding the fearful look on my face, I looked over at Heath, who had actually chosen that MOS and was grinning like a kid.

An hour later, we were on a bus to engineer school at Courthouse Bay Camp Lejeune, North Carolina. Checking in, we were put in our assigned rooms and because there was only one other female in our class, I had to share a room with the "slut of MCT". Pfc Straws had gained her reputation by sleeping with every instructor at MCT. She was out of shape and overweight. While I would be in the gym after school every day, she would be flirting with the guys and eating junk food. Because of this, her fitness sucked and she was constantly getting yelled at for falling out of our morning runs. Because I was the only other female and the Guide, I got yelled at for her fitness level.

I know I come off harsh describing this female, but there are so few females in the Marine Corps. When one decides to sleep around in order to obtain special favors or doesn't take her fitness seriously, it sheds a bad light on all females. Not only that, our work is taken less seriously. When we are promoted, it is automatically assumed that we got there from sleeping around, which is not always the case. However, sadly, it is the case in numerous situations. So when I describe her in a harsh light, it is because I took it personally because I did suffer the impact. Because of her laziness and promiscuity, I not only experienced ongoing sexual harassment because of her actions,

I also experienced a very hostile environment against females.

As you will soon see, this hostile environment would get much worse. There was a group of us, Heath, James, Seth, Graham, and Cole that became close. Seth was the only one older than I was. He was from Egypt, spoke five languages and loved his alcohol. Every morning during PT, he actually sweat alcohol and I was grateful I didn't have to run behind him. James was a very sophisticated Jamaican who was shy but more talkative. Cole was from the Bahamas with a solid build, trusting smile and was such a motivator. The class troublemaker was Graham. I took him under my wing and tried to get him to shape up. He came from a bad home and I felt for him, knowing how hard that could be. My mother used to get mad at me for befriending kids from bad homes, but I related to them. I couldn't relate to "normal" people.

On one of her weekends off, a group of us decided to get tattoos. The guys went and got some generic moto tattoo, but I had already designed mine. I had drawn a seahorse. Why a seahorse? Because it represents a significant time in my life, the moment I began to think for myself and question what I was told. Growing up, we were told by my parents and the other members of the cult that seahorses weren't real. They told us that sea horses and dinosaurs were like dragons and unicorns. At around 13, I went to an aquarium and saw a tank of seahorses. After that moment, in my head, I questioned everything my parents had ever told me and everyone else as well. Instead of believing right away, I searched for evidence defending the statement until I viewed it as true. The scientific evidence available didn't matter to my parents and the members of the cult.

They refused to acknowledge the truth.

James and I became closer and I shared with him some of my family history and how I was still so hurt about the break up with Charles. My dreams were still filled with memories of him, and I missed him terribly. I missed the intimacy, our friendship, being able to trust someone.

Graphic Content Rape Warning

One weekend, James Heath and I went to a local drag racing event. After meeting up with some of the Marines attending a different school, I began mingling and sipping on a beer that one of them had got me. After my second Budweiser, I knew something was wrong. Everything began to spin and I blacked out. The next thing I remember was waking up, getting raped. My jeans were around my ankles. The zipper had been mangled from forceful removal and my thong had been ripped off. The hot breath on my neck stunk of cheap beer and cigarettes. Starting to panic, I had no idea where I was or who this man was raping me. Hot tears started coming as soon as I opened my eyes, not only from physical pain, but the memories of being raped as a child. The room started spinning. My head was pounding and the sunlight coming in through the cheap looking curtains, made it hard to even see.

Desperate to escape I shoved him off of me and fell out of the bed. I managed to pull up my destroyed jeans enough to cover myself up. As I started for the door, looking around the room, I observed that I was in a sleazy hotel room. As my eyes adjusted, I looked over and saw James sitting in a chair watching the entire thing. The suffocating effect of the room, drug induced migraine and the need to vomit caused me to sprint towards the door and puke in the bushes outside the hotel room.

Luckily, I had seen my clutch purse on the table and grabbed it on my way out. I was thankful I didn't have to go back in that room. James came out of the room mid vomit and silently stood there staring at me. He didn't say a word until we were in the taxi on the way back to base. My sunglasses hid the tears that I couldn't hold back. Questions raced through my mind. What happened? Who was that guy? Why hadn't James stopped him? What I did know was that someone at that race drugged and raped me. In an ice-cold whisper, James told me how disgusted he was with me. Shocked at the words coming out of his mouth, I had a panic attack and could hardly breathe. As he continued to speak, he confessed his love for me and the pain he felt while spending all night watching this guy doing what he had been wanting to do with me.

By the time I arrived back on base, the gossip had already started. As I made my way from the taxi to my barracks room "slut, whore, walking mattress" were just a few of the names I was being called from the guys in the smoke pit. I had just been drugged and raped by someone I didn't know while someone I trusted and cared about sat and watched. Before even arriving to my room to mentally process everything, I was labeled a whore. All these brother Marines that were supposed to have my back, they all assumed that I got drunk and hooked up with some stranger. Who would ever believe me if I reported this? They had already found me guilty and I was labeled a Marine Slut. If I told my command, my reputation would be the whore who got drunk in school and regretted it so I claimed rape. I had worked too hard to allow this to happen. I also knew that as a female Marine, this reputation would continue with me to my first duty station.

The next few weeks leading up to graduation, I avoided everyone, spent hours in the gym, and only when the memories became too intense did, I go to the beer garden to drown out that memory. A week before graduation, I was still guide and selected for meritorious promotion. One Friday evening I met up with Heath to have some beers at the beer garden. One of the Sergeants from our class was there as well. He had always tried to flirt with me during class, but I was aware of his reputation for sleeping around. This Sergeant was around six foot five, 220 pounds of muscle and tattoos and had these evil eyes. I had brought a six pack and had two beers when this Sergeant came over and grabbed my ass trying to pull me on his lap. Panicking, I told him to fuck off and quickly left. Not one of the Marines, not even Heath, said a word in my defense. We were supposed to be family, look out for each other, but that only applied to male Marines. I wasn't there, sister. They let me get drugged and raped in front of them.

Leaving my beers with Seth. I called a taxi and spent the night by myself in a hotel room and came back the next morning. As the taxi was dropping me off, I saw my platoon standing in formation, in their cammies, outside of our barracks. It was Saturday afternoon, our day off, so I knew someone had messed up and we were about to be punished. Jumping out of the taxi, I fell into formation. Later, I found out that Graham, my troublemaker little brother, had been caught underage drinking at the beer garden.

A knock on my door interrupted our field day punishment. It was the barracks duty who informed me that I was being ordered to report into the First Sergeant's office. Here we go again! After reporting in the First Sergeant handed me photos of Graham with the Sergeant that had grabbed my ass drinking beers together. He proceeded to tell me that when the Sergeant had been called in for questioning, he told them that he didn't know Graham was under age told that I had given Graham the beer. After telling the first sergeant what really happened, he shockingly believed me. He went on to inform me that the Sergeant had been moved from another school he was in due to a sexual harassment issue, and was placed in the platoon I was in. The First Sergeant went on to give me more infuriating news. After a pathetic and meaningless apology for what had happened, he informed me that he was unable to promote me because an accusation was filed against me. This was now the third time I was not promoted, despite deserving it, because I was trying to do the right thing. Again, I told myself I wouldn't let anything would change me. I wouldn't let them break me.

Too often in the military, if you're accused of sexual misconduct and even if you are found guilty, instead of being punished, they just move you to a different unit. They don't want to deal with the problem, so they just move you. That command didn't want to deal with the problem. So instead of punishing that Sergeant, they sent him to a different unit and washed their hands of the situation. Kind of sounds familiar, like the Catholic Church. Rape a kid, you won't get punished, you just get moved to a different church where you can do it all over again.

Chapter 16

Right after graduation, Heath, James, Cole, Graham and I received orders to Camp Pendleton. I was put into a company with only one other female name, Monica. She was a five-foot two stunning Mexican with a fiery attitude. Jensen was Monica's best friend, but when he kept coming over to our room daily, I could tell it was to see me. From the moment we were let off work, the knocks on the door would begin. For women, your attraction rating increases in the military. Especially in the Marines due to the male to female ratio. For example, a female in the civilian world that was a six was now an eight or 10 in the military. Soon I found out that female combat engineers were extraordinarily rare. So rare, in fact, that I was the only female in my platoon.

My squad leader was a Sergeant that told me I didn't belong in the Marine Corps from the moment I was assigned to his squad. During morning PT, he would take us on death runs and loved to take us on the meth-trail. The trail gained its name because you would have had to been on meth to consciously choose to run it. Because of my hard work and dedication in the gym, I never fell out. Numerous times during the run, my squad leader would turn around thinking he had broken me, but I was right there behind him.

Jensen and I started becoming closer. When he wasn't drinking, he was a very sweet guy and a dedicated, hardworking Marine. Jensen had asked me out numerous times, but I kept turning him down. After I found out Charles had gotten married, I agreed to go out with him. Due to being raped, and having two boyfriends that crushed me, I rethought the idea of saving my virginity for someone that was mutually in love with me. Knowing the devastation I felt from breakups in relationships without sex, I couldn't comprehend losing a love with someone I had given my virginity to. At the age of 25, after being raped by two different people, I finally decided to give up my virginity by having consensual sex to a man I wasn't in love with. Just wanting it over, I felt numb. He was drinking and thought he needed to tell me that he loved me. It brought back a lot of painful memories. Not only because I knew he didn't love me, but saying it just made it so cheap and meaningless.

Our battalion was scheduled to go to Bridgeport, California for cold weather training. Wait, what? Cold weather training in California. That's right. Snow up to your chest and 15 below zero type of weather. It was the most dreaded training among most Marines. Prior to departure, a female Marine was transferred from her platoon in Yuma. Her reputation preceded her for sleeping with half the platoon and caused so much drama they had to ship her to a different base to get rid of the headache. Once again, the military shipping off individuals that should have been punished instead of dealing with it. Lance Corporal, I'll just call her CB short for Crazy Bitch, was an out of shape, short blond chick that constantly played the "girl card" to get out of everything. This lazy POS couldn't run three miles in thirty minutes, hated the Marine Corps and was the biggest dirt bag I had ever met.

As soon as she was told that we were going to do cold weather training, she told them that if they forced her to go, she would commit suicide. Because of her pathetic, empty threat, she was put on suicide watch and taken off the roster. They ended up moving Monica out of my room and put crazy bitch with me so I could watch and make sure she didn't kill herself. The night before we were leaving for Bridgeport, the barracks were filled with Marines getting as drunk as possible. Several others did everything they could to get out of going. One idiot had his wife kick him in the balls repeatedly until he was bleeding and ended up in the hospital. Another jackass ironed his bare foot and ended up in the hospital as well. After they were released, they were charged with missing a movement, forced to go, and were given the dreaded duty of collecting the bathroom buckets and discarding the waste.

We had been issued Mickey Mouse boots that were three sizes too big for me because they didn't have enough female sizes. We called them Mickey Mouse boots because they were large, white, cold weather, insulated boots. Not having proper female sizes was a common issue women had to endure without complaint. The hike up the mountain was around 13 miles, seemingly straight uphill. To my knowledge, every female in my battalion fell out of the hike except for me. There were gym studs that fell out, which shocked me. They were beasts that scored perfect PFTs, held every single weightlifting record, and even some of those fell out! When we reached the top, I gained respect from just about every single person in my battalion.

It was one of the most challenging, physical, accomplishments I had ever completed, even more so than the Crucible with a fractured ankle. So many times I wanted to quit and take off my pack, but I kept putting one foot in front of the other. Every step I took, when I didn't know how I can manage, I thought about Joy and Marie. If Joy could fight against MS, Spina Bifida, and all of her other physical injuries, I could too. I did it for Marie. I did it for myself. I did it to show everyone that females can be Marines. I used the anger inside me from being raped and all my past trauma, as fuel to get me up that mountain. I ended up getting pneumonia, but refused to go back down the hill or stop training.

Even in cold weather training we had Fire Watch. It was the most dreaded duty as you would have to be woken up at all hours of the night, get dressed and perform some type of duty for an hour. Most of the duties were patrolling guards where you would freeze your ass off walking around, protecting your platoon from nonexistent enemies. After hearing me nearly cough to death, Jensen kindly took over two of my night duties. Thank God for him. It was kind acts like that, that had won me over. Occasionally during the night, you would wake up to hear the shift change and thank God that you didn't have to get up. I remember hearing one person in particular. Corporal Jones, a Jamaican that hated the cold weather, refused to wake up one morning. As I was laying in my sleeping bag, still shivering, I heard him say, "fuck yoooouuuuuuu... It's too fucking cold. I'm not leaving my warm sleeping bag." I couldn't help but laugh.

One evening, Monica came and told me a secret, she was late and thought she might be pregnant. She was sleeping with a Marine in the other platoon who was married. I tried to comfort her and tell her it was going to be all right. After our intense training, we were rewarded with being allowed to go drink at the Pickle Chalet. This was a bar that was located on top of the hill at base camp.

After several beers, I looked over to see Monica arguing with the suspected baby daddy. I saw him grab her wrist and twist it, making her cry. It brought back memories of what my mother and brothers used to do and I snapped. I walked over, told him to take his hands off her and got in his face. He called Monica a stupid bitch and to get the hell away from him. My drunk ass went to backhand him, missed, and ended up slapping the squat record holder of Camp Pendleton in the back of the head. He got in my face. "What are you going to do? Hit me back? Go for it, I'm not scared of you. Your asshole friend hurt my roommate, so fuck both of you." This was very uncharacteristic of me and due to a combination of the alcohol, the altitude and the pent-up anger I had from previous traumas. Jensen came running over as well as several other members of my squad to break it up. Jensen dragged me to the door and started to walk with me down the icy hill back to the barracks. We were joined by several other members of the platoon we found slipping all over the ice. One slipped, still holding his beer and somehow caught the beer, only spilling a little. It was like a scene out of a cartoon. We all cheered.

Halfway down the hill, I heard footsteps running and turned to see the squat champion running towards me. Jensen tackled him right before he reached me, both falling into the snow. After that, it was chaos. Platoon on platoon brawl. I got knocked over and started coughing so bad I couldn't breathe. The next thing I knew, Jensen was helping me up and pushing me away from the fight back down the hill. He made sure he walked me back to my barracks. The next morning on our way to chow, the bridge to get there was covered in pink snow from the blood the night before. I found out that after I had gone back to my barracks, the fight continued.

Our unit was forever banned from the pickle. Marines had taken every single beer pitcher the bar owned and left with them. The next morning, when the command came to retrieve them, allegedly no one knew where they were. The Lance Corporal Underground caught wind that whoever was caught with the pitchers were going to get in trouble. So, our platoon sergeant told the guys to throw all the pitchers on the roof. Thankfully, no one got in trouble, but we were banned from the pickle, probably for the best.

After completing the challenging cold weather training, the battalion decided to reward us by giving us a 36-hour R&R in Reno, Nevada. I had a fairly early night and avoided the drunken shenanigans. The next morning during formation, around 90 percent of our platoon was still drunk, swaying back and forth and unable to stand up straight. One of the females in the company had on large sunglasses and was instructed to take them off. Removing the glasses revealed a massive black eye. We found out later that she punched one of the guys because he wouldn't sleep with her, so he punched her back.

We had one Marine that was UA and was going to be charged for missing a movement. This particular Marine, we found out later, had been sober for three years. That night, he decided to drink, got smashed, ordered two hookers and ended up calling his fiancée while having sex with both of them. No surprise, she ended up calling off the wedding. We had three Marines just bailed out of jail and one with a broken foot. One was sent to jail for punching a guy in a wheelchair that had been talking smack. Another had been arrested after sexually assaulting the bartender. The other was for public nudity. The marine with the broken foot had seen a pigeon on the sidewalk and did a running kick only to find out that it was a statue.

Chapter 17

One day, while I was working at a car wash fundraiser for the Marine Corps Ball, I was told that the company CO wanted to see me. After reporting in she handed me the phone with a pissed off look on her face. "Hello, this is Lance Corporal Ives, how can I help you sir or ma'am." My stomach turned "Well, hello again, this is Captain Levite." This bastard! Couldn't he just leave me the hell alone? He went on to yell about delinquent scooter payments. Before I had joined the Marine Corps, Jezebel wanted to buy my scooter from me. She didn't have enough so I allowed her to keep it if she promised to make the monthly payments. A few months before, she had called to ask me advice on what she should do about the scooter payment. She had failed to change the address when she moved and when she took it for an oil change, they refused to give it back because she didn't have proof of ownership. I was pissed off knowing that this would destroy my credit, which it did.

After finding the paperwork she needed to put the loan in her name, she said that she would take care of it. Apparently, she had not taken care of it and that was what Levite was calling about. He continued to yell at me, calling me irresponsible, an evil person, that I was going to hell and a list of other names he thought would hurt me. I had to stand there and take his abuse because my CO was sitting at her desk watching me. Doing my best to remain calm I explained to him the situation, but he wasn't listening. He wanted me to pay for the scooter and just give it to them, ignoring the fact that this was seriously going to mess up my credit, or take any responsibility. I had managed to remain calm until he said "all you do is lie. You say your brother raped you, but then you leave Marie in the same house with him. If he had really done that to you and you actually loved Marie, you would have never abandoned her in Michigan to go sleep with Marines and then try and become one." Marie was my weakness and anyone that spoke poorly about her would feel my wrath. "Listen to me clearly, you piece of shit." He tried to interrupt me. "Shut the fuck up and let me finish what I am saying. You will not get one penny from me. Calling my battalion commander to get me in trouble shows what a cowardly piece of crap you are. Leave me the hell alone. Never call me again or so help me God, I will find a way to ruin your fucking pathetic life. Then again, I hear you are homeless and you've been fired from several pastoral jobs. Is it because you beat your wife or maybe you were like one of those other pedophile priests out there? I am not someone you want to mess with." I had forgotten about the CO who was now standing behind her desk. I hesitantly handed her the phone back, Levite still screaming on the other side. The look on her face was priceless and left her speechless. After she had a minute to gather her thoughts, she sternly said, "Lance Corporal Ives, what the hell was that? The battalion CO told me that you aren't paying your bills. Do you realize that you could be NJPd for not fulfilling a loan agreement, let alone the trouble you are in for speaking to a captain in the Marine Corps like that? It's called disrespecting an officer and that display of disrespect could result in you losing your rank, restriction, and half pay."

The anger from the multiple times I had been screwed over by the Marine Corps and the smug way Levite had talked to me, was still burning in my soul! Trying my best to not let my emotions get the best of me, I respectfully and calmly replied, "I apologize for that, ma'am. That was my brother in law. He was a Marine Corps Captain, but he has been dishonorably discharged and uses his rank to cause drama in my life. I did not do those things he said I did and I am truly sorry you had to hear that." She told me that the command was going to look into the issue with my finances and I better be on my best behavior. I left the office and felt my phone vibrating nonstop. It was Levite. He had left four voicemails threatening to call the Sergeant Major and ruin my career.

I called Jezebel and tried to discuss the issue with her. Levite took the phone from her and continued to scream at me. After hanging up on him, I texted Jezebel and told her that I needed to talk to her, not Levite. She messaged me back and told me that Levite was her husband and she must do as he wishes. I replied and told her that I loved her, but what he was doing was wrong and I wanted no part of it. That was in September of 2006. We never spoke again.

Graphic Content Rape Warning

Later that week I received a call from my grandmother letting me know that my grandfather had passed away. My grandfather was an incredible man, a real cowboy who had lots of stories. He used to send me the rattles from rattlesnakes and clippings of newspaper articles he thought I would like. I did my best to respond, but I hadn't replied to his past few letters. I felt terrible. I ended up walking over to Seth and Graham's room to find comfort and distraction with some friends. Jensen was out and about. We weren't in a serious relationship, but technically we were still together. I had one Bud Light and one shot, which was not a lot of alcohol for me during those days. The last thing I remember was coming to sitting outside the room on the balcony. Could this really be happening again? I knew I had been drugged. I don't remember getting to my room. I just remember waking up vomiting in the bathroom. I was in my bra and panties and I felt my bra being taken off. I turned around to see Graham bending over me, one hand trying to stick his fingers in my ass and vagina, the other unhooking my bra. I panicked and tried to scramble to my feet.

I was yelling for help, but there was loud music and my neighbors were out for the weekend. Slipping on the floor, I fell and hit my head and everything else was a blur. I remember being on the cold ground and talking to Jensen on the phone. He said he was coming to help me. Moments of hazy and painful rough penetration, a hushed voice saying he was helping me because I was too drunk. I was not drunk. I was drugged and being raped by my friend, my brother.

The next morning, I woke up from the daylight peeping through my window and the sound of voices on the catwalk. I was completely naked and I froze when I felt the pain. I had been raped and sodomized. I had a splitting migraine, exactly like the one I had the morning after being drugged the first time. Enraged, devastated, betrayed, terrified and ashamed, I made it to the bathroom where I found the green on green PT gear I had been wearing on the floor. I knew I should have immediately gone and reported it, but the thought of a painful exam and the desperate urge to wash the filth off, took over. I was ashamed and disgusted, desperate to erase Graham's touch. This was the third man to rape me. I started blaming myself. I had been trained to never fight back, to accept what happened to me and move on.

As the water ran down me, I sobbed as the blood from my asshole and vagina washed down the drain. If it were only that easy to wash away the pain and emotional devastation I was feeling. I tried to piece the night together and figure out what I was going to do. No one would believe me and they would just look at me like a victim if they did. All I wanted was for this fucking bastard to pay for what he had done in the same manner he had hurt me. I had defended him, mentored him and considered him a friend. Was Seth in on this too? Who could I trust? I lived in a building with around 200 men and maybe three other women.

After finally finding my phone I called Jensen and left several nasty messages. I would soon find out that I never spoke with Jensen that night. Graham had called a friend and asked him to play along, convincing me that I had help on the way. Jensen never came back to the barracks and I soon found out why. Jensen, another Marine, crazy bitch, and the chick with the black eye from Reno, had an orgy and took multiple photos/videos documenting their consensual activities. The chick with the black eye had a guy that liked her who was trying to join in the orgy. When they wouldn't let him in, he called PMO (military police). After PMO arrived, both girls said that they had been raped and NCIS got involved. They confiscated the photos and all ended involved ended up getting NJPs. I despise false claims of sexual assault! They need to be placed on the sex offender list in my opinion. They all lost rank, were put on restriction, and lost half pay for two months.

Not only had I just been drugged and raped by someone I considered my little brother, my boyfriend just had an orgy with crazy bitch of all people. Because of the alleged rape, we had to have rape watch on every floor, and every corner of the barracks 24/7. Everyone was pissed and talking shit about females accusing people of rape when they regretted their choice and how females shouldn't be in the Marine Corps. I had finally gained a good reputation with my guys. What would happen if I went and reported my assault the same night this orgy took place? My reputation would be garbage. I would have to press charges and I would have to face all the shit that would come from that. My past experience and the stories I heard from other women had me convinced Graham would get away with it.

Instead, I took matters into my own hands. I took my pocket knife and walked over to Graham's room. I walked in, held the knife to the back of his throat and told him if he ever came near me again, I would kill him, cut off his balls and shove them down his throat. He never came near me again and I avoided Jensen. I wasn't going to give him the advantage of knowing my pain. My story is just one of many that happen in the military with not only females, but men as well. If you think that you hate false sexual accusations more than rape victims, you're wrong. Rape victims are extremely impacted by false allegations. My story is a prime example of that. When individuals falsely claim rape, it makes actual rape victims seem untrustworthy and it encourages them to not report. False allegations assist with the continuance of rape culture and rape in general. This is why I believe that false accusers, when actually proven false in a court of law or admit that they had lied, should be prosecuted to the full extent of the law.

"Many sexual trauma survivors, especially the ones that are assaulted more than once, start to feel as if they are to blame. Or they are ashamed and embarrassed. How could I, a strong Marine, get raped by three different men? According to research, more than one-third of women who report being raped before age 18 also experience rape as an adult. Being raped multiple times is disgustingly common and warrants further research to develop improved methods of prevention. Part of prevention requires stories like mine and millions of others to be heard!

There are certain situations where the victim cycle continues due to unhealed behavioral patterns the victim chooses. However, there are vulnerabilities that these predators look for that the survivor may not be able to avoid. In order to understand this, you need to think like a predator. Which potential victim would a predator choose: a white female from a wealthy family in a committed relationship or a Native American foster child who was just dumped by her boyfriend? The predator will typically choose a victim with the best chances of getting away with the crime.

This doesn't mean that sexual assault is ever the victim's fault! I am only telling you what the predator looks for. You can't change the fact that you came from an unloving family or you grew up poor, both making you a vulnerable target. However, there is a difference between being honest with your life and sharing vulnerabilities to the public a predator would use to target you.

Be cautious with whom you share information about breakups, financial loss, family abuse, any kind of abuse in general. I learned this the hard way! Being open and trying to help others made me a target and since I have published my story, several people have used my vulnerabilities to hurt me. There is a fine balance between sharing too much and just enough to live in your truth.

Many will blame the victim for what they wore, who they were with, and other ignorant reasons for shifting the blame away from the predator. Every 73 seconds, someone in the US is sexually assaulted. Celebrities like Madonna, Marilyn Monroe, Miley Cyrus, the popular song WAP, encourage women to embrace their sexuality and dress to show off their bodies. The danger in this is, these celebrities have security, PR, and legal teams that provide more protection than most have the luxury to afford. A vulnerable individual that embraces these celebrities and tries to be like them are going to make themselves even larger targets. We need to be mindful of what we wear. An outfit suited for a night clubbing in Las Vegas would make you a target at a local bar down the street. Sharing how much you hate your family, how you just lost your job, or how everyone you date breaks your heart, on a public social media site where millions of people have access to your information, is like sending predators an invitation to target you.

Chapter 18

Not only had Graham raped me, he had forced me to repress every emotion and left me cold hearted and not wanting to be around anyone. Repressing feelings would prevent me from that amazing feeling of being in love I knew I deserved. Due to my closed off nature and avoidance of everyone, I began to hear rumors that I was a stuck-up rich bitch. In the Marine Corps, female Marines were labeled as either a slut or a lesbian. They would be labeled a lesbian if others couldn't find one situation, such as being found alone with a male, that could be viewed as you were sleeping with them. If you had a male friend or seen more than once with them, this had to mean that you were sleeping with them. A male Marine being friends with a female Marine meant that he would have to deal with the gossip and possibly unwillingly get involved with false sexual accusations. The false reports, even though found innocent, would haunt you for the rest of your career and cause endless problems. The risks involved scared most of the quality male Marines away.

I had another PFT and I was determined to get my 300 score or at least a 290 or above. For the arm hang, my wrist injury had been giving me issues and I only made it 68 seconds. Disappointed, I shook it off knowing that I had to get my mind right and prepare for the run. Self-doubt is incredibly damaging to any type of test, especially physical ones. Even though I hated running, I knew it was part of being a Marine and I forced myself to run at least five days a week. My run-time was twenty-one thirty, missing the perfect score by thirty seconds. Knowing I had given my all, especially after vomiting after the run, I was satisfied with my score.

By the time I got back to my room to change over, I was doubled over in pain from severe cramps. I wasn't supposed to start my period for two weeks, but I knew something wasn't right. The pain was crippling and after sweating through two pairs of cammies, I called my squad leader and told him I was going to the emergency room. Unable to get out of bed, I laid there shivering and alone, unable to drive myself to the ER. Feeling the need to vomit from the pain, I attempted to make it to the bathroom, but I blacked out on the way. The next day I went to BAS (our medical station). They told me to go see a gynecologist (GYN). The GYN told me to suck it up, that it was just PMS, and changed my birth control. It did nothing for the pain.

During one of our company formations, I felt the pain from the severe cramps starting to take over. I started to black out from the stabbing pain consuming my core area. It started with sweating profusely from the pain, then seeing spots and the beginning of tunnel vision. I tried everything to stay conscious as it would be so embarrassing to pass out during the formation. I couldn't show any weakness or this would just make myself a bigger target for the ongoing harassment I had to endure! Thank God they dismissed us but my relief was short lived when they told us we had another formation to go to. We had to drive over to that one at our battalion headquarters. I parked the car and saw everyone forming up. I knew I wasn't going to last through this one and I hid in my car. Thankfully, no one noticed I wasn't there.

After going to BAS and asking to be prescribed Glucosamine for my knee, they made me get an MRI. After the MRI, I was immediately called in and removed from the deployment list and was transferred to a different platoon. They started the paperwork to medically separate me, but I fought it. I had worked too hard to become a Marine. I went to three different doctors and completed another 290 score PFT. I was sent to physical therapy and proved that I was able to hold my own despite having the knee of a 90-year-old woman and being told I should never run again.

Around the fall of 2007, we were informed that our company would be deploying to Fallujah, Iraq. I was ready to go! Desperate for a change and excited to finally do my job. We began preparing by doing field ops, weapons training and other mandatory pre-deployment training.

Corporal Jones was an attractive Jamaican with kind eyes, an Abercrombie model face, and an ability to make you feel at ease. After I got moved to his squad, I started to get to know the type of leader he was. Caring, hardworking, knowledgeable and always putting his Marines first, were some of his best leadership qualities. Not only was he one of the funniest people I had ever met, we had such similar taste and twisted humor. We became fast friends. He had this personality where everyone wanted to be around him.

In November, our company went to 29 Palms for our pre-deployment training. I was sitting by myself outside, deep in thought, waiting for our Humvee rollover training when Corporal Jones or Anthony, as he introduced himself, came and sat next to me. We were throwing rocks at different targets and chatting. He could tell something was bothering me and I brought up what had happened with my sister and her crazy husband. I hadn't told anyone and was surprised how comfortable I was around him. Knowing he would be going on deployment with me was such a comfort.

When the war started in Iraq, a pattern began to develop, forcing our military forces to make a massive change. Due to the religion and cultural beliefs, males were not allowed to touch or even look at the local women. The insurgents used this to their advantage and began to smuggle contraband into the cities with the women and children. The Marine Corps knew this couldn't go on, and because women weren't allowed in combat roles, they formed special groups of women. They formed the female engagement team (FET) and the Lioness program.

I volunteered for both. I would be attached to infantry units for different missions when we deployed. Our very limited training began in 29 Palms. While my platoon was sitting around playing on their phones, I was sent off to train with an infantry unit. I was one of the very few females in my battalion to volunteer. The first day we did a hike and simulation. We set up checkpoints, cleared houses, and did other combat training. The hike was around 8K in full gear and I had to practically run to keep up with their fast pace. I was beyond thankful for the countless hours I spent in the gym.

The gear weighed around 90 or so pounds and because the gear was designed for men, it was extremely uncomfortable! Especially for a woman with large boobs like mine. It sucked! My arms would go numb, the pressure on my chest made it hard to breathe and the waist straps would cut into my sides, leaving them raw and bleeding. Our hair buns would push our kevlar down, which pushed our ballistic eyewear into our nose, causing extreme pain and making it very challenging to see. Despite all this, I loved training with the infantry and wished I could do this instead of my regular job, which mainly consisted of construction.

The next day I returned to my platoon and found out that we were heading off to a live fire range that we had finally been cleared for. In 29 Palms, the grunt units always had priority and it was rare that a POG (person other than grunt) platoon would get to do some of the live fire ranges. That evening I was standing waiting for the safety brief. It was dark but I could see hundreds of eyes staring at me and it dawned on me, I was the only female in a massive group of around 400 male Marines. We slept in formation under the stars with just an ISOMAT (a padded sleeping mat) and a sleeping bag. I loved it!

Our first live-fire range was a fire team combat maneuver through a rock field. I was fire team leader and had to call out the commands to rush and get down. We had been instructed to time our runs and yell out instructions to our fire team, "I'm up, they see me, I'm down."

When I first arrived to 29 Palms, I had done everything required and finally was promoted to Corporal. There was another Corporal in my squad that no one liked. Several of the Sergeants thought it would be funny to put me in charge of him. It blew my mind how manipulative these guys were! By putting me in charge of him, it made this senior corporal that already had one combat tour, challenge everything I said. It also made it seem as if I didn't deserve the fire team leader position and was only given it to piss this Corporal off. They ignored the fact that I was qualified and I did a better job than most.

After returning from the live fire range, I was sent to do a 48-hour special effects training with the grunt unit I was attached to. We did raids through meat houses and other buildings, created roadblocks throughout the city and performed roving patrols. I was getting frustrated with the situation because I didn't know any of the platoon's SOPs. I didn't know their clearing techniques and I hadn't been training for months with these guys. Grunts go through a different school for months and these guys just spent the last year training together. My platoon spent our training months sitting around a smoke pit or building stuff. When they let me clear some rooms and actually allowed me to participate, I loved it! For forty-eight hours we were not allowed to take off our flak jacket or Kevlar helmet. Trying to go the bathroom with all of our gear on made it miserable!

The temperature was so cold at night, my Camelback froze and I couldn't sleep. I would try to sleep on my stomach, but couldn't because my magazines and grenade pouch were on the front of my flak jacket. If I laid on my back, I would have a hard time breathing because of the weight on my chest. My side was even worse. All that weight pressed my hip into the ground, cutting off circulation to my legs. The best way I found was partially laying back, sitting down with my back against a wall. I finally fell asleep against a Jersey barrier we had used for mock patrol stops.

The grunt unit I was attached to during training was not going to be the same unit I would be with in Fallujah and I wish it could have been. All the guys were respectful, courteous, and I never once heard any of them complain that I was there. This was very different from what I was used to in my unit. If people knew the harassment female Marines had to endure, especially in our unit, they would be horrified. Sexual harassment was common, so common it actually became normal and I often didn't even realize it. I would ignore it and believe it was just part of the hazardous work environment. I had grown tolerant to daily comments on my large breasts, no matter what I was wearing. Crude sexual remarks and constantly turning down sexual advances were the norm.

After returning from 29 Palms, I decided to go home and see Marie during our Christmas block leave. I hadn't spoken with my family much and I was missing Marie every single day. Who knows if I would ever come back and I had to hold her one more time. My parents didn't mention anything about my brother and what I had told them. Being around my father was like walking through a minefield. I avoided him as much as possible. Cain invited me to a party he was having, and there was going to be a lot of my old friends there that I really wanted to see. My protective coping mind took charge and I acted as if nothing had ever happened. As I was getting ready to go, my mother came into the bathroom "I bet you are so excited to see your brother. I hope you can spend some alone time together." I looked at her in total disbelief and right then I knew she didn't believe what I had told her.

Upon arriving to his shitty house, a wave of pot smell, stale beer, and urine greeted me. It took me several minutes to gather up the strength to knock on the door. This was no place for a child. As I firmly knocked several times, my heart was pounding so loudly I was afraid he would be able to hear it. Show no fear, don't let him see your emotions, I told myself as I waited. Thank God his three-year-old daughter answered. She looked as if she hadn't bathed in weeks, and the smell, when I picked her up, confirmed my suspicion. The living room was disgusting, stains in the carpet, dog hair from his pit bull everywhere. It reeked of cigarette smoke due to him smoking inside and beer cans were laying around everywhere. It reminded me of the drug dealers houses you see on America's Most Wanted. The pit bull scratching on the glass door to get in couldn't have been more perfectly placed.

Sounds coming from the garage indicated that several people were already there. We made small talk until his daughter asked me to read her a book. Grateful for the opportunity to get away from him, I followed her to her room. I didn't talk much at all to Cain and I made sure that I was never alone with him. I stayed for around an hour chatting with some of the guys I grew up with. They all turned out to be losers that drank all the time and did a ton of drugs. There were not only beer bottles everywhere, they smoked cigarettes and weed inside the house with a three-year-old living there. I was disgusted and couldn't stay any longer. There would have been no point to call CPS after my experience with them.

When I was getting ready to leave and go back to California, my father came into my old room. I hadn't spoken with him since I had arrived. He told me that what I was doing was wrong, that women shouldn't serve in the military, and if I died over there, it was God punishing me. "OK", I replied and went back to packing. He walked out and I took off to the airport, holding Marie's hand the entire time. We both made tearful goodbyes and I told her I would call her and writ her from Iraq. Little did I know how much this deployment would change me for the rest of my life!

Chapter 19

The flight from Kuwait to Al Taqaddum Airbase (TQ) was terrifying. We were in the back of a C-130 strapped into these harnesses seats made from cargo straps, and most of us had fallen asleep. It was cold inside and smelled of fuel and body odor from the Marines packed in. Looking around, I was grateful for being in the same uniform as I was the only female. As much as I hated the unflattering figure I had in uniform, times like these, when I had to sit across from perverted men, being the only woman, I was grateful.

After being up for almost 30 hours without sleep, I was exhausted. Just as I was beginning to nod off, the plane dropped and I thought we were going to die. The other deployment virgins had similar looks of terror on their faces. Those on their second or third tours laughed at us. This was a common procedure when flying through a combat zone and nothing out of the ordinary, but they kept this knowledge from us. It was one of the many combat deployment type of initiations we would soon experience.

When we landed in TQ, we were loaded into seven tons and transported to our base in Fallujah. The moment we arrived things were chaotic. Running around, unloading gear, finding your own gear. I had my rucksack on my back, a seabag strapped onto the front of me, another seabag in my hand, my weapon cross slung, and my other hand held my day pack.

We weren't allowed to leave the compound alone, so I would walk the three kilometers to get to the chow hall. I usually would tag along with Brutus, Davis and Jones. While we were passing the laundry facility, Brutus felt the need to point out that this would be the perfect place to rape somebody because it was too loud and no one could hear you. I ignored his comment but in the back of my mind it scared me. I had the rare opportunity of learning how men think because these three said everything and anything that popped into their heads. Even though I was grateful for the education because I could see through the bullshit lines men used to try and get in your pants, I was still disgusted and didn't trust anyone.

I received my first Lioness assignment. I made sure I had all my gear prepared. My weapon was clean, first aid kit was in my day pack, tourniquet and seat belt cutter attached, and I was as mentally prepared as I could be. I was picked up outside our compound, got in the back of the MRAP (mine resistant ambush protected vehicle), and headed out for my first time outside the wire in a real convoy. Excited and a little nervous, I climbed in and joined an Arabic female interpreter wearing a flight suit and several other male Marines. The gunner, a cute white teenage boy with a country accent, popped his head down to say hello. My first assignment was crowd control and security at an ECP (Entry Check Point) to check women and children entering the city of Fallujah.

Around twenty minutes later, I heard a loud explosion *a*nd my body went flying up. My head hit the top the MRAP and I came down hard, getting knocked out in the aisle. After regaining consciousness, I heard screams, footsteps, radio, yelling out instructions of an IED strike. Looking out the window as our vehicle maneuvered away from the blast zone, I saw the MRAP that was in front of us. It had been hit and the corpsman and other Marines were taking out bodies from the mangled vehicle. It was a quick glance, but it was definitely a wake-up call. Even though I had been knocked out and my head was pounding, I never reported what had happened. If I had, I would have definitely been taken off of the assignments.

The first day was long and grueling, standing for ten hours in full gear. Searching women all day was exhausting, but I loved it. The Sea of Black, which is what I called the line of women dressed in black burqas, seemed never ending. Standing in front of the search, I was in charge of crowd control, searching the bags the women brought in and searching the bodies of the women and children. Sweat dripping from under my Kevlar, swatting away the swarming flies, I called the next woman forward. I was quite impressed with the amount of items these women carry. Often, they would have a large bag balanced on their head and two large bags in each hand. The contents inside were often items to sell in the city or food.

Occasionally we would find copper wire and other bomb making parts, which we would have to report and confiscate. We would also assist with questioning the women and gathering intel with surveys or through Kat interpreting. I enjoyed this part. The part where we had to get up close and search the women was not something I enjoyed. Due to the lack of plumbing, most regular citizens didn't shower and the smell made me gag at times. The unveiling, however, was fascinating. It was like opening a package. When they would lift up their black burqa to be searched, you never knew what to expect. Some of the women had on full makeup, others were scary and had these death stare eyes murdering you in their mind. Some looked like supermodels and others resembled the Wicked Witch of the West.

Kat and I started to become very good friends. She told me she risked her life on a daily basis to protect her people, do the right thing for her country, and hoped to get to the US one day. I was grateful to have her around. Not only did it help pass the long hours, it helped to have an interpreter.

After a physically, mentally and emotionally exhausting day, I was dropped back off at our compound. That evening, I went to the sad little gym we had. Even though it was small with little equipment, no AC, and no fans, it still worked. The gym was my therapy, and after the long day I had, I needed a long session. After finishing my workout and a quick shower in the shower trailer, I collapsed onto my single bed. I put up a curtain for some privacy and to block out the light from my two roommates.

When I wasn't leaving the wire to do Lioness missions, I would wake up at 5:00, work out, shower and be ready by 07:30 for morning formation. While being on the main Fallujah base had its perks, I hated it. The main base had a coffee shop, a huge chow hall, PX, large gym, nail salon... However, we were living in the same building as our entire battalion command. Walking out my room, I would dread running into some Colonel or Sergeant Major with a stick up their ass just waiting for someone to screw up. Our command was filled with ribbon chasers and women that believed they needed to be as manly as possibly so they were strict and ruthless.

The head was outside the building we lived in. Not only did you have to bring your weapon with you everywhere you went, you would have to be in proper uniform. If you were sleeping at three o'clock in the morning and had to use the bathroom, you would have to put your hair up in a bun, make sure to grab your weapon and make it to the bathroom before for pissing yourself.

On my next Lioness mission, Kat was my interpreter again, and we quickly caught up on our way to the ECP. While the convoy commander was speaking with my CO, some of the other interpreters and Marines exited their vehicles to say hello. They were heading to another ECP and wanted to chat before we left. After a brief exchange of hellos and how are yous, I climbed in with Kat. This time we were going to a different ECP and I was excited, nervous and mentally preparing myself for what this one had in store. Would this be the day I had to shoot a mother or be blown up by a child wearing a suicide vest?

We had almost reached our destination when I heard a familiar explosion. This time I had strapped myself in and the impact was less than the other one. I overheard on the radio that the two vehicles in front of us had been hit with an IED. Two Marines and three of the interpreters we had just chatted with were killed. Kat's eyes filled with tears; she had been close with them. The pain in the Marine's eyes was difficult to see but I couldn't let it affect me, I had a job to do. I put on a strong face and was especially vigilant that day while checking the women.

The following day, I volunteered again and was sent to assist with crowd control and searching at a medical clinic. Our military doctors and nurses would volunteer and offer free health care to the local people. The lines were long and crazy. People were there for all types of reasons, some to get their babies vaccinated and others for much more serious issues, such as injuries from IEDs going off and innocent civilians being in the wrong place at the wrong time. Desperate mothers trying to get their children help started surging forward, pushing their way to the front or shoving the people in front of them. A few other male Marines and I had to point our weapons, rack them back and yell out warnings.

These clinics were also used for intelligence gathering. We asked questions about where they were injured, if they saw any suspicious activity and showed them BOLOs (be on the lookout). Myself and Kat would assist with this intelligence gathering. One of the dog handlers used to mess with the men that would glare at me by letting his dog just sit and stare or sniff them. When a male wouldn't listen to my instructions because I was a woman, he would bring his dog over and the man would then obey. The local men would look at me with hatred or as if they were taking my clothes off. The way women were treated in this country was eye opening and heartbreaking.

I was leaving the wire for Lioness missions at least twice a week. When I would return, I would go back to my platoon who thought I was actually sitting on office duty somewhere. They would make a roaring noise like a lion and would say, "Oh, here comes the lioness, or should we call you a Fobbit? A Fobbit is an individual that never leaves the wire, is never in any danger, and has a cushy office job. They had no idea what I was doing and would have been jealous or in awe of everything I was actually doing. They were pissed that they were on deployment and instead of leaving the wire, they had to build stupid desks, beds and gear trees for our lame ass command. Most of the higher ups were more concerned about their own comfort than they were about their Marines. Our platoon had a truck we would use to transport construction equipment. Our company Gunny and company First Sergeant would take the truck to go get coffee or their nails/hair done.

One of my favorite missions was when I got to go to ECP five. This assignment was a minimum of three days, quite often five. I loved being away for that long. Even though I missed my talks with Jones, I hated being in our compound. Our talks had become more personal and lengthier. He had offered to go running with me at night because we had to have a partner. Our gym didn't have any cardio machines. They used to have cardio machines, but they ended up breaking. One of the treadmills wasn't grounded properly so when I ran on it, it would shock the hell out of me if I touched the metal handles or it would do a stutter and I would slam into the front of it. During our runs, we would laugh and talk as much as possible while running. He was in great shape and found running easy so he would do most of the talking and I would just listen and laugh. Everyone started to assume we were sleeping together instead of running. Looking back, we did have such an incredible bond and I enjoyed his company more than anyone else. I could see why others might have thought that.

At ECP five, Kat and I had a tiny room in the headquarters. The headquarters was a building that had been taken over and was now being used as the main base of operations for that ECP. Our room looked like it had been previously used as a cleaning closet. It had electric wires everywhere and water leaking from the ceiling, which was also covered in disgusting brown stains. It was our home while we were there and we made the best of it. The compound had approximately 15 swa huts that were used for barracks and a chow hall. Swa huts are wood-framed, multipurpose buildings. I had also begun taking online classes from my university back in the States. My free time was spent in the computer tent, submitting my assignments or reading the study materials.

When I returned to base, I was told they needed to have somebody pull some night shift duties and monitor the BFT (Blue Force Tracker). The BFT was used as a communication between base and those out on convoys. We would have to monitor the communication and report to the command if anything out of the ordinary happened. We also were tasked with documenting how many of our Marines were outside the wire, who they were attached to and when they returned. Answering phones, chow runs, and numerous other duties also kept us busy.

Jones' wife was also deployed and stationed in TQ. She had an office job and would often call to speak with Jones. I would answer and felt bad when I had to go wake him up. Due to his long convoys as a gunner and the odd hours he worked, he didn't get much sleep. I had noticed that he wasn't his typical self, spent most of his time in his room, didn't go running with me and hadn't laughed in a while. He would wake up tired, come to the office and answer the call. I tried not to eavesdrop, but his wife would get so loud, everyone in the room could hear her screaming at him. Screaming at him for stupid stuff. Things like Jones broke his PCP and wanted to get another one, but they had a joint account, so he had to call and ask for permission to spend the money. Or if he wanted to buy a pair of shoes he liked, she would be screaming so loud he would have to hold the phone away from his ear. Never once did he get mad, raise his voice or give any reason to provoke this. I began to develop an extreme dislike for his wife as this continued for months. Due to these calls, I began to conclude the cause of his mood change had a significant amount to do with her.

Chapter 20

It was my May 1st, 2008. I was sitting in the phone center waiting for my turn to use the phone. I had put my name on the sign-in sheet and documented the time I arrived. The next day, Marie's birthday, I was scheduled to leave the wire for a convoy doing route clearance. I was scheduled to be sweep team leader. I would be gone all day, so I wanted to wish her happy birthday before I left. Finally, it was my turn and I dialed the number to my family's home. My mother answered and I asked to speak with Marie. My mother told me that my sister was not there. "She's been going through a really difficult time", she said. I replied, "Why? What's wrong? Is she OK? What happened?!?"

The next sentence would haunt me for the rest of my life. "Oh, she's fine. She's just been watching too much TV and has it in her mind that someone raped her and said touched her where she shouldn't be touched." I couldn't breathe. I knew right away what had happened. Before I deployed, I found out that Cain had lost his job and was now living with my parents. My mother then went on to tell me that my sister had been acting out and even tried to hurt my brother's three-year-old daughter. My little angel had not one single evil bone in her body and was the most loving little girl I had ever knew. This was not her.

As I was sitting there hearing the worst news of my life, there was repeated knocking on the door. I heard a familiar annoying voice say, "Your time's up." We were allowed one hour and I had been on the phone for less than ten minutes, so I knew my time wasn't up. She must have been looking at the time I arrived, not when I started using the phone. The knocking continued and I recognized the voice as one of my female Marines. She was a rank below me and I had spent hours with her before deployment and had gotten to know her very well. While we weren't best friends, I did consider her a Marine that I cared about. "Check the sheet. My time isn't up", I replied, fighting back the anger and covering up the phone.

I went back to hear my mother tell me that it was all in my sister's head and she would get over it. I knew that my mother had thought I had made it up all those years ago and that it was just in my head too. She didn't believe a word I had told her. If I had been Bruce Banner, I would have gone full hulk mode and destroyed anything in my path that was keeping me from getting to my sister to rescue her and take her away from the hell I left her in. This was all my fault. Why hadn't I told people when it had happened? Why didn't I tell the police he was free? Because I was too afraid my sister was getting raped by my rapist.

The knocking and annoying voice continued and I snapped. I don't remember the exact words I said, but I unleashed all hell on her. Taking out all of my anger and rage and making her cry. She was just trying to call home and talk to her parents before her convoy. I felt like someone else had taken control of my body and words. All I wanted to do was get on the next flight to Michigan and save the love of my life. My little angel, my child, was going through something worse than death and there was nothing I could do. After a few more select curse words and hurtful names, she turned away and I slammed the door.

I had already hung up the phone so my mother hadn't heard anything. I couldn't move. I sat there staring at the phone. After waiting in the phone booth for half an hour, I found the strength to compose myself enough to make it back to my room. When I arrived at my room and shut the door, I collapsed onto the floor, sobbing and struggling to breathe, not wanting to leave the room. Try and imagine the pain of having your rapist rape your child because you hadn't said anything. My roommate Billings, a wonderful Native American woman, came in and saw me. She didn't say anything, only came over and wrapped her arms around me. I lost it, sobbing into her shoulder, soaking her shirt with my tears. Finally, after I calmed down, I told her what had happened. She hugged me and told me it would all be OK.

I was supposed to go on the mission the next morning, but I needed to do something about the news I had just found out. I couldn't pretend that nothing happened. I couldn't do to Marie what everyone had done to me and just ignore it. Billings went and talked to a company Gunny and they arranged to have someone take my place on the mission. I cried myself to sleep and woke up an hour later to running footsteps, crying and voices talking loudly at around 04:00. Billings got up to see what happened. The Lance Corporal I had just cussed out hours before, had been blown up and killed by a roadside bomb along with three other Marines. I couldn't breathe as the words I had spoken to her repeated in my head.

Somehow, I gained composure and went to call my sister. It took everything in me not to cry when she came to the phone. I told her Happy Birthday and how proud of her I was. She was eleven. "Cinni Mini, mom told me that something happened to you. Do you want to tell me about it?" She replied angrily "No, I don't want to talk about it." The tears started to come. "You know, Cain did something to me when I was around your age and I was so scared I couldn't tell anyone. You can tell me anything. You know that, right?" "I know. I just don't want to talk about it" she said. "Cinni Mini, you can tell me anything. Sweetheart, can you just tell me if he did something to you?" There was a long pause and my heart hit the floor when she whispered "yes."

I couldn't fight back the tears anymore. "Oh, sweetheart, I'm so sorry. I should have been there for you to protect you. Are you OK?" I said, choking back the tears. "I don't want to talk about it. I have to go, bye Batman", she said hanging up. I felt like I had left my body and I had no will to live. This may seem strange to some, but others that have been through something similar, may relate. The life crushing weight of grief, anger and pain was too much to endure. It felt like the only way to survive was to leave my body. The overwhelming guilt for leaving her there was too much to endure. I was looking down at myself on my knees, in the closet sized phone room. Desperately trying to breathe and silence the sobs crawling up my throat.

Then the numbness takes over and you turn into a walking

zombie. Your soul leaves your body in order to sustain life and can only return once the pain subsides. For some, it never returns and you walk the earth lifeless, not alive or dead, just there. For others, your soul returns too quickly and every morning you up and remember, you feel as if you're suffocating. After around half an hour, my body stood up, opened the door, praying that someone would be on the other side with a rifle pointed at me and end my misery. I don't recall how I even got to my room. I watched myself walking to my platoon Sergeant's room, knocking, and requesting to see a psychologist. I watched myself sit in the psychologist's office telling her what my brother had done to me and what I had just been told. No tears, cold, unemotional words came out. Too afraid to unleash the demon inside that wanted to hold him down, rip out his tongue with pliers, pull off his fingernails, watch him get raped by hundreds of men and see the tears he cried in pain. I wanted to show my parents exactly what he had done to me and let them rot in prison being forced to see the vision over and over again.

After the psychologist filed the paperwork, she informed me that she would contact CPS and I returned to work. Around three days later, I received an email from my mother. Obviously, CPS had been contacted and they went and began an investigation. My mother's email was horrible. She told me that they took Marie and put her in a facility due to some disturbing information that a forensic psychologist found during their interview with her. My mother told me that Marie was terrified and screaming as they took her away, that it was all my fault. Several weeks went by and I thought I would risk calling to see if Marie picked up. Several times my mother or father answered and I hung up right away, disgusted by the sound of their voice and filled with anger every time. Finally, one day her angelic voice said, "Hello". "Hi Cinni Minnie, it's Batman. How are you?" I could feel the confusion and anger in her words "I hate you. I don't ever want to talk to you again", she said, hanging up.

I was too late. Nothing happened and the monster Cain was still free. Flashbacks of being raped, the woman being shot in front of me, the fear of living with this guilt, fear, and not trusting anyone, consumed me. The nightmares came back and the depression and anxiety took over. I was disgusted with myself for the way I talked to Lance Corporal, for denying her the opportunity to have one last conversation with her parents, for not being brave enough to report the rape, and feeling responsible for him raping my child, for constantly allowing people to hurt me, left me wanting to die.

The day of the memorial service arrived. Sitting there, seeing the boots, rifle and dog tags, hearing her name called three times and no sound of her voice responding "here", broke my heart. I was the reason her parents couldn't have one last conversation and the one that made her cry just hours before her very last breath. I was so angry at God for not taking me instead. Why did he let me live? I failed to protect my sister, my child. I had no family after that, no one to come home to, and this all-consuming wish for death. She had friends, a boyfriend, parents that loved her! Why? Why couldn't it have been me? Realizing how much I yearned for death, I still had a desire to live and be happy. However, ever being happy again seemed impossible.

As I was leaving the chapel, I saw some Catholic medallions. Never being a Catholic, I didn't know the different Saints. Picking one up, I saw it was Saint Christopher. On the medallion it said Patron Saint of protection. Not really knowing why, I picked it up and I added it to the cross Marie had given me before deployment. My desire to never return from Iraq resulted in volunteering for every opportunity to go outside the wire. I begged to go on every raid, route clearance, or dangerous mission. I prayed that God would give me the opportunity to give my life to save someone. When that didn't happen, I started doing stupid stuff.

Chapter 21

Every time I entered a house or a building we cleared, I prayed that I would be able to save someone and give my life. I wasn't planning on taking my own life, but I daily desired to sacrifice it and end my torment. The following week, I returned to ECP five again and found out that they were doing construction to repair the damage from an IED. They had run over the search hut that we used to search the women in. Because of this, we were not able to search the women and I had no job to do. I couldn't sit around and do nothing with everything going on in my head. I needed to stay busy, so I went to the First Sergeant and asked if he had any construction materials. He told me that they did and asked why. "I'm a combat engineer First Sergeant, I know how to build things." He showed me where the materials were and I spent the entire day measuring, cutting and prefabbing an approximate 20 square foot search hut to replace the demolished one.

The next day First Sergeant assigned two Marines to help me assemble the hut and put the roof on. After we had finished, I was quite pleased with my work and went back to get some chow. It was around 120 degrees that day and I was severely dehydrated and in need of water, rest and food. As I was sitting in the chow hall eating, I smelled smoke and heard rounds popping off. I ran outside.

Marines were running around, trying to put out a fire that had started. The huts were so close together, the fire started to spread fast and within minutes three swa huts were consumed in flames. I jumped into *action* and started running in and out of the huts, grabbing everything I could and ensuring no one was inside. Rounds were going off everywhere, roofs and walls were caving in. One nearly collapsed before I barely made it out. The heat from the flames was hotter than anything I had ever felt. I kept going, no concern for my own safety.

We finally got the fire under control. After losing fifteen swa huts and many of the Marines belongings, I started vomiting from the smoke inhalation and the extreme heat. Unzipping my flight suit, I tied it around my waist, which helped a little. Half the Marines on night shift had been woken up and were running around in just their boots and silkies. Billings, who had been out with me on that mission, had documented everything with my camera. After we gained control of the fire, we started to sort through the damage. Thankfully, no one had been injured. I returned to base that night and the word had already spread about the fire. My CO saw me in the hallway showing the photos of the fire to my platoon sergeant and asked if she could see them as well. I gave her the camera which only had the photos from the fire, no personal photos or anything bad. She brought the camera back to me 20 minutes later and thanked me. Around an hour later, Billings and I were called into first Sergeant's office. I thought I was going to get an award or at least a thank you.

Instead, Billings was asked to sit down and I had to officially report in. After I was done, First Sergeant pulled out a file and said

"You have the right to remain silent, anything you say" ... I couldn't believe it. "Corporal Ives, you are being charged with conduct unbecoming an NCO by being in photographs with naked Marines and for disobeying a direct order by wearing your flight suit in disagreement with battalion policy, by having it tied around your waist." I started laughing. How many more things could go wrong? I had already been pushed beyond my breaking point, and now this." You think this is funny Ives?" "Yes, First Sergeant I do think this is funny." At that moment I gave no fucks. She stood up angrily "Get the fuck out of my face Ives."

I was restricted from leaving the wire and awaiting my NJP. I started laughing as I walked back to my room. How much more could I take? Billing's must have thought I had lost my mind. Not only this, but this command had also forbidden any organized sports activities. One of our corporals got caught playing basketball and they took his rank and NJPd him. This command was such a damn joke. Can't we just do our jobs? We were risking our lives daily and they were concerned if our hair was up in a bun, if we had a proper shave, if we were playing sports. Talk about a command full of ribbon chasers!

For the next week, I was put on office duty and I hated life. After hearing about my pending NJP, the First Sergeant from ECP five scheduled a convoy to come pick up supplies and have my back. As I was standing outside my room door in the hallway waiting to get yelled at, I saw the First Sergeant come *through* the door down the hall and walk into the CEO's office. There was no need to try and eavesdrop. Even though the door was closed, everyone in the hallway could hear everything, he said. He spoke very highly of me and put her ass in check. It was awesome! After he was done with the CO, he walked over to the Company First Sergeant's office and lit her ass up as well. When he was done, he came over and said, "Don't worry, I got you." I tried to thank him and he stopped me and said, "No, don't thank me. I was simply doing my job." The Marine Corps needed more men like him. Too bad I couldn't have asked to finish up my deployment with his unit.

After that, all charges were dropped and I didn't hear about it again. I was finally cleared to leave the wire. I volunteered the next day for another Lioness mission. The province had started to become more active and we were receiving incoming at least twice a week. While I was working at one of the checkpoints, I saw a woman with a child that caught my eye. Something wasn't right. I yelled for her to stop and Kat translated. The woman was screaming and flailing her arms, her barely walking son clutching her burqa beside her. "Ives, this isn't good" Kat said. I racked back my weapon in warning and cited in on her head, my heart pounding in my ears. I did not want to shoot a woman with her kid right there. God damn it. Something in my gut told me to wait and let her get closer. The woman's sobs finally turned into words and Kat translated them. She was telling Kat that she was hurt and trying to get to the hospital.

With her head still in my iron sights, I let her approach the search hut. When inside, the woman lifted her robes to expose her breasts, which were no longer there. Instead there was burnt flesh and pieces of skin hanging, dripping blood everywhere. The smell of burnt flesh would haunt my dreams forever. Her screams and brutal injury brought such a heavy realization of how women suffer in this fucked up society. These horrific burns that melted off her breasts were caused by her angry husband because she wouldn't have sex with him!

The male Marines would often talk shit about how females only saw the inside of an MRAP or never left the office. What they didn't know is the shit we really went through. The brave woman on the FET teams, or Lioness programs were not only thrown into situations alone and quite often unwanted, we had to deal with the possibility of shooting women and children on a daily basis. We had to see children with blown off limbs being brought through the checkpoints by their mother trying to get to the hospital. Every day we faced potential women and children suicide bombers. We had to mentally be prepared to shoot women and children.

Prior to one of my missions, we received intel that insurgents were smuggling in contraband inside dead babies. Due to the intel, when I felt the cold, lifeless body of one infant, I felt sick knowing what I had to do. I made sure the room was secured and did not allow anyone inside. Alone, I grabbed a pair of blue latex gloves and lifted up the shirt of this lifeless little infant girl. I saw the abdomen had been sloppily sewn shut. As I cut through the string with my knife, I smelled formaldehyde. Upon seeing a plastic bag inside, I stopped. I wasn't trained to process intel or handle evidence, so I covered the baby with a blanket and radioed to the command post. When I got back to the base that night, some of the guys in my unit were mocking me, making insulting roaring sounds. They thought it was funny we were called Lionesses because they didn't think we really did anything. Part of me wanted to tell them what my day involved, but there was no point. Looking back at those moments, perhaps this is why I went through all the horrible things I had. What if everything I had gone through was preparing me for this? All that trauma had given me the strength to do a job most could not do.

Several days later I was back working at another ECP. A busted up white four door vehicle pulled up to the first barrier. It was around 25 yards in front of me when I saw an AK 47 pop out the window. I knew shit was about to get crazy. Thankfully, there were not a lot of people walking through that day. Seeing two women with around four children in front of me, I ran forward, grabbed them and pulled them to cover behind a Jersey barrier. They only got off a few shots before a 240 lit them up from one of the guard towers. I felt nothing seeing their bullet ridden and bloody remains. These monsters didn't care about the innocent lives they destroyed or the kids caught in the crossfire. The ECP was quickly closed and I was forced to immediately return to the compound for the rest of the day. I never told my command about what I went through or what I was doing in fear that they would never let me return again.

The job continued to get more and more dangerous. We received death threats every time I went out, I even had a bounty out on my head. I saw the horrors of war and the damage it took on the innocent. I'll never forget the kids with their limbs blown off, mothers weeping, holding their dead children. Daughters burning themselves with acid to avoid being married off. The news about my sister and the death of several of my friends had made me temporarily numb to everything. I buried the memories of getting shot at, seeing people blown to pieces, hearing the screams, seeing children killed. Those moments where you have no idea if you have all your body parts requiring you to check yourself. That moment when you enter a room to clear and have no idea what to expect around the next corner. Would it be a child with an AK in their hand or a woman strapped with explosives? These were all events I had to bury in the back of my mind until I had the strength to deal with them.

On Mawlid, the Prophet Muhammad's birthday, a rock was thrown into the area I was searching the females. It said something like "Death to all females in the name of Allah kill the whores and you will have great rewards awaiting you." It also went on to threaten the local women that were helping us at the ECPs. They were risking their lives to come and help us to make their city safer. That day they were terrified. Five IEDs went off within half an hour, just blocks away from us. We had to close the ECP due to the high threat level against us.

I volunteered to provide a security escort for the local women that were helping us. They had to take numerous different taxis in order to get home to avoid being followed. My heart went out to these women. They were so afraid to leave my side they would not go to the bathroom all day. I found out one day and put a stop to that and volunteered to escort them to the bathrooms.

Due to the fire, my platoon was tasked with returning to ECP five to help them rebuild. I was relieved to be going back and glad to get away from base. We arrived at around 02:00 and had to wait for heavy equipment unload the wood and other materials we had brought. Since there were no swa huts, we were sitting under the stars with our backs against jersey barriers. Jones came and sat next to me. He could tell that something was seriously wrong and I was surprised when I told him. Not only did I tell him about Marie, I told him about my brother raping me. I felt like I could tell him anything and that he would never judge me. "Fuck, bro, you're the strongest person I know. I would have never guessed you were going through all that. How are you not a serial killer?" He asked. "I do my best" I replied. What he said next meant the world to me. "Well, I know someone. He can be taken out tomorrow. Just say when." He wasn't joking either and for a brief moment, I strongly considered it. But I would never jeopardize someone's freedom or life, especially someone I really started to care for.

We worked for 13 hours straight in the extreme heat. We had one of the female staff sergeants that had been moved to my platoon with us. There was only one area for everyone to sleep, so we were given permission to sleep in the same room with the guys. We all passed out too exhausted to even take a shower. I was covered with dust and sweat, probably the dirtiest and most unattractive I have ever looked. My body ached from the long hours of work, but I was happy for the distraction from my mind. Jones had set up his cot next to mine. When I woke up, for a brief moment I was disappointed that I had made it through the night. Rolling over to see Jones sleeping just a few feet away, brought this remarkable calming feeling. I couldn't have asked for a better person to have in my life during this time.

The next day we were split into groups and began putting up *around* three swa huts every hour. That night I went back to our hut drenched in sweat. Brutus had a stripped down and was walking around butt naked before getting changed. I was sitting chatting with Jones. I was in green on green and had a sports bra on underneath. *Not* thinking it was a big deal, I took off my sweaty shirt and put on a dry one. The female shower time wouldn't be until much later and I didn't want to go to chow with a sweat soaked shirt. Jones looked over "holy boobs" he said a little too loud. I playfully punched him, not thinking it was a big deal. Unfortunately, the female Staff Sergeant was in the hut and heard Jones announced my boobs. She took me aside and reprimanded me for changing in front of the guys. Later that night she moved us into our own hut but it had no AC while the other one did. I hated the double standards! She thought what I had done was inappropriate but was fine with a male stripping down naked.

We completed the ECP five huts and we're tasked with another mission to build a structure for an Iraqi police outpost *in* the middle of nowhere. After the night I had talked to Jones about Marie, things changed between us and this bond would only become stronger. I was still heartbroken and numb, but he was the only thing keeping me going day after day. The outpost we had to build needed to be done in one day. We had been up since 02:00, started building at 06:00 and didn't have a break until around 13:00. Jones and I were on top of the roof, in 125-degree weather, with the tar from the roof melting to us. I was so exhausted and kept smashing my thumb with the hammer when I was trying to hold the nail and place. Our platoon sergeant was sitting in a foldout chair laughing at us. "Hey, Ives, you're supposed to hit the nail, not your thumb" he said, like a smart ass who had been sitting in the shade with a fan for most of the day. The exhaustion and rage took over and I threw my hammer at him barely missing him. Jones gave me a look of I can't believe you just did that. Shutting down with a sarcastic "sorry, I lost my grip" I went back to work.

After retrieving another hammer, I went back to work. Jones was trying to nail down some of the tar paper that had become loose from the edge of the roof. When he started to fall, I hooked one foot into the opening in the roof and dove forward, grabbing the neck loop on the back of his flak jacket. After I pulled him back, we both looked down to where he would have fallen. There was a row of rebar sticking straight up that would have surely impaled him if he had fallen. "Holy shit, you just saved my life", he said with sweat dripping down his face. He didn't realize he saved mine just by being there for me when I needed someone the most.

Chapter 22

At the end of June 2008, we had begun to tear down the Fallujah main base in preparation for the transition of the U.S. military leaving Iraq. We were tearing down our construction office on the Motor-T Lot. I was using a sledgehammer, taking out my anger in a healthy manner smashing things. Seeing a large floodlight bulb. I slammed down my sledgehammer as hard as I could. There was a loud bang, followed by a moment of sheer panic as I saw red everywhere. Red covering my boots and trousers, red on the boots of other Marines standing near me, red everywhere. My heart was pounding in my ears. Did I just kill or seriously injure someone? Where did all this red come from? We all froze and started checking for the wounds from what we thought had been a bomb.

Thinking back to that moment where I had wished to be blown up came flooding back in like a tidal wave of regret replaced by a new desire to live. Jones' face flashed through my mind. It became very obvious to me how much I cared about him.

To our great relief, it was only a red spray paint can that had exploded. It had been buried underneath the light bulb and when I hit the bulb, the can exploded. "Holy shit Ives! Dammit, these cammies are ruined." The guys weren't happy about the red paint, but at least it hadn't been a bomb.

The morning before we were to leave for a new home in Ramadi, Iraq. I had a Marine from intel until come up and find me. "Hey, Ives, do have a moment." "Yes Sergeant, how can I help you?" I responded. The look on his face was somber. My heart started beating hard, that sick feeling of dread bubbling up. My palms started sweating and everything else became quiet. No more bad news. Please, God, I can't take any more! "I'm sorry to inform you, but your interpreter Kat, they found her body in a Wadi this morning." My heart dropped and I almost vomited. Don't cry. You have been through worse, I told myself. "After not showing up for an assignment, we contacted her family and found out that she'd been missing for almost a week. We truly valued her." Not hearing much after that, I thanked him and retreated to my room.

No tears came. They had all been used up. I curse God. Why? Why her? Why not me? People say that God only gives you as much as you can take. Well come walk in my shoes. If this is true, then why do 22 veterans a day commit suicide? Why are there so many people in prison? Then again, in a way it is true. God only gives the person you were what they could take and when he gives you more, you have to become someone else. You have to in order to survive.

After dismantling our base in Fallujah, we were transferred to Ramadi. Our new living quarters were inside these massive tents around two miles from the chow hall. But we were thrilled because that meant we were far away from our command. Finally, we were away from their constant microscope, and to my relief, close to the gym. There were no more Lioness missions in Ramadi so I was left with my platoon full time. Not having any other females in my platoon caused a number of issues. Not only did they always forget to pass word to me about any changes in schedules or missions, but I wasn't allowed to go anywhere alone. We would have to have a battle buddy to go to the chow hall, store, the gym, anywhere. Even though I would constantly remind them and ask them to come and get me before they went to chow or the gym, they rarely ever did. There were numerous days I would go to bed hungry because I didn't have anyone to go to chow with and they never came and got me. I would have asked Jones, but I didn't want others to see how much I cared about him.

One day I was showering in the female shower trailer. No other females were there because they were all working. Because I worked nights and everyone else worked days, I was usually alone. It was nice to have the place to myself. As I stepped out of the shower, I went to grab my towel. The door opened and in walked around five men from the cleaning crew. It didn't register right away that they were janitors and all I saw were men dressed like the same people that had tried to kill me. Standing there naked and dripping wet, I grabbed my gun and racked it back. The men scattered with looks of shock and fear on their faces. From then on, I locked the door to the shower trailer before showering.

Even more frustrating was not being able to go to the gym when I wanted. In order to deal with the memories and stress I was under, I worked out several times a day or for at least several hours. Most of the guys worked out sporadically, not at all, or for less than an hour.

Thankfully, the gym was close and I would often risk getting caught when I ran there as fast as I could to avoid detection. One particularly long day, I hadn't eaten. I was feeling the lack of energy while I was working on cutting wood for a structure we were building. One of the duty drivers pulled up in our company truck and walked over with a sandwich. Once again, all the guys had forgotten to get me before chow, so I hadn't eaten all day. "Hey Ives, Corporal Jones asked me to tell you to eat something" he said handing me the sandwich. I tried to hide my smile, but I was so touched. When I thanked him later, I told him that was one of the nicest things anyone had ever done for me. He was shocked. From his perception of me he thought people did nice stuff for me all the time. How far from the truth that was!

When we transferred to night shifts due to the extreme heat, my sleep schedule was nonexistent. We would work all night and get back after eating chow at around 04:00. I would rack out for several hours until the sun came up. Then I would wake up in a pool of my own sweat, unable to fall back asleep. The AC units didn't work and instead kicked out hot air, so we just turn them off. Plus, they made such a loud noise and I hated not being able to hear when someone came into our tent. Some of the nights it was so hot I would take off my bra and sleep just in my shorts, laying on my stomach. My guys knew I was the only female sleeping during the day and they would never knock or announce themselves in hopes to catch me changing. One morning, Brutus came in without knocking to pass word and saw me sleeping topless on my stomach. After going and telling the others what he had saw, they would often come in and toss rocks at me in hopes that I would jump up and flash them. After that, I never slept topless again. Brutus had been trying the entire deployment to sleep with me, but I had no interest whatsoever and had turned him down numerous times.

Most days the gym would be packed full of Marines that were on night shift, not working out, but passed out all over the theater and lounge areas as it was one of the only air-conditioned buildings around. Before walking into the guys tent, after knocking I always had to mentally prepare myself for the unexpected. Sometimes you would have to duck and cover and avoid getting hit by objects launched by whatever they had constructed that day. Other days I would walk into leg beat-downs they called bapping. They would slam their knee into your quad, trying to drop you saying bap bap bap. Oh, the immaturity of these grown men. One day I walked in to find these idiots experimenting with blood transfusions, with no idea what the other person's blood type was or any medical person observing. Yep, crayon eaters at their finest. We all were taught how to put in an IV, but they took it one step further. Other times they would be giving each other homemade tattoos. When they weren't in the tent screwing around, they were on the lot, shooting each other with nail guns or seeing if they could break wood over each other's heads.

There were several occasions where we had no work due to the changeover in command in preparation for a battalion to return to the states. During the down times, Jones and I would end up sitting outside on the smoke bench talking for hours, sometimes all night long. We talked about everything for hours and it was still never long enough. The more we talked, the more I never wanted to go home.

161

Could we just stay here forever? He never made a move even though I could tell he wanted to. Both of us were trying very hard to keep from doing what we both wanted to do. The way he looked at me, reminded me of the way Charles used to, but even more intensely. No one had ever looked at me that way and it only made things harder. Even though we were only going on an hour of sleep, sleep could wait. Even though we both loved sleep, we had both found something we desired even more, our conversations. Being around him was healing. I felt as if I had known in my entire life.

Fighting the growing feelings for him, I was determined to shut them up and remain great friends. There was an undeniable attraction between us, but we never talked about it. What if I had met him before he got married? In the back of my mind, I knew being raped by Graham would have never happened. The stupid mistakes I had made with other guys would have never happened. Then again, I would not understand what an incredible man he was and how different he was than the others. I wanted to stay there with him in that shithole forever. Despite the living conditions. Despite living in a tent in extreme heat, hearing live fire going off nightly, not being able to sleep because the intense heat, RPGs whistling over our heads forever. I wanted to stay there forever with him. I didn't want to go back home to face all that was to come.

One evening after talking for hours, he had to go rack out because he had a convoy that day and needed at least a few hours of sleep. After showering and changing, I fell asleep with a smile on my face. I hadn't felt this happy in my entire life. The anticipation of seeing him that evening and the nights to come in our own little world, under the desert sky with hundreds of stars looking down on us, left me blissful.

That morning I woke up sobbing, shaking and covered in sweat and tears. The worst dream I had ever had shattered me, and I jumped up panicked. For a few moments I couldn't breathe. Was it real? Did Jones really die on his convoy? He was the lead gunner and, in my dream, I saw him die in an IED blast. During those few moments, I realized a devastating truth. I was madly in love with him. My dream had given me an experience of life without Jones and the pain was so intense, I wanted to die. My nights in Iraq were filled with night terrors of watching the child I raised get raped in front of me while she begged for my help. I was her protector, her Batman, and I was the reason she was raped. They were filled with memories of getting raped over and over again. The pain from those dreams were horrific but the pain from losing Jones was worse. It was the same fear I felt when I first realized how much I loved Marie. Life without her would not be worth living.

The love I felt for Jones wasn't an 'I can see myself dating him or even spending my life with him' kind of love. It was a soul mate connection. An all-consuming, endless, real and unconditional love. The same love I felt for Marie, but intensified with sexual chemistry, romantic love, unwavering loyalty and friendship forged in the combat zone. I had been angry at God before, but now I hated him. Why would he let me find a soul mate I could only look at it but never touch, only smile at but never kiss, laugh with but never share true intimacy. My rage was soon replaced with fear and I bolted from the tent. The dream was too real and I was terrified for him to go on that convoy.

Seeing one of the guys in my platoon sitting outside the tent, I asked him to go wake Jones up. As he exited the tent, barely awake, it took everything in me not to hug him and never let him go. Shaking, heartbeat thumping rapidly I couldn't speak because the words were still stuck in my throat. That feeling you get when you're about to cry and the pain in the back of your throat becomes painful enough to make you cry. He asked me what was wrong in a concerned voice. Swallowing hard, I got out a quiet "I had a really bad dream. Can you please not go today?" "Come on, T" (short for Athena and something he started to call me when it was just us), you know I have to. Was it really that bad of a dream? What happened?" The tears started coming and I turned my head so he couldn't see them. "Come on, bro", he joked "It'll be fine. I'll be back before you know it. Don't worry, I promise I'll be back."

I kept my back turned as I regained composure and made sure no tears escaped. After saying OK, I started to walk away. My heart sank moments later as I saw him start walking to the convoy brief. When I got back inside my tent, I couldn't shake the feeling that something bad was going to happen. After the way things have been going for me on this deployment, how everyone kept dying and not me, I thought maybe I was being punished. Or perhaps I survived because of the St. Christopher medallion I wore around my neck was protecting me. Willing to do anything to see his face again, I went to give him my necklace. Knowing I wouldn't be able to give it to him without crying, I asked of the female drivers going on the convoy to give it to him. That evening, I was sitting outside pretending to write in my journal, but I was actually waiting for his convoy to return. It was one of the longest days of my life.

Hearing his familiar laugh, I felt a flood of nervous emotions. Oh, thank God he's OK!!! Now what? Could he tell how much I was in love with him? Was it written all over my face? Good God, I started realizing just how attractive he was. No, no, no. Stop. Stop getting turned on. You can't have him or be with him. Just be happy he's back. Good Lord. I felt like I was dealing with nine different personalities and voices in my head. OK, stop thinking he's almost here. He came strolling up with a big grin on his face. God damn, he looked so good in uniform. How I would love to rip it... Stop it!! He handed me my necklace saying "I had no idea you cared so much." I did my best not to let him see my true feelings "Don't get too excited. It's just a necklace." "Yeah, but it was between those" he said pointing at my boobs and doing this thing with his eyebrows/ grin he would do to make me laugh. We both started laughing and I waited for him to shower and we walked to chow together. I prayed the nights with him would never end and hated when the sun would come up, making it easier for people to see and start rumors.

A few days before my twenty sixth birthday, I was heading to the armory to train some of the new Marines that were replacing us. Before I arrived at the lot, Brutus came up smiling and said, "Hey Ives, Jones is gone. He had to escort Sgt. Shah to Kuwait because he threatened to kill himself last night." "OK, and you're telling me why" I asked? Inside I was devastated and I prayed that it wasn't written all over my face. "Oh, I just know that you guys are close and all. I just wanted to be the one to tell you" he replied with an evil grin on his face. My squad leader, Sergeant Luke, a friend of Jones', came up to me and told me that Jones had tried to come to say goodbye. He said it was a last-minute assignment and Jones had asked Luke to tell me and that he was sorry he had to leave and was going to miss my birthday. He said Jones would make it up to me.

We finally left Iraq and headed to Kuwait. The first two days were torture. I had no idea where Jones was and I was afraid to go investigate because I didn't want anyone to know I cared. I spent my free time talking with Billing's, who I had grown very close with, and watching movies that would help take my mind off the dreaded return home and all the trials I would have to face. I think I was one of the few that didn't want to go home and had even volunteered to extend my deployment. I was sweating profusely after loading our gear into the trucks that would be transferring them to the flight line. It was around 20:00 and we were leaving that evening. As I was wiping the sweat from my brow, I looked up to see Jones walking towards me, obviously trying to hide his grin. My heart stopped. I'm in so much trouble with this one. I wanted to jump into his arms and never let him go.

He asked me to take a walk with him. We went and found a gazebo away from prying eyes. Sitting next to me in the dark, he placed his hand on mine, telling me he was so sorry he missed my birthday and wished he could have been there. What a cruel God you can be I thought. Sitting there, the feeling of his hand on mine, felt so right. It was so confusing. How could something this right be wrong? What would I do without him? The most miserable place on earth had become the happiest place because of him. My wish for death had been replaced with never wanting to leave his side. The realization of what I was returning to was hard enough and knowing I wouldn't be able to see him every day was even harder. Knowing that we wouldn't have our nightly talks seemed unbearable.

Some find me disgusting for falling in love with a married man. Why would I ever want this? He was unattainable. I was haunted by dreams of Marie calling for Batman and how I never protected her. Jones was the only thing keeping me alive. He helped me climb out of the pit of hell, but I felt like God was cutting the rope and watching me fall back in. My hell was living knowing what had happened and death seemed like the only way out.

Our moment was too quickly interrupted when they called us to load up onto the bus to get to the flight line. Walking towards the bus, his hand still purposefully brushing against mine, he quietly spoke to me "This is going to sound silly and I may not say it right, but look, I love my wife, but it took being away from you to make me realize how much I really care about you." Really, REALLY? Pissed at the world, at my life, at the cruel joke of my soul mate being married, I punched him saying, "Don't you fucking say that. Why would you tell me that? Don't tell me shit like that." "But why" he asked? He was so confused and rightfully so. He had attempted to tell me how much I meant to him and I freaked out on him. I couldn't answer because if I did, I would have started sobbing.

This man I was so hopelessly in love with had just told me how he cared about me, but in the same sentence, how much his wife meant to him. It was like saying, 'Hey, we are perfect together and

I care about you, but nothing will come of it. It played into my fear of never feeling like I was enough for anyone. That no one would ever love me back. It felt like when Michael took back his love for me, but so much more painful. Like someone told you they were in love with you, but they couldn't be with you. I knew he didn't say those things to hurt me. He couldn't have possibly understood how devastating those words were. He was going home to his wife and I was going home to an empty barracks room with no family or anything that gave me a reason to return.

We sat next to each other on the way to the flight line in silence and soon boarded the flight to Germany. Staring out the tinted windows with the bright blue curtains of the charter bus, I was thankful for the darkness. Jones hadn't said a word. The tension between us obvious, but he had no idea why. What could I have said? You're the love of my life. You're my soul mate. Leave the wife you just said you loved despite all of the marriage problems you're having. You are everything I had ever dreamed of, hot as hell, kind, fun, great body, hardworking, and loyal. There was no doubt in my mind I would never love another man as much as him, and it was devastating. I knew there was nothing I could do to change how I felt no matter how much I fought it, and it scared the hell out of me. Was I doomed to be alone forever, hopelessly in love with a man I could never be with?

My voice was silent, but my mind was screaming. WHY GOD? Why him? Why was he my soul mate? He's married. He's my best friend and all I have and now I would have to watch him with her. The same person that would scream at him over the phone for no reason. I would have to watch her, put him down and make him think he isn't this amazing man I know that he is. I will have to go home alone every night wanting to fall asleep next to him and wake up to see his face, but he won't be there. He will be with her. Why couldn't I have just died over there?

Chapter 23

Jones didn't sit next to me on the flight back to the States, and by the time we arrived back in California, I couldn't spend any longer away from him. I didn't want to waste the few hours we had left together. On the bus ride home from March Air Force Base to Camp Pendleton, Jones came and sat next to me. We fell back into our normal routine, laughing and talking about everything. The trip wasn't long enough. Our time together was never long enough. I could tell that he felt the same way.

He had been so open with me about what he felt, but I was still too afraid to let him know I was in love with him. While I was deployed, I kept a notebook filled with pictures I used kind of as a journal. While I hadn't written about my love for him, I did write about my attraction to him. He caught sight of his name and asked if he could read it. Embarrassed for him to read about my bodily reaction to his presence, I shyly turned my head away, blushing. When he had finished reading, he asked me if he could write in my book of Joy, as he called it. In his chicken scratch, he wrote 'So I'm writing in Athena's Book of Joy and I don't know what to write, maybe because I just tell her instead of writing it. I have a message for you Athena, you're a great person and you should stop hiding that from everyone."

Many of you have seen the homecoming videos of military members coming back from their deployments. The Welcome Home signs, the loving girlfriend, proud parents, wife juggling two children, smiles, tears, laughter. For some, it is one of the greatest feelings in the world. Holding their child for the first time, kissing their loved one, hugging parents that had driven over thirty hours to be there, or good friends that were there to help you get your gear and bring you your favorite alcohol. Then there was me. I had always dreamed about this fantasy homecoming, but it wasn't to be. Instead, it was one of the emptiest days I have ever known.

I felt as if I had just been buried alive and I couldn't breathe. Jones said a quick goodbye, had several other buddies of his meet him there to help him with his gear, and drove off. I remembered watching him drive away. I almost fell to my knees, absolutely crushed. Making my way through the crowd of Marines being embraced by their loved ones, I found my gear. Because no one was there to pick me up, I was the only Marine that needed to use the bus to get back from the parade deck to the barracks. As I climbed back on the bus, passing each empty seat felt like someone telling me, "You aren't enough, you aren't enough, you aren't enough."

After checking into the BEQ (Bachelor Enlisted Quarters) office, I was assigned a room. After putting my sea bags in the room, I returned to grab my day pack with George strapped on it. George was the monkey I had given Jezebel for her senior year on Valentine's Day, along with a dozen roses. When I had returned home for Christmas before deployment, I found George in the trash. Taking custody of George may seem silly to some, especially for a

172

grown woman, but he was a great snuggle buddy. George even came with me on deployment. The guys used to kidnap him and leave me ransom photos, but always returned him unharmed. George had been my sleeping companion on the countless nights I cried myself to sleep.

When I came back from my room to get my pack, my heart stopped. George was gone. It takes pushing me to the breaking point for me to get angry. Emotions still at an all-time high, I was past angry and was ready to pull out a gun and shoot whoever had taken George. Yes, I know, a major overreaction! "OK, motherfuckers, who the fuck took my monkey?" The kidnappers thought it was funny and started mocking me "Oh, Corporal Ives wants her monkey back." I saw one of the guys holding George and I grabbed him. "You touch my stuff again and I will fucking kill you. You hear me?" I got in his face and some of my guys pulled me away and told me it was just a joke and to calm down.

Before this moment, I never truly understood how someone could snap for such a stupid reason. This memory would change me forever. If you don't know what happened before that moment, you will never understand the situation. After that, whenever I saw one of my Marines snap, get so drunk they couldn't walk, or punch a wall in rage, my heart broke for them. How much pain had they gone through to put them in that mindset?

When I returned to my room, I immediately felt bad. They were just joking around and I should have never reacted so aggressively. That night Would be the first time in over a year I would have to sleep alone without someone else in the room. Despite not wanting to be around anyone but Jones, the reality of my situation was crushing me, making it hard to breathe. After running to the PX to get a six pack of beer, I ordered a pizza and cried myself to sleep. The barracks were empty as everyone had gone home or to hotels with their families. To say I was depressed is like describing someone that had just lost their child as being sad.

We had 96 hours of liberty before beginning post deployment procedures. 96 hours without Jones, without Billings, with only my demons inside my head to keep me company. I tried to stay busy. I went and got my car out of storage and called Amanda to see if she wanted to go have dinner. I went and visited her family, but I wasn't me. I regret exposing her family to the condition I was in and I wouldn't find out until years later some of the hurtful things I had said and have no recollection of. I was unaware of the PTSD I had developed on deployment.

When I received my smallpox immunization prior to deployment, it had left me with this nasty purple scar I hated. What better way to cover it up and be distracted than a tattoo? I had bought a bracelet in Iraq that represented the eye of God was watching over you. I felt it a fitting tattoo as I had miraculously come back alive despite the stupid stuff I had done. I went back to my tattoo artist that had done the tribal tattoo on my back and got a half sleeve. I wanted so badly to get a full sleeve, but I was going to wait so I wouldn't jeopardize my career.

Chapter 24

Finally, the day came where we were all to report back to work. I was desperate to see Jones again. We hadn't spoken at all since the bus ride and it felt like weeks had gone by. Knowing he was busy and getting an apartment, moving his stuff out of storage and preparing everything for his wife to arrive home in a few weeks, I didn't bother messaging him. I was doing everything I could to keep my distance, no matter how much I wanted to spend every moment with him. Trying desperately to fight the feelings I had for him because I didn't want to get hurt. Then the human instinct to survive and stop the pain took over. Being around him was the only thing that helped stop the constant flashbacks, the feeling of hopelessness, the desire to die. Being around him reminded me of what it felt like to be loved by Marie. The time we spent together were the happiest times of my life. The next few weeks were like we were back in Iraq. We would sit for hours laughing and talking, waiting for formations or in stupid lines for all the post deployment checklist items.

When I was deployed, I had found the sports car I had always wanted growing up a spider eclipse convertible. I found one in Huntington Beach within my price range. Despite the car being a manual, which I had no idea how to drive, I went and bought it. The salesman thought I was crazy, but he would have done anything for a sale. Not bad for a newbie, I only stalled once on the way home. The next day, Jones took a ride with me and gave me pointers on driving a stick, which immediately helped. If it only could have stayed like this!

For the first month after getting back, as soon as we were released, I was in a skirt and heels. I would even clean my room in heels. I wasn't doing it to show off or get attention, I did it for me. I just spent seven months dressing like a man, covered in dirt, with the only flattering girly outfit being my workout clothes. If I had to go to the store or get food, I would throw on jeans and a T-shirt, but as soon as I got back to the comfort of my own room, I'd put on that little black dress and heels. I wore the dress for me, no one else.

While everyone else was out buying Escalades they couldn't afford or drinking their paychecks away every night playing video games, I was signing up for more college classes and going to the gym. Anything to keep my mind occupied. One evening I was invited to go out with the guys to a local bar. I messaged Jones to invite him and he showed up with Sergeant Luke. Jones and I ended up sitting next to each other. He looked so good in some designer jeans, spotless white sneakers and a Jamaican formfitting shirt. I didn't realize how obvious our attraction was to each other until one of the female Marines I didn't know well came up and said, "Hey Jones, I didn't know you got divorced. Who's this?" He replied "Nope still married. This is Ives, we deployed together and she's a great friend of mine." When she walked away, there was this moment of awkwardness as both of us realized how obvious it was to everyone, but we had still not admitted it to each other.

Jones and Luke decided to leave and invited me along. After gladly accepting, Luke drove the three of us to another club. This one had a dance floor that was crowded, but not annoyingly so. Jones asked me to dance and took my hand, leading me to the dance floor. We danced for a few songs. He looked so good that night and being so close to him was a struggle. I rarely got to see him in civilian clothes and he looked so good. To add to the difficulty, the two of us were like one on the dance floor. None of that awkward bumping into or moving one way when the other person went the other, we complemented each other. We both knew how much trouble we were in and both of us were fighting the inevitable. I didn't know how much longer I could hold out. This man was everything to me.

When the bar closed, I prayed we could rewind it and do it all over again. Just an hour in his arms. Instead, I had to go back home alone knowing he was going home to his wife. I started to cry on the way to the car and Jones for the first time saw me cry. He was finally able to hug me and I never wanted him to let me go. It felt amazing. He smelled intoxicating, a hint of cologne and fabric softener. His strong arms wrapped around me, made me feel safe and loved.

Even though Jones never talked about what was going on at home between him and his wife, I could they were having serious problems. Most of what I picked up was from their phone calls or seeing the way she spoke and treated him in person. The way she talked to my best friend, made me start to dislike her. Her smothering him, untrusting attitude, and talking down to him, only pushed us closer together. Every time we were together, it was becoming more and more difficult.

During block leave for those to go home after deployment, the barracks were empty, minus a few stragglers including myself. One night I was sleeping when I heard a noise that woke me up. Ever since being raped, I was constantly afraid it would happen again and slept with a knife. The noise I heard was someone opening my window and was using the window jamb to try and unlock the door. Grabbing my knife, I jumped up, threw open the door and saw a man I had never seen before holding my window jam. He took off running. After I put a sweatshirt on, I went down to the duty hut and told them what happened. They called PMO, who never ended up showing up. Apparently, they were too busy pulling over Marines for speeding, which is far more important than making sure a female Marine doesn't get raped.

I had also been having some stalker problems which was making it impossible to sleep without waking up to every single sound. Since I had come back from a deployment, I had numerous stalking incidences with several different Marines. One happened when I was in Pacific Beach at a club with Amanda and some friends. This Marine came up to me and told me he knew all about me and how they used to talk about me in TQ. People in Fallujah and Ramadi knew who I was, but how and why the hell did this creep? I had never seen him before so why did he know about me? He told me that the guys would talk about how they like to watch me run and how my giant boobs bounced. Him and his friends followed us to three different clubs.

Another time I was standing in the chow hall line when two Marines came up to me, "Hey Ives, you just got back, right?" "Yeah"

I replied, "Why?" "Oh, no reason. We just love watching you walk up the stairs to your room on third deck. The room in the corner, right? We sit in our car in the parking lot and watch you." I couldn't believe these idiots. "Seriously, why the fuck would you tell me that? What did you think? That I would be impressed that you know where I live and watch me. You think I would be so turned on that I would want to fuck you right here, right now? Stay the hell away from me." I left without getting any food. There were several other run-ins with Marines all resulting in similar outcomes.

This break in was the last straw. I wanted to be somewhere. I wasn't afraid to go to sleep. After reporting all of this to my command, they told me to move out and they would approve my BAH (military housing allowance). It's only granted to certain ranks or to married individuals. I moved into a studio apartment off base. Jones continued to fight with his wife. Even though he didn't tell me, I could always tell. He had a long ride up north with his motorcycle club over the weekend. While his crew was inside a bar having some drinks, he stepped outside to call me. He would always call whenever he had an opportunity. We talked on the phone for a while and I had already had a few drinks at home. Liquid courage that allowed me to finally tell him how I felt. I told him I was in love with him and how hard it was not to act on those feelings. There was a moment of silence and I told him that I didn't want him to respond. Partially it was out of fear that he wouldn't say it back, but the other part was I didn't want him to say it unless he felt that way in return.

After a long pause, I laughed "Well, say something. You don't need to respond about what I said, but you could change the topic, something..." He cleared his throat, something he did right before he needed to tell me something important. "I had no idea you felt that way. You can have anyone. Why me? I'm nothing special." "Well, you are. You are my favorite person on this planet. I'm sorry for dropping all this on you. I couldn't hold it any longer." We talked for around an hour before he had to go.

The next work week, nothing changed between us. No awkwardness like I was used to when guys didn't share the same feelings. A few days before his birthday, I messaged him asking if he was free for dinner before or after his birthday because I wanted to cook for him. The day after his birthday, he showed up to dinner almost an hour late. I had made his favorite chicken and broccoli alfredo and my grandmother's favorite cheesecake that he loved. When he arrived, I asked him what took them so long. He shyly admitted he couldn't figure out what to wear because he wanted to look good for me. He always looked amazing. Even with Frank Sinatra playing in the background, the dinner was filled with tension. Even though I had started to hate his wife for how she treated him, I still felt very guilty.

I was trying to tell him how hard it was for me to trust men, and I brought up what Graham and the other Marines had done to me. Tears came pouring down my cheeks. He held me and brushed my hair back. After a good cry, I fell even more in love with him and the way he made me feel safe, happy, loved. I would have done anything to make him feel the same way. When I came out of the bathroom, I found him sitting on my bed. At that moment everything else disappeared and all I wanted was to keep this feeling of happiness and avoid the pain I felt when he wasn't there. Standing in front of him, he slowly slid his hands all over my body and finally started kissing me. He was an incredible kisser. He was gentle, passionate, and I could tell that he truly cared about me. His phone had been ringing nonstop since he had arrived. The buzzing of the phone, the knowing he would have to leave soon, and my fear of getting hurt, tried to poison this moment we shared and I needed to silence it. After we were done having passionate sex, he looked very concerned after checking his phone. Without giving me any details, he had to take off, but gave me an incredible kiss goodbye before he did.

Still lying in bed, savoring the lasting memory of his touch, my phone rang. It was a number not in my phone. I answered it in case it was one of my Marines. "Is Anthony with you?" It was Jones' wife Sarah. Almost dropping my phone, my hands started shaking. What happened? How did she know? I told her no, that I hadn't seen him. Guilt flooded in and the bliss I had just felt turned to concern and doubt. The next week during work, Jones showed up late several times and looked like he hadn't slept in days. I could tell how stressed out he was because he was smoking much more than normal. We were both busy, but he didn't speak to me for over a week. If we did talk, it was to pass word or information about work. My emotions went from being crushed to pissed off. I wrote him a letter telling him how hurt I was and that I wasn't just some person he could sleep with and toss aside. I knew that wasn't the case, but I wanted him to know that it was what I felt like because he wasn't telling me what was going on. I saw him smoking in his car and walked over and gave him the note. "Read it and burn it, OK?" I said handing it to him and walking away.

He called me that night and told me how sorry he was that I felt that way. Him and his wife were having major issues and he was trying to lay low and wait until everything passed. He told me that she had even tracked his phone and showed up at a bar he was at to get out of the house. A week later, I received a phone call from an unknown number. I answered and heard Sarah, Jones' wife crying and screaming at me. She was with one of her friends and they had found the letter I had written that had described what he had done in some detail. I almost vomited and could hardly breathe. I hung up and blocked the rest of her calls.

On my way to work the next morning, I saw Jones in Luke's car passed out in the passenger side. I dreaded what was to come. Sarah had kicked him out and he was staying with Luke. For the next week, Sarah would come to work and watch us from the smoke pit while we were standing in formation. Awkward doesn't even begin to describe standing next to him information while she sat there watching our every move. If looks could kill! Jones was avoiding me and hadn't said a single word to me. This went on for a week and I was devastated. I felt like I had been finally rescued from almost drowning, only to be thrown back in. I decided to go get another tattoo and went to visit my grandmother and aunt.

My maternal grandmother had taught me her favorite word agape, the Greek word for unconditional love. I decided to get this word as a tattoo. Not only in remembrance of her and for my sister, but also for Jones. It was a tattoo of one of my favorite flowers the plumeria with the words agape written in Greek. When I returned to work, putting my work boots on was painful. Jones had seen me limping over to my car and came over to see if I was all right. This was the first time I had spoken to him since everything had happened. I showed him the tattoo and told him the significance of it. I told him this was for Marie and him, that no matter what, I would unconditionally love them forever. He didn't know what to say, but he didn't need to say anything. I could see it in his eyes, those eyes, how I love the way he looked at me.

Rent at my apartment was getting too expensive. Because my command had gone back on their word and did not approve my BAH I was forced to move out. I asked if I could move into my uncle's guest house, a garage converted into a studio. No one was living there, so I moved in. My cousin lived in the main house with his girlfriend. I decided to have a housewarming party and invited a bunch of Marines. It had almost been two weeks since Jones and I had even spoken. He was standing, talking with Brutus and Luke when I came up and invited all of them. I was shocked when Jones told me he would be there. That Friday, the day of my party, I was walking to my car to go home and get ready when Sarah cut me off, almost hitting me in the parking lot. She rolled down the window and told me that this would be the last time I ever saw Jones and I had better watch my back. She continued to threaten my life and I ignored her getting in my car.

Jones never showed up to my party, and I was a drunk, crying mess which pissed off Corporal Cole, who had been trying to date me for months. He had developed a crush on me in engineer school, but had never said anything until then. I couldn't tell anyone why I was so upset, and the only person I could talk to was Jones, who wasn't there and wasn't talking to me.

On Monday, Jones tried to talk to me, but I ignored him and went to my car. Looking back, this was so childish, but I didn't fully understand the impact of PTSD. I was having panic attacks, flashbacks and nightmares. Not only was I dealing with all that, but the ignorant doctor I went to for the then miss-diagnosed endometriosis pain, had me on the highest hormonal birth control on the market. I was a raging hormonal mess. Even though I was trying to ignore him Jones was determined to talk. He followed me to my car and told me to open the door. He told me that he had been getting ready to go to my party when Sarah came in and flipped out on him. He said it was World War Three at the apartment and there was nothing more he could have done to come. I felt awful. The only two people I cared about were Marie and Jones, and I was ruining their lives.

To add to my devastation, Jones had orders to Hawaii along with Sarah. We were sitting in the parking lot at Battalion one evening after work when he told me that they were filing for divorce. It was hard not to show my joy at something that was hurting someone else. Even though I couldn't stand her. I never wanted her to hurt. I would never intentionally hurt someone. He tried to deny orders to stay closer to me, but was told if he did, they would send him to Japan. So he decided to go to Hawaii, which was closer to me. I didn't want to get my hopes up and I knew it was going to be months, if not years, before we could ever be anything serious.

When Jones left, I missed him every single day. I tried to fill my time with working out and staying as busy as possible, which wasn't hard. Since I returned from deployment, I had been taking night classes every Tuesday and Thursday nights from 18:00 to 22:00 and two Saturdays a month. I would drink on the weekends to fill the emptiness that consumed me.

One day I received a letter from the CPS department in Michigan telling me that after a thorough investigation, they did not find enough evidence to open a case and it had been closed. Furious that they had failed once again, I decided to call my hometown Police Department and finally report what that monster had done to me so many years ago. This opened up another case and I received a phone call from the monster himself. He wanted to come and see me and talk about everything. I hung up on him and never spoke to him again. The PD told me that due to statute of limitations, there was nothing they could do.

I missed Jones so much. I needed him! I missed seeing his face every day. I missed laughing for hours and working with him on a daily basis. I was so lost without him. One morning I was doing room inspections when Brutus came up to me, "Guess who's pregnant" he said with an evil grin. "Sarah." My heart shattered. "Oh, good for Jones. Happy for him," I said, and barely made it to the bathroom before I lost it. I knew at that moment that we would never be together, that he would never leave her. She found the one thing that would keep him there forever. I knew Jones. I knew what kind of man he was. I knew what his father had put him through and I knew that he put his responsibilities and his word above his own happiness. My dreams were shattered. My idiotic hope that one day I would be able to be with the love of my life was over.

For the next month, I don't remember smiling once. I went through the daily motions, work, school, gym, and home to cry myself to sleep every single night. Jones hadn't called or messaged me in weeks. I suspected he was too scared to tell me what happened. This is the problem with falling in love with your best friend. I had no one to talk to. No one to give me any type of support.

My younger brother John messaged me one day and asked me if he could stay with me when he came out to San Diego to visit. He had stayed out of everything involving my sister and I was shocked and excited that I might have one family member left. I picked him up from the airport and had taken a week off of work. Brutus messaged me and asked me to come to a goodbye party he was having before he left for Japan. I told him my brother was in town and I couldn't go. The next day I had gotten Sea World tickets and I was on my way there when my phone started ringing nonstop. After I paid for parking and gave John his ticket, I checked my phone while standing in line. I had messages from Cole, Seth and several other individuals that I used to call my friends. The first message "whore" the next "you fucking whore" followed by "slut; homewrecker; we know everything." Then one that heard about me transferring to counter intel, "if you try and lateral move, they do a background check and interview your coworkers. I'm going to tell them you're a home wrecking whore." They continued "slut; bitch; I hope you die; burn in hell; you chose Jones over me; I hope he was worth it; hypocrite."

I told John I needed to go find a bathroom and left him at the Shamu show. How did they find out? I hadn't spoken to Jones since I heard the news about Sarah and my hands were shaking as I dialed his number. He answered after several rings and there was a brief pause. I asked him if he had told anyone about what had happened between us. After talking to him the puzzle pieces came together. He told me that while he was living with Luke, after he had gotten kicked out, they were talking about everything at work in the office. They thought they had been alone, but Brutus had walked in and heard enough. When Brutus hadn't said anything and weeks had gone by, Jones thought he was in the clear or Brutus didn't hear anything. Saying Jones felt shitty was an understatement. He didn't know what to say and ended up having to get off the phone because Sarah had just walked in.

I had also found out from a trusted friend of mine that a large group of guys, including Brutus and everyone that had just sent text messages to me, had a bet going on in Iraq for who could sleep with me first. Hearing that my brothers had thousands of dollars riding on who could have sex with me was devastating. The same guys I vowed to protect, plucked their eyebrows, comforted after breakups, helped pick out engagement rings, and nearly died next to, didn't see me as anything more than a sex object. They didn't see me as a sister or even a Marine. After everything I had done to hold my own, remain professional, cook for them, be their friend. Was it a coincidence that Brutus had been trying up until the day he left to have sex with me? Was it just a coincidence the night before he left, he was with the very group of guys that had sent me all those nasty messages? The same guys who shared with me all their stories about banging married women. The same guys that came to me for advice about their wives and girlfriends who they had just cheated on but now wanted to make it work. Was it just a coincidence that Brutus lost a bet and suddenly everyone knew about what had happened with Jones and I when he was the only person in that group that knew? What a pathetic excuse for someone to try and sabotage my career. You coward, vengeful, insecure little boy! Men think women are pathetic. I just had my career irreparably damaged, my life threatened and treated like a prostitute because a pathetic, jealous little boy had his feelings hurt. I was furious, scared and embarrassed that now everyone knew. What they didn't know was the truth. This wasn't a fling; it was so much more!

With all this information was running through my brain, my little brother was waiting for me. How the hell was I going to act normal after just finding out all that? I couldn't talk to anyone, least of all John. The only person I could talk to was Jones and talking to him just made me want to be with him even more. I did everything I could to keep it together. I was grateful for the shows and transferring the responsibility of entertaining my brother to someone else. While sitting at the dolphin show, I was also grateful for my sunglasses, that were somewhat hiding the tears streaming down my face. I was even more grateful for the dolphin that soaked us, hiding my tears even better.

I cooked for John, took him to Sea World to a pub dinner for some drinks, drove him everywhere, let them stay with me, took him to Six Flags and paid for everything. Not once did he say thank you. Not once! I would bring him a plate of food I had cooked and after he was done, he would hand it to me to go wash. After the third time, I told him I wasn't like mom and he could wash his own damn dishes. I couldn't believe what a spoiled prick he had turned into. He was my father. I was beyond relieved to drop him off at the airport and could care less if I ever saw him again. He was selfish, rude, had no manners and was just using me for a free place to stay.

Chapter 25

When my leave was over, I dreaded returning to work. I had no idea how people were going to react or treat me, but I knew it wasn't going to be pleasant. I was right. I was harassed daily. The survivor's guilt, Jones leaving and the pregnancy, PTSD, the high doses of hormones from my birth control, and being treated like a home wrecking whore at work, left me wanting so badly to go back to Iraq. I would end up spending most of my time in my car listening to Korn or at the gym. I played one song in particular over and over again.

The words from the song running through my head: "Pick me up, been bleeding too long. Right here, right now, I'll stop it somehow. I will make it go away. Can't be here no more. Seems this is the only way. I will soon be gone. These feelings will be gone. These feelings will be gone. Now I see the times they change. Leaving doesn't seem so strange. I am hoping I can find where to leave my hurt behind. All the shit I seem to take. All alone I seem to break. I have lived the best I can. Does this make me not a man? Shut me off. I'm ready. Heart stops. I stand alone. Can't be on my own. I will make it go away. Can't be here no more. Seems this is the only way. I will soon be gone. These feelings will be gone. These feelings will be gone. Now I see the times they change. Leaving doesn't seem so strange. I am hoping I can find where to leave my hurt behind." -Korn

Luckily, I was soon transferred over to the construction shop and put in charge of my own squad. Despite everything I had been through, I was an outstanding Marine and I did not allow my personal life to turn me into a dirt bag. Because of my outstanding performance, I was put on a meritorious sergeant board and I ended up winning. Jones and I started to talk again and I did my best to pick up the pieces, trying to keep moving on. I oversaw 30 Marines and was given most of the troublemakers. They gave me three Marines that were getting kicked out for drugs, two that had mandatory AA meetings, which I had to take them to and from, and an 18-year-old fresh out of high school.

On top of all that, I volunteered to run the battalion's BCP (weight loss program). This was a group of Marines that were overweight and required to workout at lunch every day. I offered to take it over because I didn't agree with the leadership style that the Marines in charge were using. They would sit in their chairs, yelling out orders, and not leading from the front. In the morning I would lead my squad in a workout. In the afternoon I would workout with the BCP Marines, and in the evening, I would go and work out by myself. I was doing everything I could to make myself get over Anthony, but it was like trying to stop the grass from growing without killing it.

I even started dating. I went to a friend's birthday party and met an outgoing and entertaining older man named Devon. He was an African-American who was 10 years older than me but didn't look or act it. We had a lot in common. Both Marines, fit, and enjoyed having a good time. We hit it off and soon started dating. I spent every weekend at his house and he introduced me to a new hobby Muay Thai. The instructor, Kru Mark, was incredible. I have never met a humbler, yet bad ass man in my life. He was a descendant of the King of Siam and had one of the most incredible stories I had ever heard. Inspired by him, I made the two-hour round trip three nights a week to go train with him. I started to get quite good and they wanted me to start fighting MMA, but I couldn't due to my knee. My schedule was crazy. Up at 04:00, to work by 05:30, work until 16:30, drive down to school or Muay Thai which took over an hour, and back home at around 23:00 hundred to start it all over again.

Even through my casual relationship, I was still madly in love with Anthony. There were several occasions where he would actually call when I'd be sleeping in bed with Devon and I would get up to talk to him. I never felt bad because what Devon and I had was more for entertainment and distraction to pass the time. I knew he felt the same because there was nothing truly intimate between us. We were just friends with benefits. There were a few times where I had started to talk about my past and he would interrupt me and say, "you know, you don't have to tell me about it if you don't want to." I knew he didn't care about who I was or what I had been through. He lived in the moment and there was no room for anything deeper. So, in a way, we were using each other.

After finally paying off my car, I decided to buy a motorcycle. I messaged Anthony and asked his opinion on a good first bike. He told me not to get a 200 because I would get bored. He suggested the Suzuki GSX600, which he learned on, and the Honda CBR 600. The best advice he gave me was to go sit on several different bikes before I decided. He told me that every rider is shaped differently and you don't want to get a bike you aren't comfortable sitting on. Best advice ever! The Honda CBR was too wide for me, but the *GSXR600* fit perfectly. After filling out the purchasing paperwork I asked "Do you guys deliver? I don't know how to ride yet." They were shocked. "Wait, so you just bought a new bike and have never ridden before?" The salesman thought I was joking. "That's how I roll" I said laughing. The best way I learn is by doing. Even though I was terrified, I went for it.

They delivered my bike and I took it around the block that same day. I was scared, but even without any help, I forced myself to learn on my own. The first two days I took my bike around my neighborhood and slowly started to get more comfortable. In order to ride on base, they make you take a riding course and I signed up for one the week after I bought my bike. The first day of the course began during an unusual downpour for San Diego. It rarely rains, so when it does, San Diegans lose their minds, forget how to drive, and there are car accidents everywhere. Not only had I never ridden on the freeway, the gods were challenging my riding skills by dumping rain on me in the process.

After making it to the main gate, I noticed the turning lane to get to the class was flooded out. There were trucks going through and the water came up to the top of their tires. There was a long line of cars behind me, so I couldn't take a moment to gather up courage and go for it. Was I going to die, falling over and getting trapped, drowning in a puddle? I knew I wouldn't. I was just trying to be funny in a very scary situation and make myself laugh. I was more concerned with flooding my bike. Gathering up the courage, I went as soon as a big truck went through, clearing some of the water out. Smiling triumphantly after making it through, I felt very accomplished.

I was the only female in the class and one of the four new to riding. The course was a week long and I picked it up quickly. The instructors were shocked that I had ridden through the rain on my first day. The other two new riders had borrowed bikes that were already at the site so they didn't have to ride through the rain. Four of the other experienced riders brought their bikes on their trucks. After hearing that I had ridden through the rain, they told me I had bigger balls than any of the guys at the course. I passed the course and got my class M added to my license. It was a proud moment and I sent Anthony a photo of it. He was very proud of me and told me to be safe.

We had a new female Sergeant check into our shop. At first, I was hesitant because I didn't usually care for female Marines. However, this one was much different. Her name was Maria Hernandez and she worked her ass off, pushed herself during every PT session and we hit it off right away. She wasn't assigned to any squad yet, so she joined my squad during Morning PT where she developed a love hate relationship with my workouts. She hated them because she almost threw up every time, but she loved the results. We also had a new Master Sergeant check in my Master Sergeant Munoz. I wish I had had the opportunity to spend my entire career under his leadership. He had full sleeves and was a bad ass.

Master Sergeant Munoz would come out and watch as I worked out the overweight Marines. I believed in leading from the front so I worked out with them. I would take them on long runs, have them flipping tires, fireman carry, and whatever else that we were working on that day. I loved it. I told everyone in my squad that I could either be one of their greatest allies or their worst nightmare. Some learned the hard way.

One field day I was inspecting rooms and one of my junior Marines hadn't cleaned the toilet. I called him into the bathroom. "Hey, PFC Arturo, did you clean your toilet?" "Oh, yes Sergeant Ives, I cleaned it." I looked inside and saw the poop stains. "Really? So please tell me what this is?" I said, pointing inside the toilet. "Um, I don't know Sergeant." I hate being lied to! "So, you don't know what your own shit looks like?" "Sorry, Sergeant. I guess I forgot to clean it." "Hmm. OK, go grab your toothbrush Arturo." He grabbed it and ran back into the bathroom. "OK, you are going to clean the toilet with your toothbrush. Obviously you couldn't clean it well enough with a toilet brush. Make sure you get a new toothbrush when you're done. If you don't have the money, I'll give you money to go buy one at the PX." "Yes Sergeant" he said.

Sergeant Murphy and I left and started going through the other rooms for field-day inspections. After a few rooms I went back and checked on Arturo. He was cleaning the toilet with the toilet scrubber. "Oh, hell no!" I walked in, grabbed the brush out of his hand that he had just been using to clean the toilet with and said,

196

"Does this, Look, Like, A toothbrush, To you?" I yelled, with every few words followed by an emphasis with the toilet brush. Each time spraying dirty toilet water on his face. He stood there sputtering "No Sergeant. I'm sorry Sergeant", he said starting to cry. "What the hell is wrong with you Marine? What now? You want to start crying because you have toilet water running down your face? I gave you a simple instruction and you didn't follow it. What happens when your ass goes to Afghanistan and your squad leader tells you to stop and you don't listen? You die Marine. You better start fucking listening now. Stop crying. You've got to be fucking kidding me. Get the hell out of my sight." He ran out of the room and stood at attention by the door with his roommate, still crying. Sergeant Murphy was dying laughing in the corner. "Fucking hell Ives, that was some funny shit, man."

What I didn't realize then but realize now, is how much I had changed who I was in order to 'fit in'. Being a female in the Marines is not easy. Every single day you are under a microscope. If you mess up or show any kind of weakness, it's like bleeding in shark infested waters. My actions with this Marine were more about humiliation disguised as a teaching moment. Military culture embraces and teaches an authoritarian style leadership. That "pain is weakness leaving the body". Thinking for yourself was discouraged. Blindly following orders was seen as a positive trait. It took me getting out of the Marines and away from that culture to realize the impact military culture had on me. This was not an example of a good leader. It was an example of trying to fit in and going against my true self.

We went on to the next room where Lance Corporal Bess stayed.

This kid was not only a constant suicide risk, he had told everyone about his zombie apocalypse conspiracy theory. When Murphy and I walked in, it looked clean, but the entire room reeked. We found rotting food under his rack with several fast-food bags filled with maggots. Murphy and I gave each other a look and we went to town flipping over his bed, throwing shit everywhere, dumping out his full trash can and whatever else we could find in the room. Another one of my Marines hated me so much that he went UA (unauthorized absence) to avoid me.

I also had a caring side. I would cook for my squad, make sure that they were always taken care of, make sure on field day that they had food. I would order pizza and bring it to them. I also mentored the female Marines in my company and was a sexual assault advocate. I sat the females in my company down one day and shared with them about some of my past and what my brother had done to me. I shared this with them because I wanted them to know that they could talk to me about anything. I told them these things to show them that they didn't have to let their past break them. They could move on and do amazing things. Sharing my past was also a form of therapy for me. Even though I wasn't ready to talk about being raped by those two Marines, I was able to talk about my brother. It turned my pain into something good, something healing.

After my talk one of them broke down and started crying. I found out that she had been raped by a Marine that was in our unit. Similar to myself, she did not report the assault. I told her that if he ever tried to come near her to call me. That I would be there as fast as humanly possible and I would beat the shit out of him myself. At

01:00 one morning, Master Sergeant Munoz called me and asked if I could drive the 45 minutes to base. There was a female Marine threatening to kill herself. I got up and was there within an hour. She was sobbing uncontrollably and I just hugged her and waited for her to talk. She went on to tell me that she had been raped a year ago and she had never told anyone about it. I waited with her and took her to the hospital the next morning to see the shrink.

To my surprise and joy, I received a call from Jones. He was going to 29 Palms for training and really wanted to see me. I drove the two and a half hours there and it was all worth it just to see the smile on his face when he saw me. God, I loved this man. He was with a friend named Ben who needed a ride off base and I didn't mind dropping him off. I dropped Ben off and Jones and I went to go find a hotel room. We talked for only a few minutes before the close came flying off. It was incredible, the best sex I had ever had. The hours that we did sleep, he held me the entire time and I woke up in his arms. It was one of the best feelings I had ever had and will never forget it. God, I wanted to wake up every morning with him. It was still dark when I dropped him off and he risked kissing me before he got out of the car. I went back to the hotel and slept until checkout and drove back with a permanent smile on my face.

It was April 2010 when our platoon sergeant called us into formation to pass word. He informed us that there was a new Maradmin (Marine administrative rule) that had just come out on the tattoo policy. To cut back numbers due to the war slowly winding down, they were making the tattoo policy much stricter. The Gunny told us that if we had our tattoos documented before June 10th, 2010, they would be grandfathered in, and if we wanted tattoos, we should go get them while we still could.

After weighing out my options, I had decided to do a lateral move to a different MOS. I wanted to go CID (Criminal Investigation Detective) and would need to do a lateral move. I had many things I needed to get done in order to transfer, and I would have to pass their extremely challenging board. I had to get tons of signatures from my command giving me permission. It took me several months to get everything, including fingerprints, criminal background check, service record check, fitness check and several other things. I passed a written exam as well as the board and was offered a position!

I would have to pass the school of course, but I was very excited. I had been told that only three percent of Marines get accepted into this prestigious job. I asked the Staff Sergeant about their tattoo policy and he told me that they liked us to have tattoos as it made it easier to go undercover and we blended in more. I went and got my sleeve tattoo that weekend after telling my platoon Sergeant and Master Sergeant Munoz, they were both supportive. I had the tribal tattoo from my back wrapped around to form a sleeve. I loved it and couldn't wait to show everyone, especially Jones.

Later that week, Joy called me and told me that she was getting married and had just found out she was pregnant. I was so happy for her, but prayed for her safety as her condition made pregnancy life threatening, but she was determined to have her child.

Chapter 26

Things were going well, and I was finally starting to feel normal and happy again. I loved my new tattoo, I was going to become an investigator as I had dreamed of doing since I was a child, I was almost finished with my Bachelor's degree, and Jones and I were talking every night. Finally, it was my turn for good things to happen. One morning I was in the construction shop showing some of my Marines how to use the circular saw. "Good morning, First Sergeant," I heard from one of my Marines and looked up to see our Acting Sergeant Major, First Sergeant Grey walking through our shop. "Morning, First Sergeant," I said and went back to work. She left without a word. Several hours later Sgt Murphy, one of my fellow squad leaders and a good friend, yelled to me to come into the office. I thought they were going to pass word to head to chow. Boy was I wrong. My fantasy that my life was going to get better was demolished. MSgt Munoz pulled me and my platoon Sgt into his office and closed the door. Shit this couldn't be good, which one of my guys screwed up?

I was informed that First Sergeant Grey had called CID and told them that I was being NJPd for getting an unauthorized tattoo and I was to report in to her at 13:00 with MSgt Munoz. Moments later I received a phone call from CID telling me that I was dropped from the program and not to bother trying again. MSgt was furious! He immediately got on the phone and started calling everyone he knew to try and help me. After numerous calls he had been informed to watch his own back because this woman was out for blood. I had heard rumors about her from other Marines. On her deployment, she had endangered the lives of numerous Marines in order to take a convoy to deliver a page 11 to a Marine that was five pounds overweight. Everyone hated her, and she was being force-retired because of it. I had never had any issues with her because I was an outstanding Marine who had never once been in trouble. She was even on the panel that had promoted me to meritorious Sgt.

I had no idea what was going on and I knew I hadn't done anything wrong! I got a tattoo in accordance to Marine Corps Policy after being given permission from my Company Gunny! I had documented my tattoo and had a page 11 in my SRB (service records) file. At 13:00 MSgt and I reported in. For the second time in my life I was being read my rights! She also began to read off a bunch of Marine Corps Articles, but I didn't hear a word she was saying. I was in shock. How was this happening again? I did everything right, I waited to get a tattoo until I cleared it with CID, I had read the article and to me it gave me every right. HOWEVER, according to her, the language was vague and allowed wiggle room for interpretation. Her interpretation was the only one that mattered, and I was about to pay for it with my career. The article stated if you document your tattoos prior to the date you would be grandfathered in. She said this was only for Marines that already had tattoos and not permission to get a new one.

My re-enlistment was on her desk and she handed it back to me refusing to sign off. I had 10 days until my EAS (end of contract). It was a Friday and MSgt told me to go home, clear my head, and we were going to call a lawyer on Monday. Jones had gone back home so I couldn't call and talk to him. I was devastated and confused, but still hopeful. There was still a possibility that I could fight this! I wasn't going to let this bitch ruin my dreams.

On Saturday, I went to the gym and tried to stay busy. My phone rang; it was Sarah. I had saved her number in my phone just in case she had ever tried to call me again. She had found the notes I had written Anthony and left me a message with devastating news and numerous threats. I called Anthony right away, but he wasn't answering his phone. I wasn't sure if it was because I was calling on my phone, so I went to a payphone and called numerous times and left messages but no response. I had to call MSgt Munoz and tell him what had gone down. I wasn't going to let him get blindsided by a phone call from Sarah. He didn't deserve that! He was heartbroken for me and told me that I was one of the best female Marines he had ever had the privilege of knowing.

In the message, Sarah had told me she was at her lawyer's office with the letters I had written Anthony and was going to give the letters to both of our commands. Not wanting to have his career destroyed, I called Sarah back. I tried to play the "I don't know what you're talking about card", but she read me some of the note to prove that she had them. She told me that she was going to fly to San Diego just to watch me NJPd and Anthony and my careers ruined. So, I did the only thing I could think of; I made a deal with her. I told her that if she would spare Anthony, that I would get out. I gave her my word that if she didn't go to his command that I would end my career even though I had just been accepted into CID. Somehow, she had already known that I had been accepted into CID and she knew what a huge opportunity this would be. She only agreed because she didn't want to go through the embarrassment of people finding out, plus she was overjoyed that my career was over.

That Monday I returned to work and broke down crying in MSgt Munoz' office. He wanted so badly to help me, but both of our hands were tied. I started checking out, returning all my gear, the medical checks, the stupid mandatory classes that are to prepare you for the civilian world, etc. These mandatory classes teach you how to write a resume that not one single company would ever look at twice and a ton of other useless information. The only good thing that came out of it was I had some assistance in filling out my disability paperwork. The Marine Corps had definitely taken its toll on my body and my mind. I was diagnosed with PTSD, a jacked-up back, the knees of a 90-year-old, hearing issues, and a number of other injuries. I also claimed the excessive pain and menstrual related issues, but after numerous tests, they couldn't find anything wrong with me.

The weekend before I got out, I went up to visit my paternal grandmother. She had been diagnosed with breast cancer and hadn't told me; my Aunt Amy ended up telling me months later. I went to visit because my Aunt had called me the week before when everything was crazy with checking out. She told me that the cancer had moved to my grandmother's brain. My brave grandmother had gone through chemo for the breast cancer and she refused to do it again to treat the brain cancer. She didn't have long to live, and I needed to see her.

Not wanting to break my grandmother's heart before she died, I never told her the truth about her son and what Cain had done to me and Marie. While I was visiting, I told my aunt what was going on with Anthony, getting kicked out, and all the other shit with my family. She had no contact with my family and hated my father, her brother. Before I left, I told her she needed to call me if my grandmother took a turn for the worse and she promised she would. Dealing with my career ending, my grandmother dying, and Anthony unable to talk, I felt hopeless. The day I received my DD214 (documents releasing you from your military active duty), I stopped by to get one last document from the career planner. He saw me, yanked me into his office, and told me to get the hell out of there after giving me the paperwork. This fucking cunt First Sergeant was trying to track me down to extend my duty so she could NJP me, take my rank, two months pay, and put me on restriction! Talk about a thanks for your service!

A month later, I checked my email on a Monday. The first email in my inbox was dated the Friday before and it was a mass forward from my father. He said that they had just arrived to say goodbye to my grandmother. Most of my family had come down to say goodbye. I checked my phone for missed calls from my aunt, nothing. I opened the next email, my grandmother passed on Sunday morning. I was furious and called my aunt. She told me that my parents said that they contacted me, but I didn't want to come. My grandmother died thinking that I didn't want to see her. My aunt told me that it was a good thing I hadn't been there because I may have ended up in jail. She told me that my father and their brother had been going through all her jewelry and other valuables before she passed. She also told me that my father told her that she was going to hell if she didn't repent. This didn't surprise me at all. In my grandmother's will she didn't want a funeral or a service, only for my aunt to spread her ashes in the mountains. Two months after I got forced out, I finished my last class and graduated with a Bachelors in Domestic Security Management. It was a major accomplishment for me due to my difficulty taking tests! Wishing more than anything for Anthony to be there, I knew this would never be.

Maria and I had birthdays one day apart from each other and I asked her if she wanted to go celebrate in Hawaii. Anthony was stationed there but we both wanted to go. I was missing his face more than I can express in words. When we were on the phone one night, he was out in the field doing training, so we were able to talk for over four hours until his phone died. He told me that he was having a baby girl and he wanted to name her Koda. Sarah didn't like the name and wanted a Native American one. She told him it was a stupid name and wouldn't even let her middle name be Koda. That night I finally told him the truth about why I got out of the Marine Corps. Very unlike him, he got choked up and teared up apologizing for how much he had put me through. I felt so bad, it wasn't my intention to make him feel bad. I was trying to show him how much I cared about him and how I would do just about anything for him. He told me that hurting someone you care about is so much worse than hurting yourself and how sorry he was for hurting me. After our talk, I ended up looking up the name Koda and found out that it meant "Mother's chosen one". It was my way of showing him that there was nothing to forgive.

A few months before getting out of the Corps, I had been told by one of their brilliant (extreme sarcasm) doctors that I had an inverted uterus and my chances of ever getting pregnant were slim to none. My dreams of being a mother were crushed! I had told Anthony about this and he told me to never give up and anything was possible. I didn't tell him then, but I decided that my first child's name was going to be Koda, my chosen one. After we had talked and before I left for Hawaii, I went and added onto my sleeve tattoo. I got the Greek words Eros (love for your lover) for Anthony and Philia (love for you family) for Marie. I also got the words Loyalty, Faith, and Koda. To this day, Anthony is the most loyal person I have ever known! I have never regretted any of my tattoos especially any ones that I got that had special meaning for Anthony and Marie.

Ben and I had become friends and I messaged him that we were coming to Hawaii. He picked Maria and I up from the airport with beautiful leis and dropped us off at our hotel just across the street from the beautiful Waikiki beach. That night we met up with Ben for dinner and I asked him how Anthony was. I had messaged Anthony to let him know I was in Hawaii, but he was off in the field doing training. Ben was trying to arrange to get him out on the evening of Maria's birthday. The next day, one of our mutual friends had surprised us and paid for a parasailing trip. Maria and I were having an incredible time! She was one of the very few people I had ever met that didn't get on my nerves after a full day of being together. We also went on a snorkeling trip and waterfall hike. On the night of Maria's birthday, we were going to a club and Ben told me that he and Anthony would be there. I put on a new dress I had gotten and looked amazing in; I knew Anthony would be more than pleased. Before leaving for the club we had some Monster with Vodka which I called my new crack drink. I didn't normally drink energy drinks and I was wired by the time we got to the club.

While Maria was dancing and making out with some guy she met on the dance floor, I had several guys come up and try and get me to talk or dance. I turned them all down telling them I was waiting for someone. I was watching Maria laughing at how easily she could find someone and start making out when I felt a hand on the small of my back. "Not interested, waiting for someone," I said turning around. "Oh really?" Anthony said with a grin. I hugged him, and tears started trying to breakthrough I was so happy. He grabbed me and kissed me. Even though I wanted to dance with him I wanted to talk to him more. He held my hand and led me through the crowd to the bar. He bought me a cranberry vodka, a Corona for himself, and led me to the section where the booths were. Ben hadn't made it and Anthony left him to come see me. We talked and talked until 3am. The club was closing, and we found Maria making out with a different guy. The three of us walked back to the hotel room and like a true friend, Maria told us she wanted to go for a walk. Anthony and I started making out and we were just about to lose all our clothes when Maria walked back in. She came in covering her eyes, "I didn't see anything, keep going. There's a homeless man I want to go cuddle with, but I need my sweatshirt," she said and then quickly ran back out. Anthony and I started laughing but then it was game on.

We couldn't go as long as we wanted because we didn't know when Maria was going to come back, and I didn't want to do that to her. Maria came back as we were walking out. I walked with Anthony to his truck and it felt so good to hold his hand. I had never been a PDA person, but with him, I couldn't keep my hands off him. I didn't care if the entire world saw us. I was proud to be by his side and I wanted to shout it to the world how much I loved this man. I hated that we usually had to hide it! He drove me back to the hotel and I didn't want to get out of his truck. I wanted to drive away with him and never spend another day without him. He held my face in his hands and kissed me telling me he would do everything he could to come see me again before I left.

Maria and I had an incredible vacation, and our last day there we stored our luggage at the hotel and spent the day at the beach. I was checking my phone every half hour praying Anthony had texted me back and I would get to see him before I left. Ben told me that he was stuck out in the field with no reception. I was heartbroken. I wanted so badly to hug him goodbye. I didn't know if or when I would be seeing him again and I cried the entire way to the airport.

When I returned, I received news from Nell that Joy was in the hospital and had almost died giving birth to her baby boy. I was so thankful that she was alive and now had something she had always wanted, a son! Despite her numerous health issues, I was so happy that she found someone to love her which she had always wanted. Even though we weren't as close as we had been before, I still loved her like a sister.

Devon and I began dating again and fell back into our old routine. We had stopped seeing each other after he stood me up during my graduation. We started training again at the gym, but I knew it wasn't going to last. He was fun and great to party with but there were no real feelings between us. One evening I came to the gym and Devon was unable to come because of work. As I was warming up, two of the professional fighters came over and started to talk to me. They had never spoken to me much, so I was surprised. They went on to tell me that they always thought that I was Devon's girl, but we had never had titles in our relationship and he only introduced me by my name. I didn't say anything and let them continue. "We thought you were his girl but then we met his girlfriend this weekend." He was allegedly out of town on business. They told me the girl's name and I remember Devon had mentioned her name before but had said they broke up because she was psycho. Devon had been in a relationship the entire time and I had no idea. I deleted his number and thankfully he stopped coming to the gym and I stopped as well a few months later to avoid running into him.

Chapter 27

I had taken the month of August off from school and decided to return in September to pursue my master's degree in forensics. I was applying to numerous jobs, but had no luck. The economy had tanked, making it almost impossible to find employment. So, I would workout during the day and go to night classes. One morning I received an unexpected message from Anthony. He was in 29 Nine Palms again and told me he would be deployed to Afghanistan soon. To my surprise and joy, he called me the next evening and asked me what I was doing. I was watching a movie by myself at home and he asked me if I wanted company. Thinking he was joking; I didn't think much of it. He showed up minutes later and told me he was all mine for the next 36 hours! I couldn't believe it. I hadn't spent that much time with him since Iraq.

Anthony also told me that he would be returning to San Diego to the drill field after he was done with his deployment. I had passed the FBI investigator exam and was given a date to depart for school contingent upon passing the physical fitness test, which wasn't going to be that hard for me. After a lot of soul searching, I declined the offer because I knew that I would likely be sent to some remote duty station and I wouldn't be able to see Anthony. I gave up a career I had dreamed about since I was eight because Anthony was what I wanted. He made me a better person and whenever I was with him, I was the best version of myself. I craved the happiness I felt with him. After a long night of incredible sex, I cooked him breakfast and we went back to sleep for a few more hours.

Later that day, we went out to get Chinese food at one of his favorite places. Then he told me he wanted to go shopping for some new sneakers. While walking through the mall, he passed numerous stores until he found what he was looking for. He spent less than a minute looking at the Men's shoes before moving over to the Women's shoes. He commented on a few different ones, and I told him which one I liked. He asked the salesman to bring me a size 7.5. It was easy for him to remember because we had the same size feet. He had 7.5 in Men's and I had 7.5 in Women's. He then helped me try them on and made sure that they fit right. He told me that he knew I would never have agreed to let him take me shopping, so he had to trick me into letting him buy me something. He knows me so well.

It was such an incredible day and I never wanted our 36 hours together to end. I got a taste of what being with him would be like, and my happiness was only lessened by knowing that he was leaving that day. There was no hiding, no being afraid of someone seeing us and doing everyday things together. We didn't stop talking or laughing the entire time. It reminded me of the movie Pirates of the Caribbean where Will Turner and Elizabeth Swan were only allowed to be together once every ten years but that time, they had made it worth it.

For dinner, he took me to this cozy Italian restaurant and we tried a few different types of wine. The next morning, he had to make the drive back 29 Palms, but I was planning on going out there to see him that weekend. It was the best 36 hours of my entire life.

The next weekend I drove up to see him and we shared another passionate night in a hotel room. We had the type of love and romance you only see in movies, and I couldn't get enough of him or him of me. Anthony had to be back on base early in the morning. He told me he was going to come down and see me again before he returned to Hawaii and then off to Afghanistan. After I returned home, we talked every day for hours. The next week, he told me I should get ready for another long night and I couldn't wait to see him again. The next day I didn't get his typical good morning message, which was odd. I thought that he was on a field op or probably busy. Then a week went by with no word and I started to get worried. Another week, no word. I called him to see if he was all right and his phone rang, so I knew it was on.

I was so worried and had a feeling that Sarah had found out again. She should be a private detective because she always found out. In a way, I was relieved when she found out. I hated hiding and feeling like I was lying. Every time she did find out, she chose to say and eventually it felt as if she was accepting the relationship.

Not only was I worried that I wouldn't be able to see Anthony before I left, I was also two weeks late. I didn't think too much of it because my period had always been a irregular and the doctors told me it would be a miracle if I ever became pregnant. When the third week went by, I thought maybe I had skipped a month due to the stress and my intense workouts. I never had one in bootcamp, and during college I would occasionally miss a month here and there. After seven weeks with no word, I stopped calling Anthony because I knew that something was going on and by that time, he had returned to Hawaii. I still hadn't had my period and my breasts had never been that swollen. Something just felt different and I knew I was pregnant.

Murphy was deploying to Afghanistan and I helped his wife throw him an early birthday party at Hooters because he was going to be in Afghanistan for it. I had bought a pregnancy test the day before and was going to take it that night when I got home. I was an emotional wreck trying to hold everything in at Murphy's party. Just as I was walking out to my car to go home, I got a Facebook message from Sarah.

In the message, she quoted some things that I had only told Anthony, and it crushed me to think that he shared those details with her. Only later would I find out, she had broken the password on his phone and found all our messages. He hadn't told her anything. In the messages I had told him about my fears of not being able to get pregnant, which she threw in my face. Her message told me that the only reason he talked to me was because he felt sorry for me because I couldn't have kids. She called me a diseased whore, a home wrecker, and said everything she could possibly say to hurt me. She used the information she found in our text messages to hurt me. While she did have every right to be angry at me, she stayed.

Looking back, I know I shouldn't have believed a word she said, but I was a hormonal mess. As I was reading her messages, Anthony texted me on his phone telling me to delete his number and never call him again. I lost it and started sobbing uncontrollably. Murphy came over and hugged me. He had never seen me cry before and was very concerned. I couldn't tell him anything. I returned to my empty house, alone with a pregnancy test awaiting me. After taking three and all were positive, I felt this remarkable sense of peace. Even though I felt like I had just lost the love of my life, I was happy that I would always have a piece of him. I would never have to be alone again and that was comforting. That sounds crazy to some, but the only time I didn't feel alone was when I was with Anthony. Now I would have a part of him with me for the rest of my life.

The next day, my brother's ex-wife messaged me on Facebook and we started chatting. Messaging was getting too long, so I called her and we got to talking about Cain. She had never received the letter I had sent her all those years back and now they had a six-year-old daughter together. Cain had found the letter and destroyed it before she could read it. When I told her what had happened to me and what I believed happened to my sister, she started sobbing. She went on to tell me that their daughter had been acting out at school, was wetting her bed, was embarrassed to change in front of her, and many of the other warning signs indicative of child sexual abuse. She immediately contacted her lawyer and their daughter was removed from that monster's house.

I was devastated. Not only because she was my niece, but I still felt responsible for every individual he hurt after me. I called

Amanda crying and begging her to call me back. I had so much on my mind and I needed to talk to someone. I called Maria. No answer. For a month, after numerous calls and messages, I hadn't heard anything from either of them. Then my phone started blowing up from my family who all left horrible, threatening messages. I deleted the messages and the emails and went back to feeling numb again. The only thing keeping me going was this little miracle growing inside of me. While driving to the gym and school twice a week, I started noticing the same tinted old Chevelle following me.

My neighbor came over when I was walking my six-month-old husky Mason. I had gotten Mason a week after Anthony disappeared to help with my loneliness. My neighbor asked if I was doing OK and if I had gotten involved with the wrong crowd. I wasn't sure how to respond. I had no idea what he was referring to. "Well, the reason I ask, I don't know if you have noticed a car following you, but I have. It belongs to one of the gang leaders in this neighborhood." I started to panic. My hands instinctively and protectively went to my stomach. "Oh, no, I have no idea why they would be following me. Maybe it's just a coincidence." "I don't think so," he said. "Watch your back, these guys don't mess around. They were part of that shooting a few days ago."

The next day, my cousin Sean came over to talk to me. He was drunk and crying. He just found out that one of his friends had been shot and killed in the gang related fight my neighbor mentioned. It was all over the news. Nine people had been injured, stabbed and shot, and three were dead. The gang leader of the same gang involved in the shooting, was now following me. The road was closed off for

216

hours and police were everywhere. Trying not to panic, I was shaken back to reality by what he told me next. He told me that when Cain lived with his family years ago, Cain had raped him. I had never told my cousin anything about what Cain had done to me. How much more will this fucker get away with? Months later I asked Sean about what Cain had done and he panicked. He didn't remember what he had told me when he was drunk and he refused to talk about it. He was terrified of Cain.

On my way home from the gym around a week later, I saw the body of a dog that had just been ran over on the side of the road. It hadn't been there on my way to the gym. I would have noticed. I was much more observant after finding out the information from my neighbor. I was driving so I didn't get a good look at the dog, but it did have a familiar looking fur. I felt sick, I knew it was Mason. Immediately when I got home and I checked Mason's kennel. It was empty. My heart sunk. Someone had opened it, secured it closed again and unlatched the fence. I didn't have the heart to go see his body. He didn't have his collar on because I had just given him a bath that morning. Before the gym I secured him in his kennel to try and keep him from rolling around in the dirt like he always did.

The next day when I got back from the gym, the same car followed me home, and this time a man got out and started walking towards me. He looked like a typical gang member you would see on the news. As I was taking the gym bag out of my car and trying to walk quickly to the house, he told me that my brother said "hi" and unless I wanted to end up like my dead dog, I better shut my mouth and not testify. I was supposed to testify against Cain about what he had done to me in his upcoming trial. What was I going to do, go to the police? What were they going to do? I had no proof and I wasn't going to wait around to get killed and lose my baby. This gang had just been involved in shooting nine people and we're still on the streets. The justice system had never done anything to protect me or the ones I cared about. Anthony was gone, I was pregnant, and had no support from anyone.

I got online and found a few apartments downtown and far away from the area I lived in. I called one place, drove down there, rented it the same day, and that night I packed up everything I owned. I rented a U-Haul, packed up everything that night and moved before anyone woke up to notice that I had gone. I was trying to get out of there as fast as I possibly could. I wasn't going to tell anyone where I was going. I didn't feel safe. I didn't trust anyone. I had almost finished when I was moving my queen-sized heavy oak bed frame, tripped over a box and fell hard with the frame landing on my stomach. I didn't feel any immediate pain and my adrenaline was pumping, which masked the injury. It was Saturday and people would be waking up soon. I had to push through. I kept going, finished and drove down to my new home. Not only did I have to come back for my car at the U-Haul facility, I had to come right back in a taxi, get my bike and ride back to my new apartment. During the ride back, I started experiencing the worst abdominal cramps I had ever had. Something was seriously wrong!

Graphic Content Warning

By the time I made it to my new apartment, my jeans were soaked in blood. Unable to stand up straight, doubled over from the pain, I somehow made it to the bathroom. There was so much blood and tissue, I knew I lost my baby. Sobbing uncontrollably, I collapsed onto the floor. Memories of Anthony telling me we would make a beautiful child together filled my mind. Now, I would never know. Was this all my fault? God, why? Why the hell did this happen to me? I didn't deserve this. Knowing I would never be able to see our child made me want to die and I prayed that I would just bleed out and never wake up again.

It was like the scene from a horror movie, Blood all over the floor, bloody clothes and a naked body wrapped in a towel, laying on the cold bathroom floor. Coming to at around 02:00 I was disappointed I hadn't bled out. Everything hit me all at once. I wanted to die. I started looking for pills but I didn't have enough in my day pack. All my knives were packed. I had no gun and I wasn't strong enough to get up and unpack. Why didn't I just let those gang members kill me? Or better yet, why didn't I just go kill my brother and then go to prison? At least then he would not hurt anyone. I managed to stand and made it to the kitchen and grabbed the bottle of tequila. I drank it straight while in the shower, letting the water wash the blood off of me. I drank until I passed out and woke up and drank again. The next morning, I ordered a pizza and didn't move from my couch for a week. I emailed my grad professor and told him that there was a death in the family and I needed to miss some classes.

I made an appointment with the VA Women's Clinic several months later after I told them I had a miscarriage. The doctor was fairly certain that I had a disease called endometriosis, which could only be diagnosed through surgery. He also did an exam to see if I was healing properly after the miscarriage. The doctor told me the miscarriage was possibly a combination of the fall, stress, and endometriosis. It didn't matter what he told me, I still felt responsible and held Cain accountable for the part he played. He asked me if I wanted the depo shot or if I would be trying to get pregnant again. "Well, Doctor, the man whose baby I just lost is married and just told me that he never wanted to see me again. So no, I don't think I'll be getting pregnant any time in the near future." The silence in the room was awkward and I asked him to order the shot.

The depo shot didn't work and the pain was unbearable. My doctor scheduled me for surgery and I was finally diagnosed correctly with endometriosis. Maria, who had finally started talking to me again, dropped me off for surgery in the morning and her mother ended up picking me up. Recovering from surgery by myself was depressing and made me realize how alone I was.

Chapter 28

Less than a few months after I had moved in, Delilah called me up one day and told me she was moving to San Diego. She came for a weekend to look for jobs and an apartment. I had managed to get a job and had been there for two months working as an administrative manager for a security company. The company was a joke, but it was something to do and some extra money. Delilah didn't even ask if she could borrow my car. She automatically assumed she could and I had been through so much, I didn't have any strength to enforce my boundaries. It was brought up when she said, "Hey, I'm going to drop you off tomorrow and go look for places to live." After telling her my few apartment requirements: clean, safe, a garage, and laundry, she dropped me off at work. She called me multiple times throughout the day while I was busy at work and was already driving me nuts. She called to ask how to take down the convertible top on my car, what I was eating for lunch, about this guy at this apartment she met and thought was hot, and a long list of other aggravating topics that could have waited until I got home.

Being 20 minutes late added to my frustration. On our way back to my apartment I had just gotten on the freeway when my hood, flew open, hitting and cracking my windshield. Pulling to the side of the freeway, managing to not get killed, I yelled, "What the hell

Delilah?" I knew, like an idiot, she opened the hood when she was trying to figure out how to take the top down and didn't bother to make sure the hood was closed and secure. She said she was positive that she didn't pull the hood release. I knew she was lying right to my face. Lying was something that she was doing more and more.

That Friday evening, we went out to a bar that wasn't too far away, and Delilah met some guys. On the way back to my studio apartment in the taxi, Delilah was texting on her phone and asked me what my address was. I thought she was ordering food or something, so I gave it to her. I walked into my tiny studio apartment and turned on a movie. Moments later, I heard a knock on the door and Delilah went and got it. In walked the guys from the bar. I was pissed that she had invited total strangers into my apartment without asking me! My home had become my only safe area and this was like locking a claustrophobic person in a tiny closet. I was very uncomfortable, but I was so tired from arguing with her and I didn't want to make these guys feel uncomfortable. They hadn't done anything. So once again, I didn't enforce my boundaries and I just let it go. My childhood had groomed me to have no boundaries. I was punished for standing up for myself and trained to believe I had no choices.

Delilah asked one of them to give her a back rub and the other one came and sat on the couch next to me. I got up to get another drink and when I returned, I sat as far away from him as I possibly could. No one had a clue what I had just gone through in this apartment and I didn't want anyone near me. Delilah passed out moments later and I got up and told them that they both needed to leave. Thank God they left. I passed out on the couch and let her have my bed. The next morning, Delilah took me to the apartment complex that she had found and they were perfect. She was going to drive down from Michigan with her dad and move in a month later. I put down the full deposit because she didn't have the money and we signed the lease.

When I dropped her off at the airport, I had very mixed feelings about living with her. However, the memory of the miscarriage in that bathroom haunted me, and I needed a fresh new start in a new apartment. It was everything I wanted and more, but I couldn't afford it on my own. I loved the person that she used to be and prayed that that person would come back. We had been best friends since we were 14. As much as she drove me crazy, it was better than being alone.

Delilah had taken over dealing with the apartment because I was busy working and she was relaying the information to me. She told me the exact date we could move in and I gave notice to my apartment. Was I making the right choice? I just lost a ton of money to break the lease for a studio I could afford on my own. Was I making a huge mistake?

Three days before the moving date, I was talking with Delilah and asked her what time the apartment manager would be meeting me. I then found out that she had screwed up the dates and the moving date wasn't for another week. I became even more pissed when she told me it wasn't a big deal. That I could put everything in storage and stay in a hotel for a week. Was she high? Oh wait, she comes from money and would have hired movers or get some of her male friends to move for her because she is totally helpless on her own and uses her body and looks to get her whatever she wanted.

Needing some space and time to think, I turned off my phone for the evening. When I turned my phone on the next day, there were over 100 text messages and numerous missed calls from her. This worried me. She seemed deranged and extremely unstable, but she did end up resolving the move in date. I felt like it was much to late to turn back. She told me that she had begged the apartment complex to see if we could move in early and they obliged. I found out weeks later from the apartment manager that Delilah had told them I was a crazy Marine suffering from PTSD, and she was afraid of how I would react if I couldn't move in on time. It all made sense then why the apartment manager was walking on eggshells around me. He and I became fast friends after a few weeks and ended up telling me what Delilah had said about me.

I moved all my things in by myself with no help. This was the fifth move I had done solo and it was getting more difficult each time due to the accumulation of more belongings. It took me over six hours and I had to pay a fee for being two hours late returning the U-Haul. Delilah moved in a few weeks later. When she arrived with her dad, who I got along with very well, I saw that her windshield was badly damaged. I asked what happened, and she told me after they stopped for gas, the hood had flown up and smashed the window. Hmmm. Sound familiar? Didn't pull the hood release my ass. Luckily when she did it with my car it only caused a small crack, her windshield was totaled.

Delilah's dad and I did all the heavy lifting while she carried bedding, her clothes, some small boxes, and the rest of the time she spent unpacking as her dad and I brought in all of her shit. To thank me for helping move his daughter's things, he treated us to a nice dinner. The next day he took us to IKEA and Delilah and I picked out an entertainment center and a table she liked. He paid for them, of course, as he always paid for all of her things. He had to get back to work and flew out the next morning. Delilah was completely useless and I ended up putting together all the furniture by myself, even her bedroom furniture. She never once said thank you for helping her move her own shit in or for putting everything together for her. It was as if she expected it, like I was the help.

I had kept in touch with all my relatives and was looking forward to spending the upcoming holidays with them. Then one day, while I was on Facebook, I was leaving a comment on my cousin's page. That's when I saw it. A friendly post and back and forth comments from Cain and my closest cousin. I was shocked, devastated, and crushed. She knew everything! Him raping me and what he had done to Marie and his daughter. I hadn't told anyone about the gang hit or the miscarriage. Why would she be talking to him? I checked my other relatives' pages and found the same thing. This monster had reached out to every single one of my aunts, uncles and cousins. They fell for his lies and manipulation. I deleted them all from my Facebook page and haven't talked to any of them since. Not one single relative has reached out to see how I was since. They didn't even try.

I was alone. Not one single family member left in my life. The reality of that hit me so hard. Never will I be able to understand how they could take his side over mine. It seemed as if the world was crushing me down, that it was burying me in a pit so far from the surface I would never be able to climb out. However, I was still my stubborn self. The more evil that tried to break me, the more I was determined to use it to make myself stronger. I would never let them win, and I would use this pain and rage to push me to become better, stronger, and never let them win.

Several weeks went by and I was rarely home. Delilah's parents were getting tired of paying for her rent and were going to cut her off so she found a job taking care of an elderly man. She had failed her RN exam and didn't have a lot of options. She was CNA, making very little money and she was struggling not being able to have the lifestyle she was used to.

On the weekends, Delilah spent her time flirting and sleeping with every single man she could get her hands on at our apartment complex, mall, bars, or wherever she found them. She was sleeping with our next-door neighbor, who lived with his fiancée. Once again, she lied to my face, but I saw them having sex on our patio. There was a revolving door of random men I had seen a few times in the apartment complex in passing. I would see them come out of her room in the morning and she still denied it! I couldn't have cared less who she slept with. I just hated that she was lying to me and I didn't appreciate so many random strangers coming in and out of my home.

Delilah had been trying her best to sleep with the apartment manager and tried to turn him against me, but he turned her down.

He knew she was a crazy, racist, slut, sleeping with everyone in the complex. He told me that the first time he met Delilah, he was showing a family the different rooms available in the office. When he introduced himself to Delilah and asked her to wait for him to finish, she said, "Henry? I wasn't expecting that. I was expecting your name to be like Tyrone or Jamal or something." Henry was Jamaican and not only was that such an offensive stereotype, she said it in front of his clients.

It didn't end there. Delilah had a black lab named Jetta. One day, while we were moving in some groceries, Jetta bolted out the door and into the hallway. Delilah yelled loudly down the hall, "Hey N***ER, get your black ass in here." I was disgusted and mortified. "Delilah, did you just really say that? What the hell is wrong with you?" She laughed and thought it was funny. On another occasion, Delilah came with me to Maria's baby shower. I stopped by a market to pick up some Maria's favorite things, mangoes and some other stuff for the party. While we were walking around the crowded market, Delilah loudly says, "Jesus Christ, what are we in Mexico or some shit? I thought this was America. Why are there so many Mexicans here?" Growing up our school was 95% white so I never realized how racist she was.

On my birthday, Delilah messaged me asking if I wanted to get some friends together and go out. I agreed and invited Henry. I told Delilah the few people I had invited and she flipped out when I mentioned Henry was coming. She was so butt hurt that he had turned her down and was more interested in me, she wouldn't even talk to him anymore. She told me I couldn't invite him on my birthday. She was trying to tell me who I couldn't invite! I was so sick of her. I ended up canceling the party and told her I was just going to chill in the hot tub. By that time, she had already gotten home from work and I went into my room and shut the door. From the time it took me to put on my bathing suit, grab a towel and pour some wine in a plastic cup, I had 85 new text messages from Delilah!

It was becoming more and more clear that she was seriously unstable and I felt that she needed to be put into a mental institution to deal with some of the anger about her divorce, and God knows what else. I didn't recognize any part of her. The friend I had was gone, destroyed by jealousy, anger and severe low self-esteem. There was nothing I could do for her.

Chapter 29

I just paid off my motorcycle, had a month off school, and I just walked out of my job. I was over dealing with my ignorant boss and when I found out he had been taken to court multiple times for not paying his employees, I was ready to leave. In the past, I had always given a two-week notice, but when he had me doing accounting and I found out he was being audited for not paying taxes for the past several years and was lying about his income, I walked that same day.

I had been wanting to travel the world since I could remember, and this was the time. I couldn't find anyone to go with me so I decided to go on my own. After hearing advertisements on the radio for a tour company called Contiki, I did some research online. On the top of my list was Greece, Rome and Egypt. There were tours going to each of these locations. How was I ever going to choose? I found ones for a week staying in beautiful hotels and seeing the Colosseum, the Parthenon or the pyramids. Then I saw this month-long camping trip through Eastern Europe that started in Athens and went to Thermopylae, ancient Troy, Oktoberfest in Germany, Vienna, Amsterdam, numerous other countries, and ended in London. I was sold!

I got on the phone that day and use a travel agent to book my flights and started packing. I was leaving in two days. Talk about a last-minute trip! Delilah owed me for groceries and utilities, so I told her that if she would take me to LAX, I would call it even. My flight was at 09:00 and she had the day off so I knew she would be able to. However, she didn't want to wake up so early, so she dropped me off the night before. My travel up until then had been through the military or strictly domestic flights. I didn't realize that I wouldn't be able to check in until three hours before my flight. I had to spend the night on a bench in the airport lobby. It was miserable, but I was so excited for my trip.

During that time, New York had experienced one of the largest earthquakes they'd ever had and it had caused numerous flight issues. We were stuck doing circles for over an hour waiting for our turn to land. I was very worried I was going to miss my connecting flight to Greece. As soon as I got off the plane, I literally sprinted to the next gate, which was like a mile away. There was another couple that was on the same flight and I arrived at the gate five minutes before them. They came running up behind me as I was begging the service agent at the gate to let me on. The door was closed, but the plane was still connected. The three of us begged the rude agent who glanced up at us from her keyboard every few minutes with a bitchy expression. She told us rudely that there was nothing that could be done and it wasn't her fault, we were late. She was rude and condescending, but I never once got an attitude with her because I felt that would only make matters worse. She told us we better get over to the ticket counter to see if there were any other flights. I wasn't getting anywhere with this lady, so I ran over to the ticket counter and waited anxiously as there were two people in front of me.

When it was finally my turn, I told the woman behind the counter what had happened and she began looking for any possible flights to Greece. There were none, so she began checking other airlines. No luck. I began to panic and wanted to cry. When I looked back to talk to the couple that was also in the same predicament, I didn't see them in line. They must have stayed at the gate for some reason.

I had the travel agent book my flight so I would arrive one day before the tour was departing Athens. I wanted to spend a full day there before leaving with the tour. If there were no flights to Athens that night, I was going to miss seeing the Parthenon and Athens. The Parthenon was the main reason I wanted to go on this trip. The agent could see how devastated I was. "Honey, are you sure they wouldn't let you on? My screen is saying that they are accommodating passengers." Oh, hell no! I sprinted back to the gate just in time to see the plane pulling away and the couple was nowhere in sight. "Ma'am, did you get that couple on?" I asked as calmly as I possibly could to the same lady that had been so rude to me. She didn't even bother looking up. "Excuse me, ma'am. I said, did you let that couple on?" I was about to snap. I looked over to the long line of passengers waiting to board at the neighboring gate that had been there when we had first arrived. I asked the group, "did she just let that couple board?" Several in the line shook their heads yes in disgust at what this lady had just done to me.

I almost jumped over the counter and beat the hell out of her. She just cost me my once in a lifetime trip. "Hey, lady, pick your head up and look me in the face, you inconsiderate, rude bitch!" I didn't care anymore. I had missed my flight. "Who's your manager? You need to be fired." This was the first time in my life I had ever used that type of language to an elder. She didn't say a single word to me and just pointed to the man at the end of the counter who was on the phone. I walked up and stood directly in front of him. He gave me the hold on finger, which didn't help matters, and sounded like he was on a personal call. He kept talking for around five minutes to what sounded like his girlfriend, and kept giving me the one moment finger motion. I was about to grab his finger and break it when he finally hung up. "How can I help you?" I calmly explained everything and he told me that there was nothing that could be done, no apology, nothing. He blamed me for being late to the flight. Then he gave me the information to file a complaint online. After that, I knew it was pointless to waste my time. I started crying and turned away so he didn't see my tears. I pulled down my sunglasses and headed back to the ticket counter.

Since I was a child, I had dreamed of going to Athens. Seeing it in person was the reason I chose this trip and they had just taken that from me. I was devastated! I was rerouted to Edinburgh, Frankfurt and finally Athens. When I arrived in Scotland, they had me on a different airline and I had to go leave customs and check back in at the ticket counter. They didn't have my information and couldn't find my luggage. Could anything else go wrong on this trip? I stood there for over an hour. I wish this had been under better circumstances because I would have loved to see where my ancestors had come from. My mother's father was from Scotland. They finally found my information and luggage and gave me my next boarding pass to Germany. I had three hours to kill, so I went and grabbed dinner and some Guinness. While sitting at the bar, I got to talking with a Scottish man I was having a very hard time understanding. He asked if I was in the military because of my military backpack and USMC sweatshirt I had on. I told him I had been and we got to talking about deployments.

This handsome Scottish man broke down and started crying. He shared with me about how two of his best friends had never come back from war and how he regretted not being there to have their backs. Right before I had to take off to get to my gate, he asked me to marry him and move to Scotland. I told him if it was meant to be we would bump into each other somewhere in the world and gave him a hug goodbye.

I had the same issue in Germany and spent another hour at the ticket counter. After being up for around 38 hours, I finally arrived in Athens. Leaving the airport at around 22:30. I ran to the train station, which was going to be closing at 23:00. It was only a few blocks away, but when I got to the ticket counter, I forgot I needed the correct currency. Running back to the airport, dragging my rolling suitcase behind me, I found the currency exchange counter and after getting the correct currency, I raced back just in time to catch the last train. Being a very inexperienced traveler, I was without a phone and only had a direction print out to find the way to the hostel I was staying at. At the time I wasn't aware I could use wifi on my phone.

To make matters even more challenging, the directions on the map were the English spelling of the Greek names.

When I entered the train, I looked up and felt a sense of panic. Not only was it my first time taking public transportation, I couldn't read a damn thing. Looking around, there were several people on the bus. I nervously asked if anyone spoke English. Thankfully, there were several helpful locals that did and were able to tell me where to get off.

As I wheeled my bright red with multicolored polka dot suitcase down the cobblestone streets of ancient Athens, Greece, I tried to take in as much as I could. I knew I would be leaving in less than seven hours. After wandering around asking some local prostitutes for directions, I found my hostel, The Zeus Hostel. I was greeted by a friendly young man with an Australian accent. He told me I was in the female dorm room, Medusa, and gave me a drink voucher for the rooftop bar.

After dropping off my suitcase, I went up to the rooftop bar and ordered a glass of white wine and chatted with the bartender. It was around 01:00 and after telling my horror story of getting to Athens, he gave me some great advice. He told me that the Parthenon at night was one of the most beautiful sights and filled me in on a local treasure. The secret was Mars Rock at night. I thanked him, and even though I was exhausted and ready to fall over, I was not going to leave Greece without seeing the reason I had come all that way. It was around a mile and a half away. The bartender had given me a map and it was easy to find as it was located up on top of the hill, lit up by hundreds of lights.

When I arrived, I was overcome with emotion. I had tears streaming down my face as I looked up at the most beautiful piece of architecture I'd ever seen. I had been dreaming of this place since I could read and fell in love with Greek mythology. Suddenly, I was that thirteen-year-old little girl walking the streets of ancient Athens. These stories were the very ones I read to escape the reality I lived in. To escape from the evil, all the abuse, and imagine another life. I saw the ruins of an amphitheater and several temples all lit up looking like Mount Olympus. I closed my eyes, imagining I was actually the goddess Athena looking out over my city and how beautiful my temple was. Looking across the great city of Athens, I fell in love with traveling and knew I was hooked. I wanted to see all the wonders of the world and experience the same incredible feeling of awe.

I made it despite everything and everyone that had tried to break me! I was not only in utter amazement with the beauty and history of this place, I was in awe of myself. Look how far I had come and everything I overcame to get to this very place! No one was around and I screamed at the top of my lungs, "fuck you!" I screamed to finally let out all the heartache I had been holding in. The devastating pain from my miscarriage, from my brother raping me, friends stabbing me in the back, being raped by men I trusted and so much more. I screamed for Marie, for my unborn child Koda, for all those I had lost. I screamed for all the bullshit I had been through my entire life. It was my warrior cry to show the world nothing could break me, no matter how hard it tried. It may have brought me to my knees and slammed me to the ground countless times, but I always kept going. I always got back up and fought. I cried for joy and pride in the woman I had become.

I found Mars rock and began the climb to the lookout point. When I got to the top I saw several people sitting down, looking out over the city. After taking in the breathtaking view of Athens at night, I walked around the Acropolis and found a cart that was selling jewelry. I found a gold and turquoise bracelet that I could imagine Aphrodite or Athena wearing. This would begin my collection of bracelets from every country I visited. To this day, it is one of my favorite bracelets.

Jet lag was starting to take over and I made my way back to the hostel. It was around 04:00 when I finally closed my eyes and I woke up to my alarm two hours later. I took a shower and went and hailed a taxi. The ride took around half an hour and the sun was just coming up. When I arrived at the campground, I didn't see anyone, so I sat down and fell asleep leaning up against my suitcase. I woke up half an hour later and saw people starting to wake up and come out of their tents. A short lady with dirty blond hair and a big smile came over and said, hello. Her name was Kristen and she was the tour guide. I told her who I was and she was surprised to see me. "I have you coming tomorrow, but you are welcome to join us today." To my amazement and absolute joy, I found out that my tour agent had failed to overlook the time change and had scheduled me two days before I needed to be there, not one as I had thought. I had a full day to spend in the amazing city of Athens!

We had our own tour bus driver, cook and tour guide. Kristen invited me to breakfast and began introducing me to my new travel companions. The majority, around 85%, were from Australia and New Zealand. There were three other Americans, two Canadians and two from Korea. The group had already spent a full month together. This tour was split into two months, the first month Western Europe and the Second Eastern Europe. Almost everyone had signed up for both months, but there were a few of us that signed up for one month. We wouldn't meet the other new members until the next day when I was supposed to have arrived. I was so thankful that my travel agent had screwed up in my favor.

The tour bus took us to the Acropolis right after breakfast, and Kristen took us on a tour of this incredible place of history. As I stood looking up at Athena's famous temple, I was in amazement of the architectural skills and the beauty of the sculptures. It is hard to describe what it meant to me to be standing there. I started to tear up with overwhelming joy. The only thing missing from making that moment perfect, was Anthony.

When we were done with our tour, we had a free day in the city to do as we pleased. The two American girls, Lauren and Jordan, invited me and three other Australians, Sarah, Megan and Ellen to join them for lunch. We found a beautiful outdoor restaurant with a spectacular view of the Acropolis. I am a very adventurous eater and couldn't wait to try the authentic Greek food. I ordered moussaka, a Greek dish made from eggplant, and it tasted amazing. After a spectacular lunch, we used the maps Kristen had given us with a list of places of interest and walked to the Grand Bazaar.

I had numerous locals come up and start speaking to me in Greek. They thought I was Greek because of the Greek words in my tattoos. Then every couple of minutes people would yell out, "Hello, tattoo lady", or they would come over, take my arm and look at my tattoo. The air was filled with intoxicating smells of spices, food, leather and sounds of numerous languages. I passed a shop that drew me in with the leather smell and I could see the shopkeeper making incredibly beautiful handmade sandals. I purchased a pair of sandals that cost me more than any other shoe I'd ever bought, but they were so worth it! They were dark tan, adjustable, gladiator style sandals that came up several inches below my knee. I ended up wearing the sandals so much I wore out the soles and had to have them replaced a year later.

Our trip lasted a month and was incredible therapy for my damaged heart. I became close friends with numerous individuals in our group. Choosing one favorite place would be absolutely impossible. Dubrovnik, Croatia shocked me with its beauty. The bath house in Istanbul was magical. Oktoberfest in Munich, Germany was unforgettable. I had brunch in the Alps, walked the rainy streets of Prague sipping hot plum wine, climbed the narrow stairs of the Anne Frank's house, saw a sex show in Amsterdam, and stood next to the King Leonidas statue and memorial in Thermopylae.

Sadly, the day came when our tour ended, I took a few photos of the White Cliffs of Dover from the bus, but we arrived in London too late to go exploring. We had a group dinner at a local pub and we all gathered to eat and say goodbye. I had a flight out from Heathrow at 07:00. I was so sad to see everyone leave and was a little jealous of the ones that had decided to stay and find jobs in London. I was so intrigued by the Australian walkabout that had resulted in Australian youth finding themselves through exploring the world. Over the years, I have met some of the most incredible travelers and most have been Australians.

Chapter 30

After returning from my European trip, I came home one day after a workout to find several massive piles of dog diarrhea on the living room carpet. In order to get Jetta to obey, Delilah would give her peanut butter, which the poor dog was allergic to but loved. Talk about animal cruelty. She fed her dog something she knew Jetta was allergic to just because she wouldn't take the time to train her properly. Delilah never really played with Jetta and only took her out to use the bathroom, but never on a walk. I cleaned up the mess and did my best to get the stains out. Not once did Delilah vacuum the living room, clean the kitchen, sweep or put any dishes away.

At that time, I was a full-time graduate student. I was finishing up my thesis in order to graduate, so I hadn't started looking extensively for a job as I managed the bills with my GI Bill, BAH and disability pay. Several days later, I came home from the gym and again I found another pile of diarrhea on the floor. This time I didn't clean it up and I left it for Delilah. The entire apartment smelled, so I stayed in my room. When Delilah came home from work, she got mad at me asked why I hadn't cleaned up and let it sit on the carpet all day! I told her I wasn't going to clean up after her dog's shit anymore and she should stop feeding her peanut butter.

The next day, I was cleaning the kitchen when Delilah came home. I was about to take out the trash when I decided I would bring it up. The trash was overflowing because I was trying to hold off as long as I possibly could in hopes that she would take it out on her own for once! "Delilah, do you think you could help a little more with cleaning and taking out the trash? I feel like I'm the only one doing it and Jetta is a lot to clean up after." I said it in a very calm, friendly, non-confrontational manner. She got up from the couch, turned off the TV and replied, "What the fuck? I'm not a Marine. I can't be all strict and do all the Yes, ma'am shit you do." This lady had lost her damn mind. "What are you talking about? Cleaning isn't a "Marine thing". I just asked if you would help take out our trash and vacuum up your dog's hair that's all over the place. You have never vacuumed once since you moved in here!" She had this crazed look on her face. "Well, I vacuumed when you were in Europe and took out the trash while you were off having fun. So, you're wrong. I have cleaned and vacuumed. So there." I started laughing. "Hold on. What did you want me to do, come back from Europe to vacuum your dog's hair and take out the trash that you made?" How could someone be this stupid?

I had started to notice that when Delilah felt uncomfortable or in a slightly confrontational conversation, she got nasty and hurtful. She replied, "Well, you don't have a job and I work all day. It's your job to clean up the house because I have a job and you don't. Your family was poor. So, this is your place. My family is rich and you came from nothing. Cleaning is your job. You're the maid." I couldn't believe what she was saying! She came into the kitchen so

I went and sat down on the couch to calm down and try to ignore her by turning on the TV. I knew this conversation was only going to get much worse.

"When my dad came here, he paid for your food and bought the couch that you're sitting on. So get the fuck off the couch. You should be grateful. I am not going to clean, that's beneath me. If it weren't for me, you wouldn't have anything you bitch." I turned off the TV. My pressure was about to boil over. "Call me bitch again and see what happens." "Bitch", she whispered under her breath. When I stood up from the couch, she took off running and locked herself in the room. I almost kicked in her door and would have loved to drag her out by her ratty hair, down the hall, and throw her in the garbage. But I didn't. I told her she wasn't worth my time and went to the gym to cool off. The confrontations grew and I couldn't take it anymore. I texted her and told her, "I don't care where you go, but you can't live here anymore." I had gone and spoken with the apartment manager and he told me that there was a girl that had been looking to move in and needed a roommate. I had a roommate lined up and Delilah started packing.

One evening I was watching a movie when Delilah came home with boxes and started packing up her kitchen items. Jetta loved me and had her head laying on my feet. Delilah kept calling her over and I told her that Jetta wasn't bothering me and I didn't mind. I was doing everything I could to be cordial and adult about our situation. Delilah got out the peanut butter, bribing Jetta to come over because Jetta wasn't obeying. After Jenna finished eating the poisonous treat that was making her sick, she would come back to me. Delilah tried it again. "Jetta, come here. Come on. You don't want to get tainted by that bitch." What was wrong with this psycho? "Delilah, can we please just be adult about this? I don't mind if she sits here. She's being good. Can we just try and get along? Please?" She pretended to ignore me. "Come here Jetta. I got peanut butter. Want a treat? Oh, good girl. You don't want to be by her anyways. See Jetta, everyone hates her. Even her entire family. She left her sister to get raped..." I jumped up. I had never been that angry in my entire life. I wanted to kill her. I wanted to wrap my hands around her throat and watch her cry and try to scream. Then I wanted to take my fist and break every bone in her face.

Delilah knew just what to say to truly hurt me and she went there. "Stand up, you fucking cunt. I said, stand the fuck up!" She was sitting on the floor and looking up at me with a deranged evil grin. She kicked me from the ground and I laughed at her. "Was that supposed to hurt, you evil bitch?" I grabbed her by the arm, pulling her to her feet. I started to back her into the kitchen and she looked terrified. "Fuck you" she said as I shoved her into the wall. To this day, I don't know how I held back from beating the shit out of her. I wanted to smash her face into the wall repeatedly. Maybe it was her saying she was going to call the cops or the pathetic look of terror on her face, but I held back.

Then a memory popped into my head. One of Delilah's many crazy stories about stalking her ex-boyfriend. She had told me that after her divorce, she had been dating a dentist who had a son. She fell for him and he found out just how crazy she was. She began stalking him and he had to get a restraining order when she showed

244

up to his son's school because he refused to introduce her to his son. After they broke up, this poor guy ended up in a relationship with a girl Delilah worked with. Delilah found out. She flew into a rage when she found out that this new girl had been introduced to the son. She tricked the girl into bringing her along on their date, saying that they had been great friends and he would get a kick out of seeing her again. When they arrived at his house for the date, Delilah got out of the car with a thermos of water, threw the water in his face, laughed, and ran away.

I smiled and filled up a cup of water and threw it in her face saying, "Now you know how it feels, you crazy bitch!" She began sputtering and crying. I just laughed, filled up another cup and threw it in her face as well. "OK, I'm done. Don't ever fucking talk to me again and you're shit better be gone by tomorrow", I said and left the room. Her dad paid for a moving truck with movers and I never saw that bitch again.

Joy's mom called me one day. Choking back tears, she told me that Joy was in the last stages of MS and was under hospice care. They told her family that Joy wasn't going to make it through the night. She asked me if I would be able to call Joy and say goodbye to her in 20 minutes. I was heartbroken. I wasn't sure what to say. When I got on the phone, I reminded her of our childhood and at the time her brother Nick played a trick on us during a sleepover one night. He had made us think that he was a burglar and we had locked ourselves in the bathroom with a butter knife. I told her about how I told Anthony all about her and how she was my inspiration to get through so many obstacles in my life. She couldn't talk and all I heard was gurgling and nothing I could understand. Her sister picked up the phone and told me that Joy was crying and had to get off the phone. I was so thankful that her family had given me the opportunity to say goodbye. A week later, my jackass of a father sent me her obituary, thinking I didn't know she had passed. What a prick! He had no idea what real love was.

After almost two years of not talking, I couldn't take it anymore and I gave in and messaged Anthony. I missed him every single day. Moments later he replied and asked, "Who is this?" I responded, "It's the person you promised you would never turn your back on." He knew right away and asked me for my address. He showed up an hour later at my job and I will never forget the smile on his face. It reminded me of the look on his face in Kuwait all those years ago. He ended up staying for around twenty minutes and we picked up right where we left off. We had a lot of catching up to do, but I was still heart broken and not sure how to get over everything I had been through. I didn't know how it'd be possible to forgive and move on.

My hands were shaking when I returned to my desk. Anthony messaged, asking if he could come and see me that evening so we could talk and I agreed. Later that evening he messaged me telling me he was there looking for parking. I walked out front to meet him. To my surprise, he was walking towards me holding his sleeping three-year-old daughter I didn't know he was bringing. "Here, hold her. A closer parking spot just opened up" he said handing me his sleeping daughter. As soon as she put her head on my shoulder, the tears came running down my cheeks. I could feel her sweet breath on my neck and her fingers clinging to my back. Our daughter would have been just a year younger, and I can only imagine what she would have been like.

By the time Anthony came back, I had dried my tears and composed myself. I was getting good at this, but Anthony could read me like a book. He knew something was wrong and kept asking me, but I told him it was nothing. We talked for several hours and he apologized for all the pain he caused me. He told me the reason he didn't contact me was because he thought I would never talk to him again. Sarah had threatened his career and taking away his daughter, and that was why he didn't come and see me two years ago in 29 Palms. He had never sent me that text. She had taken his phone and messaged me telling me to delete his number and never contact him again.

After talking for hours, I still hadn't told him about the miscarriage and he could tell I was hiding something from him. I didn't want to tell him because I knew it would hurt him. There was this massive wall I had built up trying to protect myself from getting hurt again. I knew I needed to tell him, but I wasn't ready. A few nights later he messaged me and asked if I'd come visit him on base because he knew something was wrong and he wanted to talk. I agreed and went to meet him. We sat in his car for around two hours, not saying a lot. I couldn't even look at him or I knew he would see right through me. I asked him to drive over to a gas station to go to the bathroom. When I got back in the car, he asked me what was wrong. I was about to burst into tears, but instead I told him I couldn't be there anymore and I had to go. I got up and walked over to my car and left.

The next day I messaged him, but he didn't respond. I knew he was hurt by what I had done and I needed to tell him what was wrong. I wrote him a letter because I couldn't tell him in person. It was too much and I knew I wouldn't be able to get it all out without being a crying mess. After I had gotten that off my chest, we had another battle to face, the sexual tension that was growing more and more every single day. We tried for weeks, but the sexual chemistry between us was undeniable and we soon started hooking up again. Once again, Sarah found out. Even though she had known about us for years and still stayed with him, I still felt guilty. I decided to talk to Anthony and we both agreed that we would try to just be friends. One day we slipped up and couldn't keep our hands off of each other. That's just how we were every time were together. The sexual chemistry was uncontrollable.

The next morning after hooking up, he messaged me. It was surprising because he was at home and he never messaged me while he was at home. He said Sarah was gone all day and he missed me. I told him how much I wished he could have spent the night. He replied how much he loved the rare mornings we got to spend together. After texting back and forth, I received another message, "you whore! This is Anthony's wife. You are both going to hell. Enjoy Anthony. I am done with him." Sarah had taken his phone and had been messaging me all morning pretending she was Anthony.

Hours later, Anthony messaged and asked me to meet him at the CVS down the street from my apartment. I told him he needed to call me because I didn't trust text messages after what had just happened. He called me and I met him an hour later. She had kicked him out and he spent the night with me. I was trying not to get my hopes up, but I prayed with everything in me that maybe this time he wouldn't have to leave. Maybe this time he could stay. Maybe this time he could be with me every night, as I had been praying would happen for the past six years. As I feared, Anthony went back and I didn't hear from him for three months.

During those three months, I was laid off from work, school was kicking my ass, and I received more devastating news. While I was with Maria and Smith. Smith was a very good Marine friend of mine and Maria's. Smith was hopelessly in love with Maria but she didn't feel the same. We were at Maria's daughter Molly's baptism when I received a text message from Delilah. She sent me around 30 text messages telling me that I was a liar and I made everything up about Cain. She told me that she went and found him, had lunch with him, and that he told her I lied about everything and she believed him.

This psycho bitch from hell also went to my family and told them that I was kicked out of the Marine Corps for being a whore and because I was crazy and had PTSD. She told me that she also went and saw Marie and that Marie hated me and wished I was dead. I went to the bathroom and vomited. When I came out, I cried in Smith's arms and Maria brought me a shot and told me if she ever met Delilah again, she would punch her in the baby maker.

A few days later, my ex sister in law contacted me and told me that the judge had dropped the case. Delilah and my parents had gone before the judge and told him all the lies that Delilah had told them about me. They dropped me from testifying as I now was deemed a non-credible witness. The evidence in support of removing my niece from my brother's custody was highly dependent on my testimony. My sister in law had told me that she had recorded the monster on the phone telling their daughter to not tell anyone that daddy touched her private parts, that only he could touch her there. This recording was inadmissible because the monster didn't know he was being recorded. With my parent's financial help and their and Delilah's testimony about me, he was awarded primary custody while his ex was granted partial.

The months following, Cain started to train their daughter to psychically abuse and torment her other step siblings. He told her different things to say to try and convince her other sisters to commit suicide. Fearing for her other children's safety, his ex couldn't have their daughter around the other kids and she gave the monster full custody.

In an attempt to get over Anthony, I decided to give dating apps a try. I was pleasantly surprised by one man's profile and went out on a date with him. He was a six foot three, African-American, personal trainer, and EMT with an amazing body, named Matt. I viewed dating as a distraction because deep down, I knew that I would never love anyone more than I loved Anthony. I realized early on that Matt was just using me for somewhere to stay and I was just using him as a distraction.

Chapter 31

During this time, I was still dating and going out with other guys. There was one attractive man from New Zealand named Jack that I had been exchanging messages with for a while. He asked me to go salsa dancing with him, but I didn't know how and I didn't want to look like a fool on our first date. This man was intimidating on paper and in his photos. He had two master's degrees, was a pararescue diver, covered in tattoos and traveled the world. He invited me out for dinner and I had to turn him down again because I was helping throw a goodbye pool party for a friend of mine that was deploying. I invited him and he said he would text me the next day of the party for the address. As he said he would, he messaged me the day of the party and told me that he would be over in an hour.

The party had started and Jack still hadn't showed up yet. It was over two hours since he said he would be there. I didn't think he was going to show up. So when Matt messaged me and asked me if we could talk, I said yes. Matt and I hadn't talked in a few weeks. When he would text me at 22:00 asking if I was home, I knew he was just looking for a place to crash. I started coming up with excuses and saying I was out. There was no chemistry between us and the conversations were incredibly dull.

Trying to be up front, I told Matt when he arrived that I had invited a date, but I didn't think the guy was going to show. We gathered for a group photo on the stairs and in the middle of it, I heard a man say in a strong New Zealand accent "Oi, is Athena here?" Oh, shit, I had two dates. This wasn't me! Up until this point, I didn't really even date and today, of all days, I had two.

Doing my best to act cool, I walked up the stairs and was immediately taken with this man. He was average height, wearing a pink tank top, blue track pants, different colored socks and covered with tattoos. Yes, I said socks, no shoes. He was one of a kind. I introduced Matt to Jack and was relieved when Jack started mingling and talking with everyone at the party. I bounced back and forth from Matt to Jack and the girls at the party were drooling over both of my dates. I won't lie. It felt good to have these two incredibly talented, successful, sexy, smart men there for me. Matt didn't talk to anyone and when he had to go back to work, I walked him to the gate. I hugged him goodbye, knowing it would be the last time I saw him.

When I returned, I saw Jack in the pool area. He had taken off his track pants, revealing these leopard boxer briefs and an incredible muscular body. The confidence of that man was remarkable. I grabbed a drink and went to the hot tub where he joined me. While I was getting in he said, "Oi, nice ass" loud enough for everyone in the pool area to hear. I laughed and said thank you for his bluntness. It was refreshing compared to the lame pickup lines and fakeness which seemed to be everywhere. I had already fallen for Jack's physical attributes and his accent, and then we started talking. If falling in love with someone's intelligence is possible that's what was happening and I knew I was in trouble. In less than an hour, this man had me terrified. I was a disaster, drinking almost every night, no job, confused, still in love with a man I could never be with, and putting on a big show that everything was perfect. This man, covered in tattoos with the vocabulary and eloquence of Shakespeare, saw me. He looked past my insecurities and saw me as I see myself.

A quote from The Great Gatsby popped into my mind. "He had one of those rare smiles with a quality of eternal reassurance in it, that you may come across four or five times in life. It faced, or seemed to face, the whole external world for an instant and then concentrated on you with an irresistible prejudice in your favor. It understood you just as far as you wanted to be understood, believed in you as you would like to believe in yourself."

I wasn't ready for him and I was too drunk to realize what a complete bitch I was being. Jack was doing a year sober and he didn't know anyone at the party, but he stayed to try and get to know me. What did I do? I went and smoked weed in my room with a friend and left him to fend for himself with a drunk group of Marines he had just met. I don't know why he even stayed after how I treated him. He told me he had to take off and I walked him to the gate. For the first time in my life, I made out with someone I had just met.

He called me the next day. He didn't text, he properly called me up and asked me to join him for an evening downtown. He didn't tell me what he had planned and I only found out when I picked him up and he gave me directions. He knew I was into forensics and he signed us up to do a mystery dinner event downtown. The event was ridiculous, but we were having so much fun together. We turned what could have been a terrible date into a great evening. We talked about everything. Our conversations could have been written into a screenplay. I was falling hard fast and my mind was trying to slam on the brakes because I didn't want to get hurt. This dating thing was supposed to be a fun fling, nothing serious. I wasn't ready to meet the real thing. I was terrified.

After the event was over, he took me to a few different bars and one that had board games. We played a giant-sized game of Connect Four, he kicked my butt in mortal combat and I beat him at air hockey. I invited him back to my place and we just made out because I really wasn't ready to have sex. The next morning, I got up and made us breakfast, and we spent the entire morning in bed. I was watching one of my favorite movies, Pan's Labyrinth. I had my leg draped over his and he kept falling asleep and would wake up and ask me what was going on in the movie. When I moved my leg to readjust, he said "Oi, thank God you cut off all the circulation with that leg of yours." I started laughing "Screw you. What, you want me to have some skinny ass legs?" He grabbed me and kissed me, telling me he loved my legs. It was such an odd feeling to be so comfortable with someone I hardly knew.

Adding to my fear, Jack had told me that he didn't want any kind of serious relationship. When I looked him up on Facebook, he had hundreds of photos with women all over the world, not just being in a picture with them, but making out with them. This raised a lot of red flags. I had already fallen for him and ignored all of these things.

During this time, I had conquered one of my greatest fears, my lack of self-esteem and weight issues. I knew men thought I had a great body, but I always felt fat, ugly and unattractive. To face my fears, I decided to do the thing that terrified me, a photo shoot in a bikini. I was shocked by how well some of them turned out, and it helped boost my self-confidence.

I invited Jack over for dinner one evening and showed him some of my photos. He was honest and gave me great feedback. He told me they were great photos and he wanted to take some to the bathroom with him, but he said I was holding back. He said I was still not showing who I really was. We talked for hours and for the first time someone called me babe. Some of you may think that is silly to get excited about, but when you have waited almost thirty-three years to hear that, it means a great deal. We talked about our dreams and when I said I would love to have an orphanage in a different country, he told me I was him with a great pair of tits.

He said he had a retirement plan already and he wanted to buy a place on the beach in Indonesia and learn how to play the guitar. We even talked about having kids. When I brought up how difficult it would be to move my shoes and books, he told me, "Babe, you won't need all your heels in Indonesia. I'll just buy you all the sandals you want and you can't bring your books. The humidity will ruin them, so we'll just have to get you all e-books." If he had asked me to marry him and run away with him at that moment, I would have. After only a few dates, I was in love with this man. Nothing compared to the love I had for Anthony, but I was madly in love with Jack.

I felt so strongly about Jack, I actually told Anthony about him and told Anthony that we had to stop sleeping together. I could tell it really hurt him, but he told me that he wanted me to be happy and if it meant not seeing him or being friends anymore, that he would put my happiness first. But I wasn't willing to let our friendship go and we continued to be friends.

Not many people understand the kind of love I have for Anthony. Yes, we were more than friends, but he was what made me believe in soul mates. He was part of me. It was the same kind of love I had for Marie. A kind of love that surpassed romance. He was the only family I had left. Since that day in Ramadi, almost nine years ago, I knew he was my soul mate, my best friend. Not time, distance, war, or anything else would ever change that.

After dinner, I asked Jack what it would take to be in a serious relationship with him. My fears came true when he told me that from the beginning, he didn't want anything serious. I was so confused. We had talked about a future and kids. He told me that he had been in love before and had serious relationships, but the women couldn't deal with him leaving for his job all the time. They would move on and find other people, leaving him hurt and alone. He told me that in a year I would have forgotten about him and would be in a real relationship. I told him he was wrong and I would just have to prove it to him.

After he told me that he didn't want to be in a relationship with me, I started to push away because I knew I was going to be crushed when he left. I just wasn't ready to let him go and I wanted to be the one that changed his mind. I wanted to show him through my actions that I saw him. That he was worthy of love and worth waiting for. We started making out that night and just before we were about to have sex, I hesitated. I was scared. Can you blame me? He told me that he didn't want to be in a relationship with me and I was already in love with him. Sleeping with him would only make it more painful when he left. He took this as me pushing him away and he got up and left.

I messaged him several times with no reply and finally, after several days, he responded. He invited me out to a surprise night of painting and wine. On our dates, he never told me where we were going and would surprise me. I loved that about him and our dates were always incredible and so much fun. I drank a few glasses of wine during the painting event and asked him if he could drive my car to get some food at Pieology, one of his favorite places to eat. Not only had it been years since he drove a stick, he didn't like to drive because he was always in other countries on different sides of the road. He did amazing and we had a few laughs about his driving my car.

I also found out why he had showed up three hours late to my party. Because he travels so much he only uses Wifi and doesn't have a cell phone plan. He had rented a car to come up to my party and had gotten so lost, it took him three hours to find my apartment and he almost crashed several times. Damn. Looking back, I was such a bitch to him that day.

When Jack ordered food, he did it custom and never off the menu. Yet another thing I loved about him. He had great taste in food and I would always try some of his. That evening we finally had sex. He told me I was the complete package, beautiful, killer body, could cook, smart, and incredible in bed. Jack took off to Washington, D.C. for some training, and I was heading to Jamaica with Ben for his friend's wedding. Ben knew I loved to travel and when he told me that the room was already paid for and I just needed to buy the plane ticket, I was in! My time in Jamaica was amazing and I met some incredible people. I learned so much about what made Anthony the way he was. It made me miss him so much. Even though I was in love with Jack, I would never stop loving Anthony. After returning from my trip, I messaged Jack when I got back, but he never responded. Over a month went by and I was scared that Jack had left and wasn't going to come back. I cried myself to sleep so angry at myself for giving my heart to someone that had told me from the beginning he didn't want it. My heart was conflicted. Even though I was single, every time I slept with someone other than Anthony, it felt as if I were cheating on him.

Jack was the only person that I could see being able to really be with, and I loved him already. A different love then with Anthony, but I still could see myself being happy with him. Did I screw up? Did I fall for another person that would never love me back? Was I picking all the wrong men or was there something wrong with me that made them never want to stay? That fear of never being good enough crept back in and I was desperate to fight it off. At that time, I didn't fully comprehend how much my past had distorted my view of relationships. I was extremely immature as far as dating went. Most go through these kinds of experiences in their teenage years and I also didn't realize the extent of damage the chronic child abuse had on me.

While I was getting more ink, a beautiful Hades tattoo on my thigh, Jack called asking me to join him at the Hard Rock for one of their famous pool parties. I was so disappointed I couldn't go, but I was mid-session in my tattoo. I saw his photos on Facebook the next day. He was surrounded by beautiful, barely clothed women all over him. I wasn't jealous of the girls; I was jealous that I missed out on such a fun day. I became even more hesitant on allowing my feelings for him to creep back in.

The next weekend, he told me to get dressed up and surprised me with a comedy show dinner date. Jack told me that he was leaving for an assignment in the Pacific and I invited him over for dinner. I got all dressed up and went to pick him up. I was wearing a knee-length, flowy dress with no underwear, as I was only planning on being home with him. When I got there to pick him up, he told me that he had a surprise and he took me to go race go karts. I wasn't dressed at all for the occasion! They had to stop the race because my dress kept flying up and I was driving with one hand to keep from flashing everyone. We both couldn't stop laughing. It was such a fun evening.

I was hoping to spend one more day with him, but he got stuck at work. I had made him his favorite cheesecake, a drawing, and a book of challenges to do while he was gone. He told me that he was too busy packing and didn't like goodbyes. He only agreed to let me come see him after I promised it would be quick and I just wanted to give him his gifts and kiss him goodbye. I jumped on my motorcycle and rode over to his hotel. I showed him the gifts I made and explained them. He was in the middle of packing and I didn't want to make him miss his flight. Plus, I had given him my word and was trying to respect his wishes. So, I gave him a kiss goodbye and started down the stairs. I felt that my kiss hadn't been adequate, so I walked back up the stairs, knocked on his door and gave him a proper kiss goodbye.

We exchanged emails a few times and he sent me an edible fruit arrangement for my birthday. I wasn't used to getting gifts and it was such a special treat. Jack had opened my eyes to many things and he pushed me to stop making excuses for myself. He may not want to be in a relationship with me, but I wanted to show him that I was someone that could live his way of life. My entire life I had always dreamed of living in a different country, and I decided to make a massive leap of faith and go for it.

Jack had been all over the world and he had told me that Indonesia was his favorite place. I wanted to discover for myself, what it was about that country that made Jack want to retire there. I found an internship teaching English at a school in Indonesia. I was terrified! I had a good job working as an investigator for an insurance company, a great apartment, friends, a car and motorcycle both paid off, and was financially comfortable. Was I about to make the greatest mistake of my life? I was also a forensic psychology doctoral student and I was trying to decide the topic of my dissertation. I wanted to study sex trafficking and how culture impacts resilience in sex trafficking survivors. Asian cultures are so different from ours, and

I was fascinated with learning how their culture impacts resilience. I needed to see this firsthand, so I took a giant leap of faith and I jumped.

Chapter 32

I arrived at the Surabaya, Indonesia airport without any issues and was picked up by the contact field support member of the internship program. According to the internship contract, I was supposed to be placed in one of Indonesia's most prominent cities, Surabaya. They told me I would have my own apartment, work regular school hours, have weekends off to travel, arranged trips to tourist sites, and a monthly stipend for food. Before I signed the contract, I told them one of my main requirements was to have access to Wifi because I was a full time PhD student and I needed internet access for my dissertation. Before I left, they guaranteed me that this would be set up in an apartment they would provide for me.

The internship field coordinator took me to my hotel and told me he would be back in the morning to introduce me to the director of the school that I would be volunteering at. The next morning, the two teachers arrived. They didn't speak much English at all, which worried me, but I was so excited to be in Indonesia and I tried to stay positive. After loading up my suitcases, we started driving through the lush and exotic looking Indonesian countryside. The ladies didn't talk much at all and told me that they needed to stop and pray.

They stopped at a mosque and told me to get out of the van and then they locked the door, leaving me standing there without a word. I watched as they walked over to the washing area and then go inside the mosque after washing their hands, face and feet. They were inside for almost an hour and I was getting devoured by mosquitoes. After waiting for around 20 minutes, I finally decided to sit down on some steps leading into the mosque. When the prayers ended and people started coming out, I started receiving a lot of nasty looks. I realized that I had accidentally been sitting on the Men's side and the women were pointing at me and laughing and the men were giving me death stares.

I was told that I was going to be taken to my new apartment before we left the hotel, and I was surprised when we made another stop. Once again, they didn't say anything and we pulled up to a military base with armed guards out front. They asked me to get out and I was starting to get very nervous. Was I about to be sold to some sex traffickers? What the hell was going on? I followed them into an office and was introduced to the General of the base. They invited me to sit down and for over an hour they spoke in a language I didn't know and were constantly saying Athena and laughing. I started to get irritated. I would have never treated guests from another country that were there helping in this manner. However, I knew I had a lot to learn about Asian cultures.

After a torturous hour, severe jet lag and countless mosquito bites, they left and told me we were going to visit the school. When we arrived, they took out my luggage and wheeled it down the street to this shit hole they called a school. It was around eighteen hundred and I hadn't eaten since breakfast. They brought my luggage into an office and one of the ladies went and got a sleeping pad that was around an inch thick. I was so confused and kept asking them when I was going to my apartment. The director didn't understand what I was asking, even though she was the head of the school.

As I was moving my suitcases into the office to get it out of the way so people can come and go, the director came in and said, "See you tomorrow". I thought it must have been some mix up with the language barrier or something. So I continued moving my things. Then I heard the chain on the door and when I went out to go look, they had locked me inside the school! What the hell had just happened? I was starving. The room was filled with mosquitoes. There was no shower, no pillow, nothing. Thankfully, the computer room had a faint Internet connection and I messaged Smith, Murphy and Maria. They all told me to get the hell out of there and come back home, but I wasn't going to give up that easily.

At 11:00 the next day, I heard the chain being removed from the front door. I hadn't been able to sleep all night and I was delirious. The director told me that she was taking me to my new apartment. I followed her past some beautiful little homes and numerous nice-looking apartments with for rent signs. We kept on walking. The streets became shadier and the houses were in shambles. She stopped outside a sketchy looking building and said with a big smile, "Your home." She opened the front door and the first thing I saw was the laundry hanging up with a hole in the ground for the bathroom and a large bucket of water to shower and a curtain you can pull shut for privacy. They wash their clothes and dishes right next to where they use the bathroom. A wave of shit and piss smell almost made me puke. She wheeled my suitcase over to a closet sized room with no window, no AC, no fan, no dresser and a sleeping mat. It looked like a prison cell in a third world country. I laughed and said, "Is this a joke? I'm not staying here. Would you stay here?" She responded "No, I wouldn't live here. I have family, my family, you no family." She asked me what was wrong with the room. I told her it was disgusting and I would not be staying there. She looked angry and without a word, led me back to the school and left me in the room, chaining me in again.

The next day, the director arrived again and took me to another place that was worse than the one before. I told her that if she couldn't find me a safe place that was suitable, that I would be leaving. I messaged the internship liaison and he called and talked to the director. He came the next day and took me 45 minutes away to a studio the size of a walk-in closet. It was nice and new, which I could have cared less about, but it was safe and clean, which I required. Then they told me it was going to cost me around 200 dollars a month to get back and forth from school. Because I was volunteering and was living off my savings, I couldn't afford to stay there.

After almost a week of sleeping in the school, they finally found me a suitable small studio apartment around 10 minutes from the school. Before I agreed to stay, they promised me that Wifi would be installed that day. The internship description was also far from what had been described. I was told that I was going to be in Surabaya, a large city, with lots to do. Instead, the school was in a town called Sidoarjo which had nothing around for at least 30 miles. Then I was given my work schedule and found out I was working Monday through Friday from 13:00 to 22:30 and Saturday from 09:00 to 17:00. The contract had said I would be working regular school hours.

On my first day, they had me teach eight classes that lasted an hour. The classes ranged from first grade through adult and the English level was terrible. In the contract I was told I would be the assistant because I had never taught English before. I had no idea what I was doing. I was supposed to be the English aide at a local school. What they left out was this was an after-school teaching English school, where the teachers barely spoke enough English to have a conversation with a three-year-old. They also didn't tell me I was part of their marketing scam. They charged an excessive amount of money, telling parents and others that I would be teaching all the classes. They didn't tell me that I would be paraded around and asked to stand outside local schools as a form of advertisement and told to hand out flyers. They would leave me alone in this tiny classroom the size of a large walk in closet, and would pack in fifteen kids with no working AC and leave to go check out their Facebook page in the computer lab.

The walk home at that time of night wasn't safe, but I sucked it up and I did it anyways. I still had no Wifi and I needed the software on my laptop to do some of my homework for my classes. I was also almost failing my class because I wasn't able to submit my assignments on time. I had to ask the director every single day about the Wifi and she always said the same damn thing "Tomorrow they install."

When I asked them to give me the topic that they were going to be covering that day in class, they would give it to me an hour before class leaving me no time to prepare. Try coming up with eight one hour long English lessons with less than an hour to prepare. The books they had me teaching out of were not only age level inappropriate, but the topics were idiotic. They couldn't understand that I needed to get the topic or the book days before the class so I didn't have to wing it every time. I needed time to prepare! I knew plenty of kindergarten games, but the book lesson would be done in ten minutes and I would have to pull something out my ass for the next 50 minutes. I was beyond frustrated!

One evening in my fourth-grade class, I only had two male students. The book lesson was Love at first sight. The first activity: have your students talk about their feelings of love at first sight and share an experience that they had. For fourth graders that hardly spoke English! The two fourth grade boys were staring and laughing at the cartoon pictures of a little boy and girl kissing. They had no supplies, no flash cards, nothing. Now, keep in mind, this wasn't an extremely poor area. They had expensive clothes, drove nice cars and lived in beautiful homes. They only had a whiteboard and a marker that didn't work. I would have to walk two miles to the store to get supplies and I had to pay for them with my own money. The amount of money they were charging compared to the services they advertised was wrong!

Thankfully, I met the young man whose parents owned the apartment I lived in. He spoke the best English out of anyone I had met and he told me he learned by watching the Twilight movies. I had asked him if he knew where I could find a gym. I was losing my mind here and I needed to work out badly. He took me on his motorbike to the gym. It wasn't that bad, but they had no AC, no fans, smelled terrible, and it cost over sixty dollars a month, which is extraordinarily expensive for there.

Something I quickly learned while living overseas is that they charge Americans and other foreigners much more than they charge locals. If it's written in English, it's going to cost you. They charge you more for rent, for gas, for electricity, for gym memberships, for just about everything. The gym was over two miles away and I would end up running there, workout, and run back. The sidewalks were so badly damaged and dangerous that I would have to run in the streets. Most of these sidewalks had large holes in them so large, you could fall and break your leg if not being careful. Walking at night was even more dangerous, so I would stay off the sidewalks all together.

Once in the gym, I realized that women here did not lift weights. I soon had a large group of female spectators, that were chatting in the pool area, taking pictures and waving at me while I was sweating my ass off working out. Running on the streets was like playing the video game Frogger. With motorbikes, bicycles and cars coming at you from all directions.

I would run to the gym almost daily and started to make loyal fans that would follow me on their motorbikes, waving and asking me to marry them. I would pass the local schools on the way and they all waved and said "Hello, Mr.", upon which I smiled and waved back. Not everything was bad. Some of my students were so funny and kind. I was informed by some that they had heard I was a famous singer in an American rock band.

I soon learned that most of the time when Asian people point and laugh, it wasn't about being rude or unkind. It's simply because they had never seen a tall white girl covered with tattoos doing something crazy like running in the streets. The most difficult lesson I needed to learn was that sometimes you just have to ask for help. Asking for help is not always a sign of weakness, but that of strength. Another lesson I learned was that nearly all the local lotions contain high SPF as well as whitening treatments. I had noticed that my skin would burn slightly after putting on a lotion and I discovered that this was the whitening product. I stopped using any of the lotion in the stores. I didn't need to be any whiter than my Casper the Ghost skin already was.

After two weeks of no Wifi at my apartment, I checked my email at the school and had a message from my professor telling me that I might be dropped if I didn't start turning my assignments in on time. The computer lab did not allow me to access my online classroom or the software I needed. I could check my email, but nothing else. I couldn't submit any of my assignments. I told the director that I wasn't going to continue working until they fix the Wifi issue. She didn't understand so I said "no Wifi, no work." True to my word, I stayed at home and after three days she came with one of the other female teachers and gave me this wireless device. However, I would have to purchase data minutes because I had to watch several videos every lesson and I was burning through ten dollars of data a day. I

270

couldn't afford to pay two hundred and eighty dollars a month. The owners of the apartment had Wifi, but I would have to sit at the very corner of the balcony with my phone up in the air to get a signal and it wasn't strong enough to reach my laptop.

There were several times where a few of the teachers would show up at my door telling me that I needed to come to work early to help them with work. As if a nine-hour teaching day with a half our dinner wasn't enough. One of the days I was returning from the gym and trying to shower. When I opened the door they just walked in and started looking around my room, opening drawers, and looking at my photos. Then they told me that I needed to come into work.

I was doing my best to make it work, but I was sleep deprived and overworked and was doing this with no pay. I was sleep deprived because I didn't get off work until around 22:30. I didn't fall asleep until around midnight and then I was woken up at 04:00 by the call to prayer. These weren't just regular calls to prayer. There were around six mosques surrounding my studio apartment and they had loudspeakers blaring the prayers so loudly it shook all the windows in my apartment. They woke me up and I could never fall back asleep. In Iraq, I didn't mind the prayers. They were actually kind of oddly soothing. The prayers here, were a different story.

They had me scheduled to work on Christmas, so I called in sick. I didn't want to leave my apartment. I was sick and tired of the stares, the tattoo comments, being pointed and laughed at. I was so thankful that Smith was in Japan and in the same time zone. We talked almost every morning and evening. I called in sick the day after as well and returned to work on the following Monday. I had been there 12 weeks and I hated every single day I was in Indonesia.

One Sunday, my only day off, I went to get some nasi goreng, a common street food in Indonesia. After the man who cooked the street food handed me the food and I paid him, he grabbed my crotch and said, "I buy. Fuck you. Yeah, fuck you. I pay tattoo bitch, fuck you." I told him to go fuck himself and I almost broke his wrist. He grabbed my ass when I went to walk away. I wanted to beat the shit out of this creep, but I didn't want to end up in an Indonesian prison. I had heard horror stories about their justice system. This bastard followed me with his cart and saw where I lived. The next few nights I saw him following me.

That was my breaking point. I wrote the internship company and told them what had happened and that I needed to be placed somewhere else. The next day I received an email telling me to grow up and this was just because I was a spoiled American experiencing culture shock. This jackass went on to tell me that it was my fault the man assaulted because I wasn't dressed as a Muslim woman and they had every right to do what they did. When this happened, I was in teaching clothes. I was wearing long sleeves and a long skirt. I wrote them back and told them that I had lived in Iraq in a tent with no AC, with no toilets getting shot at daily, and I would rather be there than in this place another night. I told them that they broke everything in the contract and I was going to contact the BBB, tell them what had happened to me, and start telling everyone on social media to stay away from this organization. They wrote me back and told me that if I felt I needed to report this, then they would call the

Police and have me deported or held for questioning.

I panicked and called in sick so I could figure out what the hell I was going to do. I Googled different internships that started right away. The only one I could find was one based in Thailand. It was going to cost me around thirteen hundred dollars, but I would be a certified TEFL (teaching English foreign language) instructor. It wasn't beginning until February, so I was still stuck. I was talking on Voxer with Smith and he told me to get my ass on the next flight and I could stay with him. I never asked or brought it up, he freely offered. I purchased both the ticket and the internship and flew out the next morning.

On my way to the gate, I saw signs everywhere saying that if caught with any amount of drugs, it was the death penalty. I knew I had made the right choice to get the hell out of there. The last Facebook post I made was indicating that I was going to go to Singapore for New Years. I was planning on meeting Jack there, but he hadn't responded in time and I made plans to go to Japan instead. Jack would pop up every couple weeks with Facebook posts in the Philippines, Korea, Singapore and other countries, always with girls and at wild parties. His messages had become brief and lacking what we had before. He told me that he was disappointed with me for not making it work in Indonesia and it hurt me deeply. He traveled with an unlimited cash flow, multiple passports and military assistance when and if he needed it. He was traveling through the tourist areas, not in remote locations like I had been. I thought he would have been proud of me and see that I could be the woman he would want to be in a relationship with. How wrong was I? I tried to explain to him why I left and I noticed a pattern forming. If he didn't like what I said, there would be no reply for weeks. The only times he would respond is if weeks later I would message him regarding something he approved of. I had moved to Indonesia because of him. I did it for myself as well, but I had taken a huge leap of faith and I landed flat on my face.

What I should have told him was that my experience in Indonesia had taught me a great deal about myself. The old me would have allowed them to continue taking advantage of me, and in fact, I was extremely proud of myself for leaving. Not only was I extremely unhappy, I was being used and lied to. Why should I stay in an unhappy situation where people were using me? I know you're all probably thinking that's exactly what Jack was doing, using me. Like I said before, I was still learning and not always aware of the damage that my past had done, especially with relationships. It's very challenging to know your value and demand that out of a relationship when those that were supposed to teach you those lessons, made you feel worthless. English teachers doing the job I had been doing made more money than almost any profession in Indonesia, and I was working there for free. Being brave enough to go against what I was told I needed to do, was a major accomplishment and I should have told him this.

Chapter 33

After spending a month in Okinawa, Smith dropped me off at the airport and I flew into Bangkok International Airport at 23:00. I had no idea what I was doing and I didn't know where to get the tourist visa. I saw a sign that said Visa on arrival. So, I got in the long line and waited for two hours, only to be told that I was in the wrong line. I was told to just go through customs and I stood in another two-hour line. After finally making it through and retrieving my two suitcases, which had everything I owned, I found an outlet and tried to get comfortable. The internship shuttle wasn't going to be there until 07:00 and I was exhausted.

After finding the internship organizer, we waited for several others that were just getting through customs. From Bangkok, we drove to the old capital Ayutthaya. The countryside was beautiful and I loved seeing all the temples on the way. The hotel we were staying at for the orientation, more than exceeded my expectations. I had bought coffee, an apple, and yogurt for breakfast at the airport, but was starving by the time we arrived. After checking in, I went to find some food. On my short walk to the 7-Eleven up the street, I knew I was going to end up living in this beautiful country. The bridge I had to cross to get to the store was something out of a fairy tale. The water was filled with lily pads, lotus flowers and a rowboat with a fishing pole hooked onto the side. Everyone I came across smiled and waved, such a huge difference from Indonesia. The country was magical and definitely lived up to the name Land of Smiles.

The orientation was a breath of fresh air compared to what I had experienced with the last one. We were given classes on culture, classroom games and other teaching related topics. They organized a trip to the old temples and an incredible dinner. The hotel had a proper gym and I went for a workout while everyone took a nap or headed to the bar. We were soon assigned our schools and I looked forward to seeing my new home. For the next seven weeks, I would be paired up with one other female teacher from Barcelona, Spain. We were the first ones to be dropped off at our new school and it was amazing. We had seen pictures the day before during our orientation, but nothing could prepare us for what was to come.

We arrived at our school located in Sena, Thailand, and were immediately greeted by around 30 peeking heads from the kindergarten windows. The director of the school came out to greet us, as well as some of the other teachers. The school was located directly next to a temple that looked as if it could have been in a National Geographic magazine. I saw monks wandering the grounds, playing with dogs and children waving from the classrooms. After a short tour of the school, we were shown to our new home for the next two months. It was a tiny two-bedroom wood shack with a kitchen bathroom and two individual bedrooms directly located next to the river. Despite no hot water, the mosquitoes, and gaping holes in the floor you could see through, I loved it! Thankfully, they had Wifi all set up that was adequate to prepare lesson plans and complete my homework for my dissertation.

The staff took us to get lunch at a local restaurant that had a menu only in Thai. They ordered for us after asking if we liked spicy food and what we would like to eat. I loved the way they ordered food in Thailand. It was kind of like family style. They would order several different dishes you could choose from and always rice. For every single meal. If there wasn't rice, it wasn't considered a meal. The restaurant was located on the roof overlooking a beautiful river. It was bizarrely playing an English Christian radio station. My roommate and I had a good laugh over that and enjoyed our first meal with our new coworkers. These women were so kind, gracious and spoke enough English to communicate.

We were then taken to the local Tesco shopping center to get more supplies for the house. They graciously got us everything we needed, including a hot pot, microwave, and some other kitchen supplies. After they dropped us off back at the school, we were invited by the director to his home for dinner. Before dinner, I heard a knock at the door and after opening it, around eight teachers and other staff members rushed in. They were eager to talk and watch us unpack. As we were unpacking, teachers were sitting in our front room and wandering around our rooms, looking at our things. This was something my new roommate and I were not used to, as we are from a culture that values privacy.

Dinner at the director's house was an adventure in itself. We were invited to sit at picnic table next to the river, but we're only joined by the women. My roommate and I spotted the bottle of whiskey that some of the men had taken from the table and moved to a different location in the yard. We both fancied a stiff drink after the long day we had, and quietly joined the men. We soon found ourselves having whiskey and club soda, chatting with Thai men about Muay Thai and the military.

Our first day of teaching began the next day and I fell in love with my kindergarten class as well as many of the other classes. I was teaching five classes a day with an occasional outdoor game of soccer and tag. The nightlife in our little compound was quite the happening place. We were entertained nightly with around 25 stray dogs, 15 cats, an occasional monkey, birds that sounded like squalling infants, an abundance of indoor lizards, and nonstop visitors from teachers, students and the random curious neighbors. One evening, my roommate ventured out after dark to retrieve a desk for her room. I heard a scream and a laugh as she came running back. She had been running away from a curious sniffing dog.

One of my favorite moments took place when I took my evening run/workout. As I ran down the street, two of my grade five students joined me. One was running and the other one was riding on the back of his friend's bike. On my run, I was greeted by waving neighbors saying, "Hello, Dr. America." Apparently, word travels fast in a small town and the teachers must have informed their students, who told their parents, that I was going to school to get my doctorate. I noticed some boys coming out of their homes with their soccer gear and they jumped on their bikes. As I look backed, I realized I was leading a pack of soccer players all pedaling furiously on their bikes behind me. It was one of the most surreal experiences I have ever had. It reminded me of that seen in Ali where he was followed by a crowd of fans on his run.

When I got back to the school, I was joined by around eight of my students and they participated in my cross-training workout. As sweat was pouring into my eyes, I looked across the school grounds to see a monk waving hello in front of a temple, sparkling gold in the setting sun. I was overcome with honor and gratitude for this incredible experience. I ended my perfect evening with a pickup game of soccer and crawled into my mosquito netted bed with an overwhelming feeling of bliss.

Jack messaged me and told me he was coming to see me in Bangkok that weekend. I hadn't seen him in almost a year and was filled with so much anticipation and excitement. Anthony and I hadn't talked much at all since I had been gone. He was busy working long hours and I was still trying to get over him. I packed up the T-shirts I had bought Jack in San Diego and had brought with me. I couldn't wait to see him and feel his arms around me again. I was also having nervous feelings as well because of the lack of communication. I told a few of the girls I had met at orientation that were in our group and they were excited for me.

I got to the bus station to go to Bangkok when I saw Jack posted on Facebook that he was flying to the Philippines. I was crushed! I wanted to go back to my room and cry. It had been so long since I had seen him. I had completely turned my life upside down for this guy who I was in love with. He told me that he was going to come see me this weekend, but didn't even bother to tell me he wasn't going to see me after all. But he sure told everyone on Facebook!

Most of the group was heading up to Kanchanaburi, Thailand. One of the guys I called little brother, saw me starting to cry. He came out and gave me a hug and told me I should come with them. I changed my plans and went to Kanchanaburi instead, refusing to let anyone ruin my weekend in this amazing country. We all met up for dinner at a lovely restaurant and two of our interns joined the band to share their remarkable skills. After playing, one of them mentioned that he would have never done something like this at home. And it struck me that this is one of the many things that is significantly remarkable about Thailand. This place had a magic about it, making it nearly impossible to be sad or not smile. Traveling in general gives you the courage to try new things you have never done before. Mainly because you will likely never see these people again. The walk home, or I should say stumble, was comical, to say the least. If you've ever seen L'auberge Espagnole, it reminded me of the scene of them stumbling home after their night out drinking. If you haven't seen it, I highly recommend it.

The next day we all took the bus to Erawan falls. I made the mistake of not bringing shoes and only had sandals. I banged up my poor feet on the hike and ended up taking them off halfway up. The crystal blue water was refreshing after the long hike up the trail of seven waterfalls. There were friends snapping photos, adventurous individuals using the slippery moss-covered rocks as a slide, a variety of fish sucking on our feet, and monkeys hiding in the trees. After the long walk down, I treated myself to some chicken skewers and pineapple at one of the numerous food shops scattered about.

Chapter 34

Needing to extend my visa, I combined it with a trip to Siem Reap, Cambodia. After getting through Customs, I hailed a taxi to my hostel. Growing up I had seen Tomb Raider and envisioned myself as Lara Croft traversing through the stone walls of Tah Prohm (Tomb Raider Temple). The temple Was in Angkor Wat, one of the many places on my bucket list. My first morning there, I met up with a friend of mine, Ross, for the sunrise at Angkor Wat. We sat in the dark, surrounded by other world travelers waiting for the sun to make its appearance. The sky slowly started to change colors. The moment it peeked over the temple; it was a magical view.

As Ross and I were headed out, I looked over at him with a huge smile and said "I think the only thing that could make this experience more magical is if there was a monkey climbing the temple walls." It had always been one of my dreams to see monkeys in the wild, up close and personal, in ancient temple ruins. Shortly after sunrise, I spotted a blur of gray fur and to my delight, it was indeed the monkey that made this experience an unforgettable moment.

Ross and I left to go check out Tomb Raider Temple before it became too crowded with the tourists. It was more cleaned up than I would have preferred, I love the overgrown look. There were giant silk trees growing inside and around the structures and had been holding up these architectural wonders. Without the silk roots, these precious gems of history would have crumbled to pieces. The carvings in the temple walls depicted the history of Cambodia and I wished I had brought a pencil and paper to capture some rubbings of these amazing carvings.

The next day we booked 'A Day in the Village' with a tour guide named Sambo. This was one of the most memorable days of my life and one I will treasure forever. Sambo picked us up from our hostel and drove us to his remote village outside Siem Reap, where he showed us how he lived. Sambo's parents had given him up as a child, and his aunt had raised him. While showing us around the little farm, he talked passionately about his desire to open a home to help teach kids for free. He also wanted to show foreigners what it was like to live in Cambodia.

We spent the day eating a home cooked lunch of fresh fish, papaya, rice and an incredible sauce for the fish that was wrapped in banana leaves and steamed. I sat in their kitchen hut watching his aunt prepare the lunch while a three-year-old child sat in my lap and was fascinated with my tattoos. After touring the farm, Sambo took us out in the middle of a rice field. We were sipping on plum wine and had some weed to smoke that Sambo had brought. I looked at Ross and we had no words, just a smile of pure contentment. I fell in love with the children in the village and wanted to take all of them home with me. These amazing boys, all under the age of ten, killed us birds with their slingshots to eat for dinner, helped catch the fish, and we're learning how to make the sauce for the fish. As they were working on the sauce, I started picking the wild green beans that were growing everywhere. We sat on a blanket and shared one of the best meals I have ever had. This was the perfect way to end one of the best weekends ever.

When we arrived back to Bangkok, it was 22:30 and the public transportation we typically used, was closed. We grabbed a taxi and gave the driver the location of where we needed to go. We were supposed to teach that morning and we needed to get back to our schools. The taxi driver started driving in the wrong direction and forty-five minutes later we figured it out. We finally arrived at Ross' school and dropped him off. The driver went to take me home. We were driving around in a circle for almost half an hour and it was clear that the man was lost.

He finally stopped and asked for directions at this little restaurant that was just closing. He got back in the car and kept on driving around, still lost. I tried to tell him to stop because he didn't know where he was going and he started yelling at me. I didn't feel comfortable driving around with this man lost in the middle of nowhere at 02:00. He finally stopped. I gave him enough money for the ride, got out and started walking down the dark and empty street. Moments later, a Thai man came up on his little motorbike and asked me if I needed a taxi. He spoke a little English and I told him I needed to go to Sena, where my school was. He told me to meet him at the police station a block away. I walked to the station, which was closed, and he told me, "I own restaurant. I take you there, my friend Police. We take you home to school."

283

I got on the back of his motorbike and he drove me back to where the driver stopped to get directions. This kind man invited me to sit down and brought out food and Leo Beers to share. A man showed up dressed in jeans and a T-shirt, and he told me that he was a police officer. He handed me the phone and asked me to tell the woman on the phone what had happened with the taxi driver. They take any negative incident with a taxi driver very seriously and I recalled that the taxi driver had also been rude to the man that had come to rescue me. I now understood why my rescuer had taken photos of the license plate on the taxi. These kind men drove me the hour it took to get me back to the school. They gave me a Buddha medallion that was meant to protect me from harm and all they asked for in return for the generosity, was photos with me and to add them on Facebook.

While I was volunteering, I started applying to numerous teaching jobs in Thailand. I applied for one that I wasn't qualified for, but I was offered an interview. The interview was supposed to take place the following Friday and I was in Bangkok when the director asked me if I could make it that Monday instead. I said, of course, and I contacted my school and let them know that I needed to take that Monday off. They didn't mind at all and were happy that I wanted to stay in Thailand. I didn't have any business appropriate clothing with me that I typically wear for interviews and my hair was still in colorful braids.

It was a job for a kindergarten position at a bilingual school and the pay was great, almost equivalent to what I was paid in my teaching job in America. I took a bus to Rayong and a taxi to the town of Ban

Chang. The morning of my interview, I took a motorbike taxi to the school. The driver was a mother who had her three-year-old daughter in the front of her motorbike. This was actually quite common in Thailand and in numerous other countries that I had visited.

A petite woman in her late 60s named teacher Mary came out to greet me and show me to the kindergarten classroom where I was to give my teaching demonstration. After the demonstration, she told me that I had done an incredible job and took me over to another building to have my formal interview. They were in the middle of construction and building a new kindergarten building. I met the director of the school and the assistant director. The assistant director, a man from South Africa didn't bother getting up or introducing himself. He was extremely rude and spoke down to the women in the office. I disliked him immediately. He was dressed in PT gear while the director was in a collared shirt and tie. I wore a shin length, flowy dress with a sweater and my hair wrapped up in a scarf. After the interview, I was asked to wait outside and 20 minutes later, teacher Mary came out to talk to me. She asked me to take a walk with her and I knew something was wrong. She told me that I was an incredible teacher and after seeing my resume, she pushed them to get me an interview. The issues the men were having were in regards to my appearance. They were concerned that I didn't fit in and she asked me why I had a scarf on my head. I told her that the only reason I didn't dress in a more professional manner and had a scarf in my hair was because this was a last-minute request and I didn't have time to go back home and get my interview clothes. I had even gone to the mall to try and find some appropriate clothing, but I couldn't find anything that would fit me. Being five foot nine and curvy in Asia does not go well for shopping. The shoes fit great though.

I told her that I had gotten braids and couldn't take them out in time for the interview. After that, she went back into the office and spoke with the men. When she called me back in, they offered me the position and I gladly accepted. The position didn't start for a few more months. So, I decided to go back to the U.S. and visit Maria and hopefully Anthony. Maria graciously offered to let me stay with her and I enjoyed spending time with her and her daughter. Her daughter was absolutely fascinated with all of my monkey photos and the pictures of elephants.

Chapter 35

After arriving in Bangkok, I took a taxi to Ban Chang, Thailand. I found a hotel and after breakfast I went to start my apartment search. I couldn't find anything online and it was my first time trying to find a place to live in another country. I took a motorbike taxi to school and started walking around near the school looking for apartment buildings. I had found the one that teacher Mary had told me about, which was going to cost around 90 dollars a month. It was much too small and had no kitchen, which I really needed. I had messaged my Thai officer friend I had met while volunteering at the school in Sena. I had only messaged him to say hello and that I had come back to Thailand. While I was walking around, sweating my butt off in the hot and humid weather, he sent me a Facebook message asking me what I was doing. When I told him I was trying to find an apartment, he told me to stay where I was and he came and picked me up in his car.

I tried to tell him that this was too much to ask, but he wouldn't hear of it. This kind man took me to around 25 different apartments. There was one that was my dream apartment. It had four stories, an incredible view from the master suite right on the ocean and a massive patio where you could entertain 45 people with room to spare. It was the most expensive in that area for three hundred and fifty dollars a month. I love the cost of living in Thailand. I wanted it so bad, but it was unfurnished and I knew that I would get lonely living there by myself.

I settled on another apartment with an equally spectacular ocean front view. My new apartment was a two-bedroom, two-bathroom furnished apartment with a full kitchen for two hundred and eighty dollars a month. The apartment also had a lap pool, which I put to use every morning before school. I gave them the first month's rent deposit and was going to move in the next morning. My officer friend dropped me back off at my hotel and I took a walk to find the veterans pub I had seen earlier.

As I was walking down the street looking at my GPS, I stopped for a moment to avoid getting hit by cars, motorbikes and pedestrians that were going in all directions, including the sidewalks. As I was looking down, I saw this massive gray trunk that proceeded to start to smell me. I looked up to see an elephant towering over me with his mahout, an elephant trainer. Before that moment, I had only seen elephants in the zoo and had no idea what it was like to get smelled up by an elephant. I couldn't stop smiling as I walked away. Even though I loved my life, there was still this huge hole in my heart and a feeling of emptiness that I knew could only be filled by Anthony.

The first day of school started and I arrived in my new teaching clothes that I had bought back in the States. My tattoos were all covered up and I was very excited to get to know the other teachers and hoped to make some new friends. I met the other kindergarten English teachers and the art and music teachers. The second day of our teacher orientation, Jesse, the art teacher, told me that one of the primary age English teachers was going around talking shit about me and showing people my Instagram photos, "saying, why is some slut like this teaching at her school?" I was going to wait for an opportune moment to confront her.

The kindergarten staff were moving into our new building that had finally been finished. There were no elevators, no dollies, and the teachers had to move everything by themselves. The teachers were no help at all, as most of them were around 95 pounds and couldn't pick up anything heavier than about 15 pounds. All the heavy lifting fell upon myself and the other male English teacher. We had to move around eighteen classrooms full of cubby shelves, desks, tables, chairs, toys and other heavy objects, up and down four stories, across the yard to the new building, and again carry them up to whatever floor they were on.

I ruined one of my new teaching shirts and was told that the next day we could wear casual clothes because we were going to be moving the next day as well. The next day I was carrying these massive bookshelves by myself and was getting an intense workout in. I had worn a baggy t-shirt that covered my butt and black workout capris. The other teachers were wearing low cut tops, spaghetti strap tank tops, and short shorts. The Thai teachers were sporting Playboy bunny pants and tops as well as booty shorts. I was the most covered teacher, but all the English teachers were already talking about my tattoos. Teacher Mary said the asshole assistant director wanted me to cover them up. I told them that would be no problem, but they would need to find someone else to do the manual labor. It was too hot to be fully clothed while moving everything, and I was pissed because uncovered shoulders and short shorts were as equally culturally unaccepted as tattoos.

The assistant principal hadn't liked me from the beginning, and he spoke to me with great disrespect, even though I had never given him a reason. Teacher Mary couldn't stand him either. She told me that he was going through an ugly divorce and had always been a chauvinist pig. The Friday before the first week of school, they had a meeting with the founder of the school, the principal assistant principal and teacher Mary, to discuss my tattoos. Teacher Mary told me what was going on and I felt like everyone hated me at the school.

That Monday I showed up to work in a long-sleeved collared shirt and a pencil skirt, which was what most of the other teachers wore. This was the most idiotic teaching attire! I was so sick of ignorant gender clothing guidelines that made no sense! It reminded me of the only female Medal of Honor Recipient, Dr. Mary Walker. She was a surgeon that worked on the battlefield during the Civil War and was arrested for impersonating a male. Due to the health risks to her patients and the impractical design of the female uniform, instead of petticoats, Dr. Walker had designed a bloomer style uniform that made her job safer and more productive. She was arrested for violating dress codes. I was sick and tired of ignorant, archaic, and gender-based norms that made no sense.

There female teacher dress codes were impractical! How would I sit cross-legged during circle time or run and jump during music and movement? They were more concerned about looks than they were about the children getting a good education. Teacher Mary explained to me that most of the men working at the school, including the assistant principal, did not like alpha females. They preferred subservient and submissive, quiet women, which teacher Mary and I were not.

After the first week of school, the principal arranged to have a staff party one Friday after school was out. During the party we were outside with no AC and I was sweating everywhere. I had to go ask permission to take off the sweater I had on and received numerous dirty looks from the assistant principal and some of the other stuck up foreign teachers. To make things even more awkward, one of the teachers from America had been drinking, and in front of numerous other teachers, including the founder of the school, told me how attracted she was to me. She told me that I had a perfect body and she wouldn't change anything about me. I would have taken this as a compliment, even though I didn't swing that way, and had a few laughs under any other circumstances. But this was in front of teachers that already didn't care for me. This just gave them more fuel to talk crap about me.

The next Monday, a few of the teachers went to get food at a local café down the street from the school. When we walked in, I saw the teacher that had been talking crap about my Instagram and modeling photos sitting and eating with her daughter. I walked up to her and in front of everyone I said, "I hear you like my modeling photos. You know, I'm also a personal trainer and if you're unhappy with your figure or want to work out, I would be more than happy to help you. Nothing better than feeling good and confident about your body." She was morbidly obese and from what one of the teachers told me, she was mostly focused on my workout and bikini modeling photo shoots. She had this shocked look on her face and said, "Oh yeah, teacher Jen showed me your photos." I rolled my eyes and went and ordered food. Everyone in the room had become silent after I said what I needed to say. Before I started teaching, I had changed my name on Facebook and Instagram to avoid any issues with my teaching career. Unfortunately, my photos with my name were in Inked magazine and she must have been stalking me on social media.

I was looking forward to one of the school breaks because Ben had told me he was coming out to visit me. A few days before he was supposed to arrive, he told me that he could no longer come. I was so disappointed. I really needed to see a friendly face. Trying to stay occupied and busy, I booked a last-minute photo shoot in Bangkok where I met a Russian model named Ivanka. During dinner, Ivanka and I started talking about going to Koh Phi Phi Island. She already had tickets to go see Cirque de Soleil in Bangkok on Wednesday so we were going to wait to fly out Thursday.

In the hotel room, we were looking over flights and hotel rooms to Koh Phi Phi. I found a flight for around thirty dollars and I purchased two tickets. When I got back to Ban Chang on Monday morning, Ivanka messaged me and told me that she couldn't go. I was pissed. Not only was Ben unable to come, now I had paid for two tickets and the flight wasn't even leaving till Thursday. I wasn't going to sit in my apartment and wait three days when I could be spending it on one of the most beautiful islands in the world.

I made a last-minute flight change to get an earlier flight, through some bathing suits and essentials into my travel bag, and took a motorbike cab to the bus stop. I was in Ban Chang, and I needed to get to Bangkok for my flight that was leaving in three hours. The trip to Bangkok typically takes around two and a half hours, so I was cutting it very close. Being able to be spontaneous is something I love about my life.

Chapter 36

When I landed in Krabi, I took a bus to Ao Nang for 90 baht (around $3USD) and we got off in an area where I saw numerous hotels and food places. Due to the last-minute change of plans I was not prepared and found out that I had missed the last ferry to Koh Phi Phi and needed to find a place to stay that night. After wandering around and only finding numerous unavailable, overpriced rooms due to the touristy area, I ended up finding a reasonable priced single room with AC for three hundred baht (around $9USD). The room was located above a massage parlor and had a separate entrance in the back alley

After purchasing a ferry ticket from one of the numerous travel agent booths down the street, I went to bed dreaming of this incredible island I had seen in many different movies. It was one of the most beautiful places I had ever seen on TV and in pictures. In the morning, when I woke up to check out and leave to the ferry, to my dismay, the front of the massage parlor was closed, holding my favorite and only pair of footwear hostage. I had to walk barefoot to the 7-Eleven across the street and purchase a pair of bright blue monkey socks, because there were no sandals. I received many laughs and stares from other tourists as I arrived at the ferry and boarded wearing these crazy monkey socks.

I took a seat near the window to enjoy this beautiful one-and- a-half-hour trip. After seeing the numerous tourists struggling with their massive rolling suitcases, I was relieved I traveled light and didn't have to wait to get my luggage when I arrived. While on the ferry, I did some research on activities to do and I found Bob's booze cruise. Not wanting to waste a moment of this beautiful island, I booked a seat that day and quickly went to find my hostel to change over into my bikini. But before I did that, I needed to find a new pair of sandals. Yes, I was still rocking the monkey socks.

After finding my hostel, the Marine house, I changed into my bathing suit and headed out to meet up with the others that were going on the booze cruise as well. There were mostly couples and friends and I felt a bit like a third wheel, but I still had an incredible time exploring these magnificent islands. First stop we made was Monkey Beach, where we got to take photos and feed the monkeys. This was not my first encounter with monkeys in Thailand and I already knew about their sneaky ways. I held onto my sunglasses so they wouldn't get snatched. Some of the other tourists weren't aware of this and lost sunglasses and other lose items the monkeys wanted. The entire cruise itself took around six hours and it was filled with snorkeling, swimming, drinking, exploring numerous islands and taking hundreds of photos. Maya Bay from Leonardo DiCaprio's movie *The Beach*, lived up to everything I imagined and more! Some of these places I had seen in movies or in photographs and I had always thought there was no way that they were that beautiful. I figured it had to have been Photo-shopped. There is no way the water is that blue or that clear. After seeing some of these places in person, I now look at those photos much differently. This place was far more beautiful than any photograph or movie I had ever seen.

A couple from South Africa got engaged in this incredible bay, bringing more magic to this once in a lifetime experience. The next morning, I found a cafe serving breakfast and enjoyed my cup of coffee while taking in all of the beauty and magic of this island. I spent the day exploring, had a lovely lunch, did some shopping, and met up with some of the cruise tourists for dinner. On my way back to the hostel after dinner, I came across a group of Thai men sitting outside their dive shop, celebrating a birthday. Among this group of men, I locked eyes with Jason Momoa's twin, and it was lust at first sight. I was a little obsessed with Kahl Drogo in Game of Thrones and this man could have been his stunt double.

I spent the evening drinking Sang Som whiskey, barely understanding any of their conversations, dancing with a 90-year-old Thai man who had some incredible moves, and a fantasy make out session with my celebrity look alike. Around 06:00, I made my way back to my hostel and slept until lunch. After finding some chicken skewers with pineapple and some fresh coconut milk off the street for 50 baht, I enjoyed my lunch sitting on the dock with my feet in the crystal blue water. I took a hike up to lookout point and found some history about the honorific tsunami that had devastated the island in 2004.

For my last night on the island, I decided to treat myself and upgrade my hostel. I went in search of a nice hotel with a great view. After an hour or so, I came across a restaurant that rented rooms for a shocking price of 500 baht. I wish I could inform the readers of the name of the place, but unfortunately it was written in Thai and I couldn't find it online. Traveling tip: There are so many places similar to the one I found that rent rooms. They have no marketing, so you're unable to find them online. Sometimes you have to get outside of your booking online bubble and go exploring.

After another long hike, I was famished and met up with Kahl Drogo and some of his friends for dinner at his friend's restaurant. Numerous whiskeys and sodas later, I found myself making out with my crush again. This man was built like a Samoan God! After a well-rested night sleep in my beautiful hotel room overlooking the bay, I woke up early to enjoy my last breakfast on the island before heading to the pier to catch the ferry back to Krabi. I am truly thankful that my friends bailed on me last minute and I had to change my flight. Sometimes the most incredible experiences will only happen when you are lost and you stop depending on your smart phone for everything.

When I returned to work, teacher Mary and I had begun planning and preparing for an incredible Mother's Day event. The typical Mother's Day events in the past were boring. They would invite the mothers to the school to make hand-print trees and call it a day. Teacher Mary came up with an Alice in Wonderland Queen of hearts day including a fashion show. The moms made mad hatter hats with their children and showed them off during the show. We put in a lot of effort into this event and when the day came, it was well worth the effort. I had dressed up as the queen of Hearts and all the Thai teachers and parents loved my costume and asked to take pictures with me. I had taken a photo with one of the Thai teachers who posted it on her Facebook page and tagged me in it. In the photo, there were high school students dressed up as the Queen's playing cards.

The week after the event, I received an email from the director telling me that he wanted to see me in his office. He had never sent me an email and I knew something was not good. I emailed him back and asked what it was in regards to so I could come prepared and bring anything if I needed to. Teacher Mary was gone in Hong Kong visiting her daughter so I couldn't ask her advice. The director emailed me back and told me it wasn't good news and it was in regards to my photos on Facebook.

I went to the principal's office and he turned around his computer screen for me to see. It was a photograph from one of my photo shoots. In the photo, I had on bikini bottoms that covered up my full bottom. Instead of a bikini top, which would have showed more skin, I had a scarf around my neck, fully covering my entire front side. Only my back was showing. The photograph was for Inked magazine and we were trying to capture the beautiful tattoos on my back. He then showed me a photograph that the teacher had tagged me. I don't quite know how she found me on Facebook. She must have Googled my name and found my alias on Facebook. He told me that I had a naked photo right next to the photo of a student, which, according to him, broke the school policy of derogatory behavior, bringing a bad name to the school. He told me that if I didn't take the photo down and resign, they would sue me. He took away my school access badge and had me escorted off the property. He said they would send me my belongings and I was restricted from school grounds.

I was tempted to tell him about what had happened one evening when I was at the VFW pub I was a member at. The assistant principal was there drunk and was hitting on me. I politely turned him down and he got very angry. Because I was a member of the VFW and the assistant principal was a well-known member in the community, they told him to leave. After that evening I rejected him was when all the trouble started. I was getting extra morning duties, dirty looks and all the meetings regarding my tattoos I believe were a direct result of me hurting his feelings by turning him down. He was doing everything he could to get rid of me. Because of my past experiences with men always having each other's backs and not knowing the employment laws in Thailand, I didn't have enough support to fight this wrongful termination. I was devastated and heartbroken! I loved my students and they wouldn't even let me say goodbye.

I ended up moving to Pattaya to get away from the small town and running into teachers and parents that I wanted to avoid. Pattaya was not a place I enjoyed, and I knew I needed to find a good place that would have a positive influence. I met a photographer in Bangkok on one of the modeling groups on Facebook. We booked a fitness shoot and I went up to Bangkok to discuss a possible fitness business opportunity. His name was Jay and we hit it off right away.

I was told by the school that I needed to leave the country within two weeks of getting fired due to visa issues. I booked a flight to Kuala Lumpur, Malaysia. Being a single woman traveling in Muslim countries was not enjoyable. I was surprised that they had separate train cars for women. Although the Petronas Towers were cool and the Batu Caves were amazing, I was ready to get out of there.

When I returned from Malaysia, I was working out one afternoon and blacked out while doing some squats from the endometriosis pain. I came to and saw one of the gym attendees hovering over me, asking me if I was OK. I told them I slipped and I was all right. I had to sit for an hour, pretending to stretch, before I was able to get up and slowly walk back to my apartment. It took me half an hour to get up the four flights of stairs to my room and I almost blacked out from the pain. The next few days. I couldn't get out of bed and I decided after bawling my eyes out, that I needed to have a hysterectomy. This was one of the most difficult decisions I ever made, but I knew that I couldn't continue living like this. I would have one week a month where I could work out with only pain from my knee. For around ten days a month, I struggled just to get out of the bed. I had been holding on so long because I wanted my own child, but this was no way to live. I was devastated but determined to end this pain that I had been battling for ten years. Jay graciously offered to allow me to store my belongings with him and I packed a carry on of workout clothes, leaving everything else I owned with him.

Chapter 37

As soon as I got back into San Diego, I made a doctor's appointment and I started trying to figure out what to do about my school situation. I had learned a great deal about myself when I was in Thailand and I decided to start giving people in my life one last chance to see if there were any hopes in saving a relationship. I even called my mother to see if there was any possible way that I could be back in Marie's life. I could give a shit about them, but I missed Marie every single day! My mother said I didn't explain enough to her about what the monster had done to me and she asked me to give her more details. When she didn't understand what giving head or going down on somebody meant, I had to describe it in detail. I had become so numb to this, I didn't even cry.

She told me that they still loved me and that she would have a family meeting to talk about what I had told her. She then told me that Aunt Sally had told her that I was having an affair with a married man. My only family member that I thought I had left, betrayed me and had disappeared from my life. The only reason I told my Aunt Sally about the affair was because she was the black sheep of the family. She was covered in tattoos and had been a stripper, but I had never judged her. She also hated my family, especially her brother (my father). Or so that's what she said. The only reason she would have told my parents is to have shifted their disgust for her lifestyle to me. I had gone to see her and my grandmother the weekend that I found out that I was getting forced out of the Marine Corps. I was devastated and needed somebody to talk to. I thought she was that person. I was so wrong!

At first, I told my mother I had no idea what she was talking about. After the words came out of my mouth, I stopped and said, "No, I lied. That is true. I am having an affair with a married man and I'm still in love with him. Now, if I can tell you the truth about that, why wouldn't I tell you the truth about this? What have I had to gain out of any of this?" The last words I would ever speak to my mother left her believing that I was a whore. However, I couldn't deny Anthony. I wouldn't deny my soul mate.

My oldest brother Jacob called me after my mother called and asked him to. I spoke with him for a few minutes and he asked me to tell him what had happened. After I did, this motherfucker told me that he couldn't take sides and that everything that was happening to me was self-inflicted. He told me that he was an alcoholic and used to drink mouthwash when he couldn't get his hands on any alcohol. He almost got kicked out of the military and ruined his marriage so he was sent to rehab. While in rehab, his counselors told him that most of the issues he was having were self-inflicted from alcohol. I flipped out and asked, "So you're telling me that I wanted Cain to rape me and my health issues all happened because of choices I made? That two of my best friends died because of choices I made?" He told me he wasn't going to argue with me and hung up.

When I had spoken with my mother on the phone, she had told me how much I meant to them and how important finding a solution was. A month went by! Thinking my mother was calling, I picked up the phone when I saw their home phone on my cell. When my father's voice was on the other line, I was tempted to hang up. It had been around eight years since we had spoken and the last words he told me in person, were he wished I had never been born. I thought those words were painful. He informed me that he loved me but in order for me to be part of the family, I would need to forgive my brother and accept what had happened and get over it. Accept what happened and get over it!!! My own father, the man that was supposed to protect and love me, was telling me that I needed to accept my brother raping me and be OK with it. At that moment, I knew he never loved me. He loved who he wanted me to be. He told me to take my time in deciding and didn't need to make any hasty decisions. I responded "No, I don't need any time. I forgive you. I don't hate you, but I do not want you in my life. Never contact me again. I have no father." I hung up before he could respond.

After an emotional doctor's appointment, I was a mess with everything and desperately needed Anthony. Things had been strained between us and I was scared to death he wouldn't pick up. I gave in and called. When he answered, I started sobbing. After I told him what was going on and about the hysterectomy, he came over and saw me the next day at Maria's while she was still at school. What we have together is something that no one in the world could change. We had gone through so much and still found a way to overcome it all. He was the only family I had left.

I started doing some research on Women's experiences with hysterectomies. The majority were horror stories and I couldn't imagine how much it would change my life for the worse. According to what I read; I would likely have to stop working out because I would lose so much bone density. I would have crazy hormonal issues and be required to take numerous medications for the rest of my life. There was also a chance I would develop seizures and was 50 percent more likely to develop heart problems. I called my doctor back and he decided to give me one more laparoscopic surgery.

The surgery was set for the day before Thanksgiving. Maria had volunteered to take me and drop me off at 06:00 for my fifth surgery. When I woke up in the recovery room, I had a bad reaction to the anesthesia. Probably because I'm a redhead and we require around four times the amount of anesthesia and other pain meds than others. This is why surgeons don't like operating on redheads. Every time I vomited, I felt like someone was stabbing me in the uterus. After an hour of vomiting, I messaged Maria to let her know I was ready. Before they operate, you are required to have someone sign a form saying they would pick you up. This was to make sure the patient got home safely. Maria had signed the forms, but when I called to tell her that I was ready, she said she couldn't because she forgot she had court with her baby daddy. I called Smith who was now back in California, and he couldn't come either. I thought having no one to pick me up from the parade deck coming back from deployment was a terrible feeling. Try feeling like you're going to die in the recovery room and not one person in your life cared enough to be with you during surgery.

The nurses kept coming in asking if my friend was there yet. I could tell they needed the bed. I started crying and went to order an Uber. Thankfully a Marine that I had served with and started to become better friends with, offered to come pick me up. He saved my butt that day. I had only known him for a few months before I got out, but we had become better friends over Facebook. He was such a good person. One of my Marine Corps friends had told me before I joined that I would meet the best people and the worst people in the Marine Corps. He was so right and so he was one of the few good ones.

After he dropped me off at María's, I slept for almost 36 hours and only got up to use the bathroom and take painkillers. I couldn't stand for long and had no one to cook or bring me anything, so I was famished. I spent Thanksgiving alone. Maria was off with her family for the night. Maria came home after doing black Friday Shopping. The next night I was still lying in bed recovering when I heard a knock at the door. It was Smith and his brother carrying Maria's favorite beer. At first, I thought he had come to see me and cheer me up, but he had only come to hang out with Maria. I was lying in bed with the door open and not once did he come to say hello.

Around a week or so later, Maria got a call from a bar asking to come pick up Smith who was extremely drunk and they needed him to leave. When Maria and I got there to drive him and his car home, he refused to leave and called me a bitch when I told him to not drive drunk again as he already had several DUIs. We left him there and, on my way, back home, he decided to text me and tell me what he thought of me. He sent me around twenty five text messages saying

"Maria told me she doesn't want you living there; You're a mooch; You use all your friends, you are useless; You bring nothing to our friendship; Mooching bitch; You're pathetic; Anthony uses you just for sex; Jack treated you like shit, but you are so pathetic you keep taking him back." I responded, "damn, tell me what you really think." He kept going, "Bitch, you're supposed to be so smart and yet you are so stupid; You're stupid; No one likes you; Your health shit is karma for what you do to Maria." He brought up Anthony again and kept trying to hurt me nut I turned my phone off and went to sleep crying.

The reason Smith's words hurt so much was because he knew how much I hated asking for help. When I stayed with him, I said thank you every day! I would go buy him dinner or see if he needed anything at the store. I did my best to make it as if I wasn't there. It was the same thing with Maria. I hated asking her for help and I went out of my way to help her. I gave her three hundred dollars a month to help with rent and I also helped pay for the groceries. Not only was I helping with money and groceries, I would babysit her kids, cook them at least two meals a day and cleaned her place every few days. Maria had been unfairly forced out of the Marine Corps. The person she used to be was replaced by someone I didn't recognize. After seeing the type of mother she was, and her not wanting me there, I left. I was homeless, had no car, still recovering from surgery, and felt hopeless.

Chapter 38

I stayed for a week in a bed bug infested hotel and spent most of my time applying for jobs and working out. I didn't have a car and I needed to get one in order to go on interviews. My VA disability was enough to get a car but not enough for an apartment. I chose a car with four doors so I could drive for Uber, which ended up being a horrible and traumatic experience so it didn't last long. Since the previous experiences with roommates I had and the situation I had just been in, I couldn't bring myself to look for someone that needed a roommate. On the weekends because hotels were more expensive, I slept in my car in Walmart parking lots, showered at the gym, and went to the library. On the week days I would put cheap hotels on my credit card.

One evening I came back from the gym to find SWAT breaking down the door that was only several rooms down from me. Most places I stayed at were too cheap to purchase fitted sheets and I would be so grossed out when I would wake up and be sleeping on the bare mattress because the non-fitted sheet they used weren't working. I went out and purchased my own cheap fitted sheets and would have to take them off myself every day when the maids came to clean.

I spent my Christmas and New Year's alone in a dingy hotel room. I wanted so badly to spend it with Anthony, but that wasn't an option. He felt so bad that he couldn't put me up until I found a job. It was one of the most humiliating experiences ever. I did all the "right" things! Even while working full time in the Marines I went to school full-time and continued when I got out. I never got in trouble with the law, was kind to people, worked harder than most, and earned a Master's Degree. All the hundreds of jobs I applied to that I actually heard back from told me I was over qualified or that I didn't have enough experience. The starting positions said I was over qualified because of my education and the jobs I was qualified for due to my education, I wasn't qualified because I didn't have the experience. It's like making just enough money to barely survive but too much to get any kind of assistance.

I was rapidly running out of money and couldn't make enough to keep paying for hotel rooms, but I had saved up enough to be able to pay rent for a few months. However, I didn't have enough income to sign a lease by myself. Anthony told me that he would help me get an apartment by signing the lease with me. He risked his career, his family, and his finances to help me. We were closer than we had ever been before. Our friendship and love for each other lasted through a war, both of us unintentionally hurting each other deeply, two years of not speaking, long distance, and so much more. Never once have we ever cussed at each other, yelled, or said intentionally hurtful things to each other. It is unbelievably hard to be in love with your best friend and not be able to have the relationship you want. However, very few people in this world have ever experienced the love and history that we share. It is an unconditional love that will last until we both leave this earth.

I finally found a job as a fraud investigator. I did so well I ended up getting two $2 raises in less than three months. I was busting my ass, working around 65 hours a week and only getting paid for 35 of it. This was because I was getting assigned cases I had no training in and I wouldn't get paid for the hours it was taking me to figure out how to do my job. I was grateful to have a roof over my head but every cent went to rent. I didn't have any kind of social life, and I knew this was not the life I deserved. I refused to settle and kept hoping and believing in a better life. One I had earned but not yet received.

Anthony and I still talked, but his wife had found out about the apartment and World War III broke out at their house so we hadn't talked for a few weeks. I had come back to the US for surgery and I stayed mostly because I wasn't complete without Anthony in my life. Being around him, even if it was only once a month, still made me feel more complete and happier than without. However, I did miss my adventures in Thailand, the cost of living there, and traveling helped me not feel so alone.

Since I had come back to San Diego, I had lost two of my closest friends, was homeless for five months, racked up a $10,000 credit card bill due to hotel rooms, and had to start over again and furnish an empty apartment. I failed at repairing relationships, was denied around 1,000 jobs, and hated my current job. My endometriosis grew back and was more painful than ever forcing me to take off days of work and I was barely making rent. My lifelong dream to have my own child pushed me to explore the cost of having one on my own. Thailand was known for quality fertility centers that were in my price budget. I resigned the next day. Since Marie was born, I had desperately wanted to have a child. I 100% support adoption and foster care but being a single woman who didn't own a home made that possibility extremely unlikely. With those situations there is also a risk that the child could be taken. I had already experienced that loss once and I don't think I could survive another. The two things I wanted, needed to feel whole, were Anthony and Marie. I felt incomplete without them and the thought of being a mom to my own child, was the only thing giving me any kind of hope.

I messaged Jay that I would be moving back to Bangkok and he was excited to see me. My disability had been bumped up and I was able to live off that due to the low cost of living in Bangkok. I couldn't afford to live in San Diego and I was unable to find a job I could survive off of due to my inability to work full time because of the endometriosis.

Once again, I put my furniture up for sale and a week before I was to leave all I had in my apartment was what I was taking with me and an air mattress. It was a miserable week and I was terrified that I was making the wrong decision. I didn't know what I was going to do without Anthony. We had become so close and I knew I was going to miss him terribly. I didn't get my visa back until the day before I was to fly out due to some idiots at this visa company I used. Anthony had promised me that he would come see me before I left but he was so busy with work and was going to have a very difficult time getting away.

My last night in San Diego, I hadn't heard back from Anthony and I started drinking to help numb my pain and drown out the nightmares. I passed out and woke up around dinner time when Anthony called me. He was still at work and asked me if I could make it up to Pendleton because he was going to have to be at work at 07:00 the next morning. There was no way I would be able to because I still had to pack up the rest of my things and drop my car off at the storage unit. He told me he would call me back and I went back to sleep devastated because I didn't think he wasn't going to be able to come.

Around an hour later I heard my front door open and in walked Anthony. He will never understand how much that meant to me! I had no idea when I would see him again and to be able to wake up in his arms meant more to me than all the money in the world. If I died tomorrow, I would be the luckiest person alive. I found a love that people only dream about and one that has only grown stronger throughout the years. As always, the sex was incredible, passionate, and lasted all night. Thankfully I had so much to do before my flight that I didn't have time to feel the impact of leaving Anthony. I didn't want to let him go when he said goodbye and drove away. It was an incredible evening with my best friend and the love of my life. I refused to ruin it with my tears and I finished packing and drove to drop off my car in storage.

As I boarded the plane to Thailand, I had one thing holding me back - Anthony. Because of all of the shit I have been through, it is nearly impossible for me to be normal. It is a daily struggle to keep the thoughts of my past from creeping in and taking over. It's funny, some guy I was dating asked me one time what I was thinking about and I had no idea how to reply. Yes, Anthony was on my mind, but so were 5,938 other things. My brain doesn't stop and sometimes it becomes so overwhelming I feel like I am going to drown. The only things that helped quiet these thoughts were Anthony, Marie, and drinking. When I'm with him the relentless turning of my brain stops. It reminds me of school where I learned different types of interrogation techniques and that non-stop music or sounds can drive someone insane. When the sound stops, there is an overwhelming sense of peace. When I am with him, there's finally quiet. The torture of my memories stops. He makes me feel that everything will be okay and nothing could hurt me. Not only do I want to be a better person for him, I am the best version of myself with him. Anthony has this incredible ability to make you feel like the most beautiful person in the world. It's changed over the years, partially because of everything we have gone through, but he still makes me feel wanted. He looks at me in this way where I could see how much he cared about and desired me.

I have been in love with other men and I would have happily married Jack and ran off to an island together. I will always love Charles and we are still very good friends. Anthony is on a different level. What we have is beyond anything I knew existed. He's my family, best friend, battle buddy, soul mate, and I am alive today because of him. We talk for hours about everything from psychopathology and twisted things to different opinions on raising kids. He is one of the smartest people I know and a father I would have wished my children to have.

So many people have told me I was weak, a horrible person, or a homewrecker to have an affair with a married man. I have had close friends tell me what I was doing was wrong and that he was just using me. I firmly believe that cheating is wrong! I believe that if you are going to sleep with other people that the other person you are with should be aware of it and if they are not okay with it, then they need to move on. If anyone thinks that I wanted to fall in love with a married man, you're fucking high. I was in love Anthony before I even kissed him. All these years later, I know in my heart he is my soul mate and nothing will ever change that.

Sharing with you all the truth about my life is one of the hardest things I will ever do. Opening yourself up to be judged is never easy especially to many of you that have been cheated on. It hurts me to know that my actions have hurt another person. I am having a very difficult time sleeping at night thinking about what this book could do to his family. Publishing this may quite possibly mean that my Cinni-Mini will never talk to me again and unintentionally hurt the people I care about the most. Yes, I do feel bad about saying the things I did about Maria because I loved her and considered her one of my closest friends. However, they were such major events in my life that I could not leave them out.

Also, keep in mind that this is coming from one person's point of view. I don't know what Sarah has been through. I don't know what Anthony has told her and she has every right to hate me for sharing the truth about my relationship with her husband. I feel sick thinking that one day this could cause his children or him pain. Maria may have a completely different view of why our friendship ended. My sister has reached out and stated that Cain never abused her and she never said he did during that phone call in 2008. She publicly called me a liar and still wants nothing to do with me. This is my side of what I went through. The courts cleared Cain of any wrong doing, but I know what he did to me. I can't say 100% if what his ex-wife told me is true about what he did to his daughter, but I believe in my heart it is.

I am sharing what happened to me, what others have told me happened to them, and what I have learned through my research to help others. To show them that they can overcome whatever trauma they are faced with and give them hope of a better life. We live in a world filled with filters, false representations of self, and a society driven by fake. It is being influenced by "influencers" who have their own agenda. The other day I was in Sacramento filming a documentary and a young woman forced her boyfriend to stop traffic so she could stand in the middle of the street to take a photograph of her. I've worked out next to Instagram "fitness models" who look 50lbs smaller and more toned in their filtered photos. I've been on photo shoots with models that look nothing like their magazine features. I've worked with famous "advocates" that say how much they care about Veterans but end up scamming them and stealing their money. I have spoken with dozens of sex trafficking survivors who are being exploited by the very organizations that are making millions of dollars to help the people they are exploiting. We live in a world filled with fake, selfish, manipulative people and it provides a false sense of reality which in turn makes many of us feel like we are not good enough. They feel alone. It is my hope that my story will help you not feel so alone.

Chapter 39

Every day I live with guilt and I feel responsible for everyone Cain hurt. Reporting sexual assault is incredibly challenging. Many have asked me why I didn't report. If it has never happened to you or someone you love, you will never fully be able to understand, but I hope this helps explain a little.

According to the Department of Justice every 73 seconds an American is sexually assaulted and one out of six women and one out of 33 men are raped in their lifetime. 59% of sexual assaults are committed by someone the victim trusts and 34% by family members. Three out of four rapes go unreported. Out of 1,000 rapes only five will see any prison time. Main reason, out of the 1,000 only 230 were reported to police, 46 led to arrest, nine referred to prosecutor, five receive a felony conviction, and four incarcerated.

Imagine rape as a stab wound and keep in mind that 93% know the person that stabbed them. Your first priority is to stop the bleeding. You aren't processing the concept of admissible evidence or being able to prove that person stabbed you. Once you stop the bleeding you need to clean it, close it, and prevent it from re-opening. Now imagine your support system are the medical staff. If you go in, the police will be called, you will be painfully examined in order to secure any evidence, and because it was someone you know, you have to fully consider the repercussions and the possibility no one will believe you. From that point on it is up to you to prove what happened.

The prosecution sends their own doctor who cuts open your stitches and causes more pain than when you were first stabbed. A week goes by and your wound is trying to heal but now they didn't get enough evidence so they open your wound again. The more times your wound is opened your scar becomes worse. You try to return to work but by that time everyone knows you were stabbed. Some have made a joke about it and said you stabbed yourself for attention or for money. You are now the most shared meme in the office. Others will walk on eggshells around you. The HR department treats you like a ticking time bomb when all you want to do is your job and be treated like you were before the stabbing. Some will even contact you and say that you provoked the stabbing and deserved it. This could continue for years while you are forced to relive this event over and over again in court. Your reputation went from a hard worker with potential to the person that got stabbed.

Now imagine you have no support system and based off of everything you know to be true, you triage yourself. After you stop the bleeding, you clean your wound, and sew it up yourself. No police were called so you won't have to be forced through the numerous painful re-opening of the wound and excruciatingly painful and invasive examinations. Your wound is left alone and you are able to heal faster. You are also able to hide it, avoiding all the other drama that this would bring. However, that scar will never go away. You must live with it every single day. Quite often, be forced to interact with the person that stabbed you.

Knowing all of this, you mentally have to make a decision just moments after you were stabbed. If you are not mentally prepared or have not had time to consult with a lawyer to determine your options/repercussions and you need more time, your chances of people believing you will become even more unlikely. The risk of not being able to prove the stabbing increase and you realize that you could go through all of this pain, risking your reputation, job and family, for nothing.

According to research from 1950 to 2002, 4,392 priests sexually abused 10,667 victims. If this was going on for so many years why did it take so long for the Catholic Church to do anything about it? Victims were reporting the abuse but due to cover-ups, payoffs, and the media, these crimes went unprosecuted. The victims were afraid that no one would believe them that a man of God would do that. Not only that, but they were one person going up against an organization that some say is more powerful than the Government.

The first victims to come forward were ignored, called liars, or caused to keep quiet by numerous different methods including but not limited to intimidation, false accusations that made them seem non-credible, and loss of key evidence. Through the perseverance of these brave individuals, others finally came forward about their assault. Strength in numbers, news reporters that believed these stories, and some brave legal teams brought this horrible scandal to light.

I have been accused of playing victim, lying, or using my trauma for personal gain. This baffles me. My entire life has been about overcoming trauma and refusing to be a victim. I did not allow this trauma to prevent me from falling in love, traveling the world, helping others, or furthering my education. When a survivor chooses not to remain a victim and doesn't fit into the victim box society has placed on them, they are accused of lying. They re-traumatize the survivor by putting the blame on them. She shouldn't have gone out with that guy. Did you see what she was wearing? I just saw photos of her on Instagram in a bikini, there's no way she got raped. Men can't get raped; he must be gay.

Being accused of lying is idiotic. This isn't a court case where I have to show proof of my trauma and I have nothing to gain. I can't tell you how much I wish I were lying. How many nights I have gone to bed praying I was crazy and would wake up realizing it was all a dream. Thinking I am going to be significantly financially compensated as a first-time author is ignorant. Most authors are not wealthy and I now have a target on my back which has not been easy to deal with. I published my story to help show people the truth about rape and give others the hope and courage to overcome whatever trauma they experienced. Shed light on what false accusations can do and what happens when people don't believe you when you tell them the truth.

Many of us choose to take on this trauma alone because the alternative isn't worth the risk. So, you didn't report your uncle stabbing you. Years down the road you find out that the same uncle stabbed your child. This is when the fangs come out and you no longer care what happens to you. You feel a survivor's guilt which is worse than your own trauma. You feel responsible and realize that no longer can you keep your mouth shut. When you come forward, you have no evidence other than firsthand knowledge, the prosecution digs into every aspect of your past and tries to make you look like a delinquent that was asking to be stabbed.

Do I agree that we should believe everyone that claims sexual assault? HELL NO! The men and women that falsely report deserve to be locked up and punished severely. They are a major part of the problem. Is there a solution? That would take years of research to be able to come up with any kind of response to that. However, reports have shown that there is a significant decrease in sexual assaults since 1993. This may be due to the buckling down on poor treatment of the victims and taking their allegations more seriously. They have changed the statute of limitations in numerous states because experts understand why it takes some so long to report the assault.

Unless you have experienced sexual assault yourself, have extensive years of experience conducting unbiased research on sexual assault, or have firsthand knowledge of an alleged sexual assault, and are on social media spewing your ignorant opinions, you are the problem! I truly hope it doesn't take one of your daughters, a loved one, or even yourself getting raped for you to wake up and take responsibility for your role in this crime.

Chapter 40

When I arrived in Bangkok, I didn't waste any time and went apartment hunting the next day. The first day was a bust as it was a weekend and there were no managers at the apartments I could find. The next day I asked the receptionist at the hotel to call the manager to ask if they had apartments available. They did and after looking at one other place, I decided the first one I had seen was the best one for me. It was right across the street from one of the largest parks in Bangkok. After moving in I went and explored my new neighborhood. The park was incredible and to my joy, I stumbled across an outdoor gym. To my surprise, things were actually going according to plan, which was something I was not accustomed to. I messaged Anthony and showed him my new home. He was impressed and happy for me, but he told me how much he missed seeing me.

I met up with Jay and we went out to lunch. It was so good to catch up with him and I was overjoyed to get my things back. I tried my wigs on as soon as I got home. I had moved to Thailand because I wanted to save up money and get IVF. My doctor told me that if I became pregnant, it would take away the pain and there's a chance the endo wouldn't come back. After a Muay Thai class with Jay, I was telling him some of my past stories. He suggested I write these stories down because they needed to be shared with the world.

I took Jay's advice and the more I wrote, the more I found myself in the pages of this book. I asked Jay if I should wait because I didn't have the "happy ending" yet. I wanted a story that would give everyone hope. An ending I deserved! He told me to trust him and keep writing. So, I did. I have for the first time in my life been honest with myself and who I am. I wrote things I experienced that I have never shared with anyone or never shared in such detail. It was an emotional roller coaster and one of the most difficult things I have ever accomplished. Once again, I faced my greatest fear head-on.

One of my greatest fears is showing someone who I really am, causing them to walk away. My past is riddled with those I've loved the most abandoning me. Before I met Anthony, I believed with all my heart that no one would ever love me, the real me. How could someone love me when the people that were biologically created to love me hurt me in more ways than I could put into words? Anthony taught me that I was wrong. So many people will make him out to be this cheating bastard that led me on for years and broke my heart. Some may want him to leave everything and be with me. Part of me has always believed that I would end up with Anthony and nothing would make me happier than to be with him. The thought of having another chance to have a child with him is something I dreamed about.

Things were finally looking up and I held onto that with everything in me. Then Murphy's law struck again. Nothing was going right. I fell into a deep depression, mainly brought on by the increasing pain from the endo. I was walking down the stairs to go get food and I blacked out from the pain, falling down the stairs. The pain was so intense I sweated through my clothes and was lying in bed unable to get up. After taking some Vicodin I had saved, I was able to stand up, but the pain was still intense.

For months, I struggled. I couldn't find work, I had no friends to go out with, I was broke and alone. The only saving grace was Anthony. He would call me almost every day. We would Facetime and talk for hours. He told me I needed to come home, that he missed me and we were always happier when we were together. After everything I had gone through, I contemplated returning to San Diego. I missed being independent and not having to depend on others due to the language barrier.

After a trip to the immigration office, Murphy's Law reared its' ugly head. On my way there, I was harassed by a taxi driver that wouldn't let me out of the car. I had to jump out at a stoplight and didn't realize that I had dropped my wallet in his car. My wallet that had my passport and all the money I had left to my name. I've been shot at, almost died while driving the crazy streets of the world, but this was one of the scariest feelings ever! It was a combination of everything added up that resulted in me crying and getting screamed at in Thai by the angry taxi driver because I had no money.

After calming down and regrouping, I was able to communicate with the driver enough to tell him to go to the police station. Instead of going directly to the station, the driver stopped at a store to get food and drove around lost for hours. I received a call from a police station over an hour away from where we were, saying that they had found my wallet. When I finally arrived at the station, I almost cried with relief when I spotted my wallet. Then I opened it. My cards, ID, and passport were all there. My heart sunk; the money was gone. All I had to my name was the $95 I had left in my bank account which I ended up having to use for the taxi, and the overstay fee for the Visa I had to pay because by the time I got done at the station, the immigration office was closed.

I cried myself to sleep almost every night, wishing things were different. I bought a plane ticket home with my maxed-out credit card. I had no money and had to sell as much of my belongings as I could to buy food. I lasted three weeks on $35, some days not having money to eat. My pride wouldn't allow me to ask Jay or any of my other Thai friends for help. Anthony called me almost daily to keep my spirits up. It amazed me that even after all this time, we could talk for over four hours a day and still have so many things left to talk about.

I arrived to LAX with no job, negative $15 in my account, and homeless. Anthony was in 29 Palms, but he could not have helped me with a place to stay. I was dying to see him and needed a hug so badly! I had to use my disability from the VA to pay for a week in one of the dingiest hotels in Point Loma. I sucked up my pride and reached out for help. I messaged several friends and told them about my situation. These so-called friends read my messages and never replied. In fact, they stopped commenting on my Facebook posts, when before they would always comment and message me back right away.

After reaching out to Master Gunnery Sergeant Munoz, he called me and told me that he had a former Marine that was willing to let me stay with him for little rent. For the next few months, I continued to struggle with feelings of depression and failure. I was 35, living in a stranger's home, broke, in debt, and alone. I knew I needed to take back control over my life. I had been losing pieces of myself along the way and I wanted them back. Instead of making more excuses, I knew something needed to change.

After months of trying to find work in San Diego, I was having no luck. Mostly because the endo prevented me from any of the jobs I was qualified for. After applying to hundreds of jobs, I received a phone call and was offered a job! The only downside, it was in Las Vegas and hours away from Anthony. In three years, I had lived in four countries, two continents, 16 apartments, two states, and never once received any help moving that I didn't pay for. I was sick and tired of moving and was hoping to settle down and find a home of my own.

After spending five months in Vegas, I had a cervical cancer scare. I was bleeding so heavily I became anemic and I was passing out at work. I called my previous doctor in San Diego and told the nurse my symptoms. After looking at my medical records she told me that I had a positive test for cervical cancer and I needed to be seen immediately. The Las Vegas VA made me an emergency appointment for that Monday.

The woman that introduced herself as a Doctor, I found out wasn't a Doctor, but a Nurse. After sitting in her office describing my symptoms, this woman who barely spoke legible English, asked me to prove that I was bleeding! She wanted me to take out my tampon in her office and show her. I was shocked and became furious when she told me I didn't need a pap to test for cancer because I just had one a year prior and I should only get one every two years! I told her the last test I had was abnormal and the nurse in San Diego told me that combined with my symptoms, I needed to be examined for cervical cancer right away. She told me she wasn't qualified to give me a pap but she could "poke around which will cause you more pain." She went on to tell me that I would have to wait three months to be seen by a GYN to get a Pap. Later on, I found out that she put on my medical records "refused pelvic exam, patient was frumpy, obese, and needs to be checked for mental health." I was livid. I spent several hours writing a letter to the Las Vegas VA and the Medical Review board. Of course, nothing happened.

Regardless if it was cervical cancer or endometriosis, the likelihood I would need a hysterectomy was high. Having no family or friends I could stay with while I was unemployed and waiting for surgery, I had very few choices. While I had been doing a lot of Veteran advocating, I met a female Veteran that lived in Texas. We had started working on getting a nonprofit going and she offered to let me stay with her while I recovered and worked on our nonprofit. She convinced me that Texas had the best VA hospitals in the States and that made sense to me because of how much they love their Veterans there. I foolishly took her word. After meeting her and her family, she seemed like a good person and I didn't have any better options. Or so I thought.

Before my move to Texas, I took a trip to San Diego to see Anthony. It had been around a year since I had seen him, and I hadn't slept with anyone else. We spent a few hours in the hotel room doing what we do so well. It was the first time someone other than myself or a toy had given me an orgasm. I cried happy tears for the joy I felt over taking back something my rapists had taken away. This amazing man not only loved me but helped heal a part of me I thought was broken forever. I'm not sure what had changed or if anything had, but something was different between us. We had never been closer and for the first time he started opening up about his feelings for me. He started calling me "my Person" and we talked on the phone an average of three hours a day.

Chapter 41

The VA in Fort Worth had no GYN so I had to see a General Practitioner. Because my medical records said that I had refused my last exam and they had flagged me, she told me I would have to wait for the next GYN appointment in Dallas which wasn't for several months. I explained to her my symptoms, my last pelvic exam results, and that I had not stopped bleeding for two months. She told me that I was exaggerating and told me to go see the front desk to make an appointment with the Dallas VA. I told her that I needed a pap test today to make sure that I didn't have cancer. She slammed down her cell phone she had been using to text the entire time I was in her office and said "fine, you want pap you get pap" in extremely broken English. I followed her into the exam room where she threw a gown in my face, folded her arms and told me to take off everything below the waist. She didn't show me to the bathroom to change. I was pissed and changed right in front of her. No other nurse was present which was unusual but I was desperate. Without any lubrication, she shoved the speculum inside me, finished the test, and then did a brief breast exam.

During the breast exam she found a large lump and mentioned allowed how that was concerning. She told me that they did not have a mammogram machine at their Women's Clinic so once again

I would have to go to Dallas. That's right, the Women's Clinic in Fort Worth didn't have a GYN or a mammogram machine. This doctor never put in the order for a mammogram and I had to call every few days to get the results of my test which showed were completed on the MyHealthEvet website. The tests came back normal and the symptoms I was having were likely due to my stage four endometriosis getting worse. Stage four is the worst kind and involves deep, invasive, adhesions causing sever pain and bleeding. Imagine superglue on your organs and each month it rips itself off, taking with it whatever it was stuck to, causing bleeding, swelling and extreme pain.

Thankfully the breast exam came back normal but I was faced with another choice. There was no available GYN appointment for four months so I was forced to use the Choice Program. Let me tell you a little about my experience with this program that was created to address the issue of Veterans dying due to the long wait for an appointment. Some people's experiences have been very good using this program, but mine have not. Several years before this, I had gone in for another laparoscopic surgery to remove the endometriosis growth. I used the choice program thinking anything would be better than the VA. I was given a doctor's office number to make an appointment. I called for two weeks, no one ever answered or responded to the dozens of messages I left. I called the Choice Program and was given another number. The soonest appointment was three weeks out. I met with the GYN and he told me that I would need an ultrasound before he could schedule me for surgery. The soonest ultrasound appointment was also several weeks out. After that I had my pre-op appointment. In the office the surgeon sighed in frustration and told me that the VA had canceled my surgery because I had passed the three-month time frame and I was going to have to go back to the VA, see if they had anything sooner, and if not, re-apply for the Choice Program and start all over again. He said he had encountered this issue numerous times and he provided a solution. He told me that he was on call that weekend at the ER and I should come in with severe pain and he would perform an emergency surgery which the VA would have to cover.

Another experience I had involved acupuncture. It was a single creepy man, in an office without any type of admin or anyone else, in a closed room. He ended up hitting nine different nerves and after the session my left arm went completely numb for almost two weeks. I know you are probably thinking why didn't I file a complaint with the medical board or why didn't I contact the Veteran Advocate, I did. I did everything I was told to. None of it helped. It took me refusing their answers and reaching out to my contacts on social media to even get an ultrasound appointment. I dreaded using the Choice Program for this major surgery but I was told by several different Veteran Advocates that the hospital the Choice Program used loved and took great care of their Veterans. After all, this was Texas. So, I scheduled my first appointment and was seen within a week. Good start, or so I thought. They told me that I needed to have a biopsy done on my uterus to ensure there wasn't any cancer. I had driven myself and the very word biopsy surprised me when he said he could do it that day. With only medication they used to dilate my cervix, they stuck an epidural size needle inside me and took a chunk of my uterus.

I drove back from the hospital alone, crying the entire way back to a stranger's garage, wishing more than anything I could get a hug from Anthony. The day before the surgery I had lunch with my business partner and did my best to hold back the tears while I told her the time for the surgery in the morning. She came and hugged me, knowing herself how emotional the surgery was, as she had gone through it herself. While we had grown distant since the months I had lived there, she was the only person I knew at the time I could ask for assistance with my surgery and I did care about her. When I had first arrived, we got along amazingly well. We both spent most of the days coming up with a business plan, networking with other Veterans, and planning a future that we felt could help make life better for those that were thrown aside by our government. Then she started to change. She had an incurable, painful disease that she took extremely potent narcotics for which transformed her into someone I didn't recognize. It felt like Delilah all over again. She began taking more and more medication, leaving her sleeping most of the day as I worked. The dream of building a nonprofit seemed impossible as I was doing everything on my own and she lost all interest.

The night before my surgery was filled with dreams of a little girl with Anthony's eyes and I woke up sobbing knowing I would never know what she looked like and I would never have another opportunity to see myself in a child. I sent a polite wake-up text to my business partner to let her know I needed to leave soon. When she didn't respond, I sent her a few more and called several times with no response. Not wanting to wake up her entire family by ringing the doorbell and crushed that she didn't care enough to make sure she was there for me; I got in my car and drove the hour to the hospital. The emptiness I felt was a crushing reminder of what was to come. I sat alone in the waiting room, watching everyone else there with their family or loved one waiting to be taken back. Looking back, it hit me, after all the many surgeries I had been through there was only one time I had ever had someone there with me in the waiting room and there for me when I woke up. It had been my mother during my first ACL surgery at 18 years old. Even though I never wanted to see her again and will never forget the horrific things she put me through, there was a moment where I would have been grateful for even her to be there. That quickly passed when I realized she never loved me, and I would never give her the opportunity to ease her conscience.

Minutes before they wheeled me back to surgery my business partner messaged me, apologizing that she didn't wake up in time, but I was too pissed to respond. I figured she would be there after I woke up and I didn't need the stress right before surgery. Due to all the surgeries I had before, I found some comfort in what to expect. The surgeon will come in and do a huddle with the others involved in the surgery. This was going to be the most invasive surgery I had ever had, and I was scared. The nurse came in and put in only one IV, but in all of the surgeries before there had been two, in case one vein collapses during the surgery. There was no huddle, I never even saw the surgeon's face before I was being wheeled into the operating room. Laying there in the frigid, sterile, room with lights shining down, I prayed I would never wake up. They told me to count down to ten and put the mask across my face. Ten came and I was still awake. I started to panic, remembering hearing stories about surgeries where the patient had been improperly anesthetized, and the patient felt everything. I felt like I was awake during a nightmare and tried to move my strapped down arms from the restraints. I heard voices say, "you didn't give her enough" and then everything went dark.

When I came to in the recovery room, I wished even more that I had died on the table. It felt as if they had shoved a claw up through my vagina and ripped out my uterus. The surgeon never came in to tell me how the surgery went, and my business partner never showed up even though she had all the surgery paperwork she had signed as my caretaker. Due to complications from the surgery they admitted me overnight and put me on Ketamine to try and bring the pain to a tolerable level. Due to my redhead genetics, this did little to help. If it hadn't been for Anthony calling and distracting me for several hours that day, I don't think I would have made it home. He was livid when I told him what my business partner had done. I had to talk him out of getting on the next flight out. I didn't tell him how bad it had gotten because I knew there wasn't much if anything he could do and there was no point in making him feel that pain of not being able to help me. What he didn't realize is he helped more than anyone ever has. I'm only alive because I have him in my life. He could be a lousy friend but for the things that really mattered, he came through like no one ever has.

I didn't see the surgeon until the following morning and even though the nurse had just upped my pain meds, he rudely asked why I hadn't been discharged yet. As much as I dreaded returning to that garage, I didn't feel safe in the hospital. There was only one nurse that seemed to know what she was doing, and she had just left after the shift change. Tears filled my eyes as I checked my bank account to see if I had enough money for an Uber, which I didn't. I contemplated driving myself, but from previous experience, I knew they would never discharge me without a ride. I had to swallow all my pride and message my business partner asking for a ride. The nurse came in to start the discharge process and tried to remove the catheter. Laying naked and exposed, I was in too much pain to say anything as a male orderly walked in, leaving the door to the hospital hall open and no curtains provided any privacy. I closed my eyes, tears flooding into my ears, wishing someone had been there for me in moments like this. What had I done so wrong to be living this moment?

The incompetent nurse couldn't figure out how to take out the catheter, despite numerous excruciating attempts. She called in a more experienced nurse who ripped it out of me, liquid going everywhere. "You didn't empty the bladder" she yelled at the nurse. "Who is this hospital hiring? I havefive other patients to see, can you discharge her without any more mistakes like this?" I heard her say as she reprimanded the nurse in the hall.

I had told my business partner when to be there according to what the nurses told me. She arrived a few minutes late, but I was still in my urine-soaked hospital gown waiting to be discharged. I hadn't eaten in almost 48 hours, I was pumped full of ketamine, just had my uterus ripped out of me, and was heading back to an empty garage with a woman I now never wanted to see again. My phone started buzzing with numerous angry messages informing me if I didn't get down to the valet area soon, she would leave She wasn't feeling well so she told me that she didn't want to park and come in so I was supposed to meet her down at the entrance. This was coming from the same woman that told me her husband had to pick her up and carry her everywhere after her surgery.

When the nurse and orderly finally came in, I told them my ride had arrived and I needed to go. They told me I had to follow the protocol and graduate from the blue gown to the green gown. The male tech was standing snapping closed the green gown slowly with shaky hands. "So, what do I need to do to get out of here?" The nurse told me I had to put on the green gown and show I could walk on my own. After numerous times of not being able to understand anything she said, I was getting angry at their incompetence. I stood up and went to grab the green gown, almost passing out from the pain of standing on my own. The male tech yelled at me "NO! I have to help you undress and put this on." "The fuck you are," I snapped. "This isn't a free fucking peep show," I said grabbing the gown. The nurse was almost in tears and the man looked as if I had pulled out a gun and was threatening his life. I managed to inch my way, hunched over in pain, to the bathroom. I put on the green gown, came out, sat on the bed and asked them what was next. The nurse replied that she had to go do more paperwork and they both left. I waited another five minutes while my phone continued to buzz.

After calling the nurses desk with no answer, I made my way out to the empty hall with my belongings in tow. The male orderly saw me when I came around the corner and yelled at me that I shouldn't be walking. I told him I needed to leave and would wait for him to get me a wheelchair. When the nurse saw him wheeling me to the elevators, she yelled at me in unintelligible English. She told the man to bring me back to my room and wait for her to finish the paperwork. As he was wheeling me back, I yelled at him to stop. When he didn't, I grabbed the wheels and stopped the chair, stood up, held onto the handrails and made my way to the elevators. The male orderly started yelling for security and just as the elevator doors were closing, I could see the nurse running towards me with an angry look on her face.

Staggering through the hospital, holding my abdomen, I finally made it to the valet, covered in sweat from the pain. She didn't even get out of the car to help me inside! I didn't have my painkillers yet and asked her if she could go to the building across the street to fill the prescription. You would think anyone that had been through the same surgery and knew how painful it was would have gone inside and filled it for me... NOPE! I sat in the passenger side seat absolutely shocked when she put the car in park and said she would wait there. Trying to not pass out from the pain, I went in to Walgreens. As I leaned against the wall waiting for my prescription to be filled and trying not to pass out, because there were no chairs to sit on, I saw my business partner come in with her daughter to get snacks and coffee. She asked me if I wanted anything, and when I shook my head no, she went back and waited in the car leaving me slumped against the wall.

By the time I got back to the garage, my abdomen was extremely swollen, and the incisions were red, swollen, and hot to the touch. Because my business partner was at the emergency room with her son, I sent her pictures and asked her if she could show the Dr. and see if I needed to go into the ER. The ER Dr. told me to go in right away. She ended up coming back to pick me up and took me which I couldn't have regretted more. Every time a nurse came in, she would use the opportunity to talk about her own health issues and try and speak for me. When the Dr. came in and she tried to tell him what was wrong I snapped. "Excuse me Dr. I am the patient. If you have any questions, please direct them towards me." After that, I asked her to leave because she started complaining about being in pain. She refused telling me she didn't want me to be alone. WHAT THE FUCK! You sure didn't care I was alone after I just went through a brutal surgery by myself. She didn't care I had to wait alone in the waiting room or that I woke up after surgery alone. She had turned my pain into an opportunity to get attention and for people to feel sorry for her. I was not only shaking from the pain but from the rage building up inside me.

I somehow managed to hold my temper and was in too much pain to yell. I informed her that there were plenty of people at the ER to help me but there would be no one at home to help me. If she stayed, she risked being in more pain and I really needed her to be there for me when I got back to the garage which she wouldn't be able to do if she was in too much pain. She didn't listen and after dropping me off after the ER, I didn't see her for two weeks!

The main reason I had moved into her garage was because she had promised she would help me get through my surgery. That she knew from her own experience I would never survive on my own and I needed someone there to take care of me. To bring me food and help me to the bathroom. For two weeks I barely ate, didn't shower, rarely used the bathroom, was in and out of consciousness from the pain and the only thing keeping me from swallowing the entire bottle of pills, were Anthony's daily calls. After almost two weeks of not showering I couldn't take it and I made my way to the shower. I ended up slipping, smashing my head into the faucet, and came to when the water got cold. Crawling back to my bed I passed out hoping I had a concussion and wouldn't wake up again. I just wanted the pain to stop and I didn't really have anything that was keeping me there, except for the one person I could never be with, Anthony.

Chapter 42

Around the third week of recovery, she showed up to "see how I was" but I soon found out she was just there to talk about one of her baby daddies and all the drama she had with her exes and kids. She asked what happened when she saw my smashed face and I told her I fell in the shower. She told me that I should have asked her husband to help. Prior to this she told me that if she died, I would be the one person that she would be ok with sleeping with her husband and how good I was with her kids. I felt like I was living in some alternate universe, where someone was experimenting on humans and how much pain, suffering, and just fucked up situations they could endure.

My recovery was brutal and due to the damage and the barbaric treatment I had received, I had unknowingly developed a urinary tract infection due to them ripping out the catheter and tearing up my urethra. This led to a bladder and kidney infection and kidney stones. I wouldn't find out until months later they had also torn up the inside of my vagina when they had pulled out my uterus leaving bloody lesions and scarring. They ended up having to cauterize the lesions. Which was, as you can only imagine, very unpleasant. Then the summer Texas heat hit, and giant wasps made dozens of nests in the garage I was staying in. I had no job, was recovering from brutal surgery, and was putting on a huge act trying to make things work with my living situation. I went into survival mode and the one good thing about recovery is it gave me a reason to avoid her. I was also relieved when her husband had her committed to a psychiatric facility for over a month and I hoped she would get the help she desperately needed. I did enjoy her family though. Her husband was one the hardest working men I knew, and he was madly in love with her. They took in a teenager that needed a home, he worked two jobs to make a good life for his family, and there was a lot of good there.

I don't know if it was the medication she was on, the fear of dying and leaving her family, or just the fear of being alone that caused her to act as she did. What I do know is that I felt used and I was desperate to escape the hell I was living in there. I started looking for jobs back in San Diego, but once again, I didn't get one interview. I even used the little savings I had to hire a resume writer and used all the Veteran Job Assistance Organizations I could find. Still nothing. Facebook became my only escape and I had become better friends with a guy I had known, but not really known, for ten years. When I filled him in on my living situation, he didn't hesitate and offered me a room to come stay in. The next day I packed up as much of my belongings into my car as I could and drove to San Diego. It took me almost two months to come up with the money to move my things back home, so I had to keep the act going and be friendly with the family I was staying with in Texas.

Science and research have been something I have used to cope with trauma my entire life. I do my best to not make choices when I am emotional. When something goes wrong in my life, I analyze everything to determine if it is something I could have prevented. Did I develop an unhealthy victim mentality that makes me drawn to certain people or circumstances? Could I have stopped that from happening if I didn't trust anyone or never took an educated chance? What if I had just kept my mouth shut or not told the truth? Why have I gone through so much hell? Is it possible I am to blame for many of the things I have gone through? Yes, and there are changes I have made to prevent those types of things from happening ever again. However, this brings up another question. How much of yourself do you change to prevent these things from happening? How much do you allow that evil, that trauma, that betrayal to change you? As I reflect on my life and the root of most of the trauma I have experienced, I believe it has been a direct result of telling the truth and doing what I believed was the right thing. We live in a world where the media alters the truth to fit an agenda; social media sites filled with filtered, fake realities showing only what people want us to see; career fields that no longer look at resumes but who you know. A world where speaking the truth can get you killed, gaslighted, alone...

The truth and doing the right thing, have cost me a price so high, I am at a loss how to end this second edition to my book. After I published the first edition to this book, I experienced even more loss and torturous pain. The truth and raw vulnerability I have shared in this book has been used to hurt me in more ways I ever dreamed possible. I have been publicly called a liar, a homewrecking whore, deserving of rape, and many other monstrous things, some by fellow Marine's and acquaintances. According to my relatives I brought shame to my parents, five siblings, 11 nieces and nephews, seven aunts and uncles, and dozens of cousins.

My former business partner felt betrayed by me sharing the trauma I went through during my hysterectomy and the role she played in that. She has come after me and those I love in the most evil, vindictive, and cunning ways you can imagine. I ignored my past experiences with people, and I took in a homeless Veteran mom and her two kids who ended up being a con artist. She teamed up with my former business partner and combined their hatred and jealousy towards me in an attempt to bring me down along with those I love.

They recruited ignorant social media contacts to threaten my life, desecrated the memories of those service members I wrote about that lost their lives, ran illegal background checks on me to find the real names of people I love, went after innocent family members including their children, attempted to destroy my reputation and career, and used the most painful experiences I have endured against me. They spread lies about me that I never had a hysterectomy, never left the wire in Iraq, that I was never raped. Their blind followers believed the lies of two women they never met and left Amazon reviews spreading lies about me and endangering the lives of those I care about. They went through my social media contacts, calling them and trying to turn them against me. They contacted podcasts and radio shows I had been on spreading more lies. Why? Why would they have such extreme hatred towards me? It's because I saw who they really were which they were doing everything they could to hide from the world.

Even though I have extremely embarrassing and shameful facts about them, I never shared that publicly. Instead I did my best to hide their identities and only shared the information I needed, to protect others from getting hurt by them. Cowards and people with truth to hide fight in the shadows and recruit others to do their dirty work. They ended up hurting people I love which resulted in more devastating loss. The fact that they celebrate this, shows what these people are. They hurt innocent people, including children, in their mission to seek revenge on me for telling the truth about them. After everything they put me through, I still don't want to hurt them. I hope that they both find some way to love themselves. That they find peace instead of being consumed with jealousy and vengeance. They both have so much talent they could use to help people and make their lives better.

Even after all of that I continued to help people. I shared my story with others, despite the harassment, bullying and threats. I kept fighting to protect children, and things were finally starting to improve. All of the decades of hard work I had put in were beginning to pay off. I was selected to be part of an undercover ops team in Asia that would be actively helping locate and rescue sex trafficked children. The last surgery I had to battle my endometriosis by removing my ovaries seemed to be working. I was in amazing shape and ready to take on the world.

Then COVID hit and another unrelated chain of events that once again brought me to my knees. A month into quarantine, I went to pay my rent and my financial aid check from school was around $4,000 short because they had screwed up and had been overpaying.

After almost becoming homeless due to the cost of living in San Diego, the gyms were closed and I faced another obstacle. I could no longer afford the hormonal medication I was paying for out of pocket because the VA pharmacy didn't have it available. Because I was pre-menopausal, and the VA wouldn't approve the higher dosage I needed because I couldn't afford the other medication, it took my doctor two months of arguing on my behalf to increase my hormone replace therapy medication through the VA, so I was forced to go without any meds. This created a major imbalance in my hormones and the endometriosis had spread to my spinal nerves, mostly attacking my sciatica. Due to quarantine restrictions, the rescue ops mission was postponed. All the training contracts and speaking gigs I had were canceled.

The worst part, was knowing exactly what many children around the world were experiencing. Many were imprisoned with their abusers. To all the combat vets, imagine being on a patrol and on a constant state of alert, with no one watching your six, no body armor, no one standing guard; for almost a year! That kind of chronic abuse, researchers have found, causes similar damage to that of combat traumatic brain injuries. There were historic increases in child abuse requiring hospitalization. It brought back haunting memories of my childhood where I had a perfect school attendance and hated summer because school was my only safe place. Memories where I would be on high alert when the floor boards creaked, the locked bathroom doorknob tried to be opened, the basement. Still, I kept fighting. I kept fighting for myself and those kids. Like Spring time, things slowly started growing back and getting better.

I started doing undercover work to help with sex trafficked children in San Diego due to the major immigration crisis at the border. Due to the nature of my work I had to stop my social media advocacy and do my best to keep my work confidential. The work was devastating. Many people think that they want to be involved in the fight against sex trafficking but they have no clue what that means. It's like taking on an Army with endless resources and money, by yourself. You get to know children that are getting raped daily and there is not a damn thing you can do to stop it. You have to see that empty haunting look in their eyes, knowing exactly what they are going through. Then I experienced two catastrophic losses due to the lies I exposed or was investigating. In order to protect others, I cannot share that information, but I can tell you, I relate to the Viking Warriors that long for Valhalla.

In elementary school I had an assignment to draw a picture of what I wanted to be when I got older. I drew a picture of a fully tattooed military superhero, that traveled the world with her six adopted children, and played professional soccer. As I grew older, the expectations society put on me and the pressures from my family, attempted to lead me down a path away from my childhood dreams. Despite their best effort, I never gave up on my dreams. The more I stayed true to myself, the harder my life became. It seemed like the more I tried, the more I failed. After losing everything I have, I didn't feel like a superhero. I felt like a failure. I started to question all my choices. Asking myself would it have just been easier if? Would my life be better if I had conformed and changed to what the rest of the world wanted? To fit in the box society put me in.

I began to search for answers, and ironically, I found my answers in the lives of superheroes. Batman saw both of his parents killed, was a millionaire, and had every reason and opportunity to be selfish and use his trauma as a fuel for evil. Captain America was invisible, bullied, kept from helping his country because the world put him in a categorized box of weakness with no potential to help. Superman lost his entire planet, had his life in constant danger for powers he never asked for, and lost those closest to him for doing what he believed was the right thing to do. All these characters became superheroes because they received abilities they never asked for or experienced a trauma that gave them a strength to be used for good or evil. Batman could have ended up being a playboy millionaire with the love of his life, or whoever he wanted, but he chose to sacrifice everything for what he believed was right. Captain America had every reason to be angry and seek retribution, but he ended up sacrificing his life to save a country that never wanted him. Superman could have hidden his strength to live a normal life and to be with those he loved. Instead he lost everyone so he could do what he believed was the right thing. I'm not bullet proof, I can't fly or shoot lasers out of my eyes, but my trauma also gave me superhuman strength and I too had a choice. I could have become a serial killer, a drug addict, a life-long victim that blamed all my poor choices on my family.

Just like those superheroes never asked for their powers or to lose so many they loved, I never asked to be raped, betrayed, or for any of the horrible things that happened to me. There were many times throughout my life I could have given up or chosen the easy way. You too have a choice. Your resilience and strength retrieved from trauma, is your superhuman ability. You can choose to use your powers for good, to help others, to become the superhero you needed. It is not an easy path and it can cost you everything.

While I do wish I could close this chapter with a fairy tale ending, the life of a superhero is often thankless and lonely. Not everyone gets a happy ever after. This isn't that kind of story. I can't end this telling you Anthony and I ended up together, that I live in a beautiful home surrounded by the people I love, or that I am even happy. The truth is, I lost everything. I will never have the life I dreamed of or even deserve. I lost the love of my life and it shattered my soul. I will never know what it feels like to have a child that shares my DNA. Most mornings I wake up covered in sweat and tears from nightmares that haunt me. Recently, after the greatest loss of my life, I chopped off all my hair because I wanted to erase who I was. I tried to give up, stop fighting, conform, take the easier path. It was like consuming poison and my entire body and soul rebelled. I may never be able to save people like Captain America, but like a superhero, I will never stop fighting for what I believe in and I will save as many people as I can before my time is up. I will go to my grave with a smile. Knowing I loved with all my heart and soul. That I risked my life to help others and fight for what I believed in. Regretting nothing. Being extraordinarily proud of the woman I became. Knowing those that sought to break me only made me stronger. Knowing I became the superhero I dreamed of as a child.